Social History of Canada

Allan Greer, general editor

New Women for God:
Canadian Presbyterian Women and India Missions, 1876–1914

The educated 'new woman' of the late nineteenth and early twentieth centuries in North America had considerable spiritual and intellectual energies in need of an outlet. Among Protestants, the foreign missionary movement came to be seen as a uniquely appropriate focus. It offered a high degree of challenge, but within a framework that did not seriously threaten woman's conventional role as guardian of moral and spiritual values. Ruth Brouwer explores the involvement of one such group of women, Canadian Presbyterians, in their work both at home and abroad.

The largest of these societies was the Toronto-based Woman's Foreign Missionary Society. Brouwer explores the background and motivation of the well-educated, generally small-town and rural women who became career missionaries in the church's overseas fields. She focuses on those who served in princely Central India, the largest of these fields so far as women's work was concerned. Brouwer demonstrates that neither the sexism of their colleagues nor the recalcitrance of 'heathenism' destroyed the missionaries' enthusiasm for their vocation. The satisfaction they derived from service to the poor, from the recognition they received from imperial and Indian officials, and from their relationships with one another made life in India richly rewarding.

Brouwer concludes with an assessment of the overall significance of the foreign missionary movement for the women who were participants in it and relates their experience to the women's movement in turn-of-the-century Canada.

RUTH COMPTON BROUWER is a Canada Research Fellow at York University.

New Women for God

Canadian Presbyterian Women and
India Missions, 1876–1914

Ruth Compton Brouwer

University of Toronto Press
Toronto Buffalo London

© University of Toronto Press 1990
Toronto Buffalo London
Printed in Canada

ISBN 0-8020-2718-0 (cloth)
ISBN 0-8020-6750-6 (paper)

Printed on acid-free paper

Canadian Cataloguing in Publication Data
Brouwer, Ruth Compton, 1941–
New women for God : Canadian Presbyterian women and India missions,
1876–1914
(The Social history of Canada ; 44)
Includes bibliographical references.
ISBN 0-8020-2718-0 (bound) ISBN 0-8020-6750-6 (pbk.)

1. Missions, Canadian – India – History.   2. Presbyterian Church in Canada –
Missions – India – History.   3. Women in missionary work – India –
History.   4. Women missionaries – India – History.   5. Women in missionary
work – Canada – History.   6. Women missionaries – Canada – History.
7. Presbyterian Church – Missions – India – History.   I. Title.   II. Series.
BV3265.2.B76 1990   266'.5254   C90-094041-7

65806

All photographs are from the United Church / Victoria University Archives
except: Outdoor medical work, United Church of Canada; Missionary types,
Presbyterian Church Archives

Social History of Canada 44

This book has been published with the help of a grant from the Canadian
Federation for the Humanities, using funds provided by the Social Sciences
and Humanities Research Council of Canada.

For Elizabeth and Matthew

Contents

viii   Contents

Preface

During the late nineteenth and early twentieth centuries, the task of 'saving the heathen' was a vital concern for millions of North Americans in mainstream Protestant churches. It cannot be pretended that a book about one denomination and one overseas field provides anything like a full picture of Canadian women's involvement in that ambitious and quixotic project. Indeed, part of the burden of the argument in what follows is that, especially in the early years, denominational identity did matter a good deal in shaping concepts of mission and that the conditions prevailing in particular receiving countries had much to do with the way individual missions developed. Nevertheless, a set of shared assumptions and common patterns cut across the woman's foreign missionary movement, making themselves evident in its rhetoric, its strategies, and its ultimate goals. This study attempts to identify the most salient general features of the movement and at the same time to convey some sense of what involvement meant for a particular group of women at the home base and overseas.

It is a pleasure to acknowledge the assistance I have received in researching and writing this book. In doing so, of course, I have no wish to implicate others in its judgments or to shift responsibility for errors of fact. Ramsay Cook supervised the York University PH D thesis on which the book is based. That statement, however, conveys only inadequately the debt I owe him for years of splendid support. Other members of York's History Department also provided guidance and encouragement at the thesis stage, as did mentor and friend Clara Thomas, now emeritus professor of English. External examiner Wendy Mitchinson prepared a careful written report on the thesis to which I have returned more than once.

Though I did not meet all of them in person, a great many archivists and librarians facilitated my research. I am especially grateful to the staff at the United Church / Victoria University Archives in Toronto, where former archivist Glenn Lucas pointed me to the rich resources on the Central India mission. These archives were – and remain – a delightful place in which to work.

In response to the notices I placed in the *Presbyterian Record* and the *United Church Observer* and to my word-of-mouth pleas for information, a number of people came forward with the personal papers of their mission-ary kin or with biographical data about them. Among this group I want especially to mention Mrs Glenna Jamieson and Mrs Choné Williams, great-nieces of Dr Belle Choné Oliver. All 'my' missionaries had died by the time I began my research, but I obtained useful personal insights about several of them, and about their field, through conversations with retired United Church and Presbyterian missionaries, most notably the Reverend Hilda Johnston and the late Dr Margaret Kennedy.

In India, Miss Lillias Brown provided warm hospitality when I briefly visited her in 1985 and introduced me to local Christians who responded helpfully to my questions about the circumstances of their families' entry into Christianity. Research on missionary involvement in their country's past is not a priority among Indian historians of the raj. For that reason I was particularly glad to meet Dr S.R. Shirgaonkar of SNDT Women's College, Bombay, who provided me with several of her articles on early-nineteenth-century missions in Maharashtra and the valuable perspective of someone writing about missionary activity out of a non-Western and non-Christian tradition.

Though I was not a part of their immediate scholarly community, Margo Gewurtz and others involved in the Canadian Missionaries in East Asia research project welcomed me to several of their workshops and gave me an opportunity to present an early report on my work. Alvyn Austin, whom I met through the East Asian connection, entertained and assisted me with his rich fund of missionary lore. At the University of Toronto, John Moir responded helpfully to questions on matters Presbyterian, while Milton Israel kindly agreed to read a draft of the manuscript in an effort to save me from glaring errors in its India content. Portions of the manuscript were also read by Katherine Ridout, to whom I am indebted both for sound scholarly advice and for a truly sustaining friendship.

In his capacity as editor of the University of Toronto Press social history series, Viv Nelles provided gratifyingly positive comments on the manu-script, along with thoughtful criticisms. So, also, did his successor, Allan Greer. Numerous authors have acknowledged their debt to editor Gerry

Hallowell; it is a pleasure to join their ranks, and also to pay tribute to his assistant, Laura Macleod. The manuscript was strengthened by Margaret Allen's careful copy-editing and by the suggestions of anonymous readers for the University of Toronto Press and the Canadian Federation for the Humanities.

I am conscious of having incurred many more debts in the writing of this book than those acknowledged in the preceding paragraphs. Over a period of several years I have received both practical and emotional support from a large and wonderful family and from colleagues and personal friends. I am grateful to all of them.

Promoting the cause: a group of WFMS members prepare an issue of *Foreign Missionary Tidings* for the mail.

The four WFMS presidents: *above* Mrs Marjory McLaren, 1876–81, 1897–9, and Mrs Catherine Ewart, 1881–97; *below* Mrs Mary Shortreed, 1899–1911, and Mrs J. Emily Steele, 1911–14

Her soulful appearance notwithstanding, Dr Marion Oliver was a combative participant in Central India's mission politics.

Left Dr Elizabeth Beatty, pioneer medical missionary in Central India and a member of the beleaguered first graduating class of the Women's Medical College, affiliated with Queen's University, Kingston. *Right* Catherine Campbell in 1902, the year she won the Kaiser-i-Hind medal for relief work among famine orphans in Central India

Dr Maggie O'Hara in regal old age. O'Hara's three great enthusiasms, according to her India colleagues, were the Presbyterian Church, Queen's University, and the British Empire. A Queen's medical graduate of 1891, she was given an honorary LL D by her alma mater in 1932.

Dr Belle Choné Oliver in 1900, two years before she became an India missionary, and in 1945, a year before her retirement. Oliver's delicate good looks gave the lie to the popular stereotype of the spinster missionary as someone too plain to attract a husband.

Dr Maggie MacKellar as a Queen's graduate in 1890 (*right*), and as a veteran missionary (*above*), proudly wearing her Kaiser-i-Hind medal

REV. J. FRASER CAMPBELL, D.D. OUR PIONEERS MRS. CAMPBELL

Mary Forrester was the first but by no means the last missionary to be lost to the WFMS through marriage. She is shown here with J. Fraser Campbell, whom she married in 1879. In later years missions publicists sometimes described the Campbells as the founders of the Central India mission, ignoring the important but controversial roles played by their predecessors, Marion Fairweather and James M. Douglas.

The special friendships that developed among some women missionaries sustained them through times of difficulty. Margaret Coltart, shown here, became Dr Belle Choné Oliver's closest friend after nursing her through a serious illness in 1916 and was with her when she died in 1947.

Mrs Johory, the superintendent for many years of the widows' industrial home in Indore, was one of the few Indian women workers whose name was well known to missions supporters in Canada.

A group of Central India missionaries, *c.* 1890. Margaret Rodger, who with
Marion Fairweather went to India in 1873, some four years before the Central
India mission was formally established, is shown, seated, in the centre of
the photograph.

A group of Central India missionaries, *c.* 1900

Dr Maggie O'Hara with a group of workers in Dhar

The mission boarding school for girls, Indore, completed in 1891

The staff of the Indore girls' high school. This photograph was probably taken in the decade after 1914.

The mission hospital for women, Indore, completed in 1891

Missionary types: *back row* Miss Maggie Jamieson, Miss Jessie Weir, Mrs Emily Thompson; *front row* Reverend W.J. Jamieson (brother of Maggie), his wife, Winnifred, and infant daughter, Dr J.J. Thompson (husband of Emily). Infants and children – 'young missionaries' – attracted friendly attention to the missionary cause and were occasionally taken along on itinerating tours.

Outdoor medical work in Central India: Dr Belle Choné Oliver and an assistant distributing medicines from the back of a wagon

NEW WOMEN FOR GOD

Introduction

In 1893, acting on her father's advice, a young philatelist in St Andrew's, New Brunswick, appealed to the secretary of the Presbyterian Church's Foreign Missions Committee for help in enlarging her stamp collection. The following year a more poignant request reached the same secretary's desk when a Gamebridge, Ontario, woman wrote to ask for assistance in locating her son, missing somewhere in the Far East and last heard from some eight years earlier. During the same decade a patent medicine company was using testimonials from a missionary wife to advertise the helpful properties of its sarsaparilla tonic. If its product could revitalize an ailing woman even in an enervating tropical climate, the copy-writer reasoned, it could surely do wonders for the average North American housewife. In 1912 the liner *Empress of China* went to the bottom of the Pacific, taking with it the complete outfit of some newly appointed Canadian missionaries. After some hesitation, the T. Eaton Company – suppliers of the goods – agreed to reimburse the missionaries for their losses. It was a somewhat unusual case in which to apply its famous guarantee of goods satisfactory or money refunded, but the company had evidently concluded that the expense would be worthwhile if it would ensure the continuance of its missionary trade.[1]

As these anecdotes suggest, foreign missions occupied a prominent place in the consciousness of Canadians of the late-Victorian and Edwardian eras. In the period before overseas embassies and modern mass media had become a part of national life, the foreign missions movement served as the pre-eminent vehicle for Canadians' contact with a distant and exotic world. A uniquely authoritative source of information and opinion about life in non-Christian lands and a congenial object for philanthropic zeal, it was also, for hundreds of young men and women, something considerably more: a siren call to a vocation and to a larger life than any they could contemplate in Canada.

The great era in modern foreign missions began in England in the 1790s and reached a symbolic if not an absolute end with the outbreak of the First World War. It was dominated by Anglo-Saxons and drew much of its vitality from evangelical Protestant churches newly awakened to a sense of missionary responsibility.[2] In Canada, the era came later, in the last quarter of the nineteenth century, and its heyday did not extend much beyond that of the movement generally. Yet during these years the foreign mission enterprise came to be a phenomenon of intense importance in the nation's religious and intellectual life. Because of its association with the nationalist/ imperialist impulse that animated parts of English-Protestant Canada, the missionary movement took on a particular significance. Some of the country's most respected figures advanced the view that the national spirit would reach its highest development only as Canadians recognized that it was their duty as well as their right to participate in the work of Empire. A sense of shared responsibility with Britain for the uplift of 'the lesser breeds' was the key element in their imperialist vision, and participation in foreign missions was seen to be one of the most vital and concrete ways of giving that vision expression.

Fired by this imperialist ethos, and in even more direct and specific ways by the example and inspiration of missions-minded Americans, Protestant Canadians became deeply involved in the foreign missionary movement. At home, wealthy and well-known businessmen joined thousands of more ordinary Canadians in devoting time and money to the cause. Abroad, the movement took participants to Asia, Africa, Latin America, and islands in the Pacific, to mission stations that in many cases were well beyond the flag of Empire. In proportion to their country's population, Canadian missionaries came to outnumber their British and American counterparts in many zones of missionary activity and to constitute, in peacetime, the largest organized contingents of Canadians living abroad.[3] As the movement developed, hundreds of thousands of dollars flowed out of Canada each year in support of missionary activities. In return, missionaries and missionary literature broadened the horizons of ordinary Canadians, providing them with the materials for a world view whose optimism and idealism would for long mask its less attractive aspects.

From the first, Canadian Protestant women played a leading role in promoting the foreign missions cause at home and in bearing its responsibilities abroad. Their early and intense involvement was consistent with the prevailing view that matters of religious and moral responsibility were ones for which women had a special affinity. Moreover, by the time their churches had decided to become full-scale participants in the foreign missionary enterprise, Canadian churchwomen were already familiar with the models of involvement established by their counterparts in Britain and the United States and with a rationale which maintained that, because of the tradition of secluding women in Eastern countries, only other women would be able to bring them the gospel. As the social service component of overseas evangelism expanded in the last decades of the nineteenth century, the need for, and the logic of, women's participation increased. Finally, at a time when changing household labour patterns and access to higher education were preparing significant numbers of Canadian women for a larger way of life, the movement provided middle-class homemakers with socially sanctioned opportunities for extra-domestic activity and leadership; while to their unmarried sisters it offered respected and challenging careers abroad and an escape from the stigma that spinsterhood often carried in their own communities. When their own opportunity to participate in the foreign missions enterprise arose, then, Canadian women were eager to respond.

/ Well before the turn of the century, single women missionaries and missionary wives outnumbered their male colleagues in many overseas fields; in some fields, single women alone outnumbered male workers. Within Canada, denominational missionary societies to promote the evangelization of non-Christian women and children became the first regional and national women's organizations, and even by the time of the First World War they remained by far the largest of such organizations. In 1916 journalist Marjory MacMurchy put the collective membership of women's missionary societies at 'not under 200,000.' By contrast, a year earlier the Woman's Christian Temperance Union had had some 10,000 members. The fund-raising and publishing endeavours of the missionary societies were attended by similar successes, with one denominational group alone recording an annual income of more than $100,000 on the eve of the First World War and publishing a periodical, *Foreign Missionary Tidings,* whose circulation rivalled that of the popular weekly *Saturday Night.*[4] Taken together, these data suggest that the foreign missionary movement had a significant impact on the lives of Canadian Protestant women of the late nineteenth and early twentieth centuries. This book investigates that impact by focusing on the women of Canadian Presbyterianism, the denomination that had become, by 1911, the largest in Protestant Canada.[5]

Their dour image notwithstanding, Presbyterians fell early victims to the romantic appeal of missions and eventually opened work in more overseas fields than any other Canadian Protestant body. The process began in the 1840s when Maritimers John and Charlotte Geddie sailed for the distant New Hebrides, but it was not until after church union in 1875 that the denomination was able to organize effectively for its 'great age' of missions. By that date, several Presbyterian women had already gone abroad to serve under Scottish or American societies, and in a few communities small groups of churchwomen had been gathering for years to pray and sew for 'the heathen.' Taking their cue from their American counterparts, male church leaders resolved to harness this enthusiasm by fostering the creation of women's organizations to finance and publicize women's work for women and children. Three regional organizations resulted. The Toronto-based Woman's Foreign Missionary Society, Western Division – the WFMS – was the first and by far the largest. By 1914 the WFMS had sponsored the great majority of the more than one hundred single women who had served their church in mission fields in mainland China, Formosa, India, Korea, and Trinidad.

Chapter 1 of this study establishes a context for Canadian women's involvement in foreign missions by providing an overview of precedent-setting missionary activity in Britain and the United States. It is followed by an account of the organizational evolution of the WFMS from its establishment in 1876 to its disappearance as a distinct society in 1914 as a result of the rationalization of women's home and foreign missionary work. Subsequent chapters deal with the missionaries themselves. The Presbyterian Church for long classified Canadian Indian missions and missions to non-Anglo-Saxon immigrants under the rubric of foreign missions, but in fact domestic activity was conducted and staffed quite differently from overseas work. This book deals only with women who were truly *foreign* missionaries. Chapter 3 considers aspects of their background and motivation. Chapters 4 through 6 focus on the missionaries who served in the princely states of Central India, much of which today forms part of the state of Madhya Pradesh.

Central India was the first field in which the WFMS sponsored personnel, and even after the turn of the century when China overtook India as the primary object of Presbyterians' missionary zeal, it retained pride of place so far as women's work was concerned. Two features in particular characterized the women missionaries' experience there: an early and continuing emphasis on institutional and social service work rather than on direct evangelism, and the emergence of a pattern of acrimonious mission politics in which gender was the central issue. Political tensions persisted until after the turn of the century, resulting in the dismissal of three particularly assertive women workers. Yet neither this feature of mission life nor the paucity of conversions destroyed the missionaries' enthusiasm for their vocation, for as Chapter 6 explains, there were compensations in the life these women had chosen that were richly rewarding and that made up for the loss of their early illusions about the romance of missions. The final chapter provides an assessment of the significance of the foreign missionary movement for the women who were participants in it and relates their experience to the woman's movement in turn-of-the-century Canada.

A vigorous free trade in religious ideas and activities took place across the Canada – United States border during the nineteenth century. Given that fact, the large body of literature on the history of women and religion that has been published in the latter country since the late 1960s has been particularly useful for this work. Some writers on the subject have emphasized the restrictive and pernicious aspects of women's involvement in mainstream religion, Ann Douglas perhaps most strikingly in *The Feminization of American Culture*. More typically, they have been interested in exploring those aspects of religious ideology and activity that American women were able to use to enlarge their own lives. In religious institutions, sexism was given divine sanction. Even so, historians such as Nancy Cott have maintained, there were abundant opportunities within them for women to find fulfilment.[6]

A specific concern with missions was relatively late in developing within this literature. Writing in 1974, feminist theologian Alice Hageman observed that missions and missionaries remained an unfashionable subject despite their importance in the history of women in American Protestantism. The reason for avoidance of the topic was not hard to find. The woman's missionary movement with its close ties to conservative denominational structures and its imperialist and racist assumptions appeared to have little to offer historians with an interest in finding congenial role models and a usable past. Fortunately, in the years after Hageman made her comment on the unfashionableness of missions as an area for study, scholarship on women and religion in the United States gained in confidence and maturity, and as that happened the woman's foreign missionary movement came to be seen as too important a topic to be neglected.[7]

Jane Hunter's *The Gospel of Gentility: American Women Missionaries in Turn-of-the-Century China* and Patricia R. Hill's *The World Their Household: The American Woman's Foreign Mission Movement and Cultural Transformation, 1870–1920* are two recent, and complementary, works on the subject that have already become important. Probing behind the rhetoric of self-sacrifice and self-effacement employed by the China missionaries, Hunter discovered that they enjoyed a remarkable degree of authority and influence through their dealings with a subject people. Indeed, she argued, so intoxicated were they by this 'more rewarding authority' that they were not greatly disturbed by their unequal relations with their male colleagues. Focusing on the home base rather than a foreign field, Hill explored what women's foreign missionary societies meant to the thousands of small-town and rural women whose lives they vicariously enlarged and to the handful of bureaucrats who directed mission affairs from regional and national headquarters. She concluded that as the latter group fell under the influence of trends towards professionalization and secularization at work in the larger society, they implemented changes that alienated their constituency and ultimately sapped the movement of its vitality.[8] In the chapters that follow it will become clear that Canadian Presbyterian women's experiences echoed some of these patterns while differing from them in significant ways.

In Britain, work on women and religion generally and on women and missions in particular lags behind that in the United States.[9] The same is true in English-speaking Canada. There is no published monograph on Canadian women's involvement in either home or foreign missions and little in the way of readily accessible article literature. An introductory essay on women's missionary societies written by Wendy Mitchinson more than a decade ago has not so far been followed by the publication of any detailed investigations of women's experience in these societies. Some historians have noted, with Mitchinson, that missionary societies took a cautious position on suffrage and other reform causes, but they have not been curious about the reasons for that caution or paid much attention to its significance.[10] As for overseas personnel, it has largely been a question of 'out of sight, out of mind': they have, until recently, all but escaped historians' notice.[11]

This book attempts to bring the Canadian woman's foreign missionary movement back into our consciousness. It is based on the assumption that an enterprise that commanded the allegiance of unprecedentedly large numbers of volunteer women at home and that offered to its full-time participants a unique range of challenges abroad is intrinsically worthy of study. In common with the American literature, this study assumes that women participated in foreign missionary work – and in other religious activities – for reasons that went beyond faith and altruism. At the same time, it argues that those aspects were important both in helping to inspire their involvement and in reconciling them to a limited sphere. At the home base and overseas, women encountered in the foreign missionary movement a paradoxical pattern of opportunities and constraints even as they brought to it their own competing desires: for autonomy and personal fulfilment on the one hand, for assurance of divine approbation and social acceptance on the other. A knowledge of their experience can add to our understanding of woman's place in Victorian and Edwardian Canada.

1

Precedents

In the nineteenth century, the North Atlantic triangle had an important religious dimension. British, American, and Canadian Protestants faced similar spiritual challenges, came together in periodic conferences, and co-operated in ongoing religious organizations. The pattern of trans-Atlantic interchange was particularly evident in the foreign missionary movement. While Britain was initially the leader in the movement by virtue of its early involvement, the United States moved, in the course of the century, towards a position of dominance in several spheres of missionary activity.[1] Given that fact, and the logic of geography, it was probably inevitable that as Canadian Presbyterians became full-scale participants in the foreign missionary enterprise in the last quarter of the century, they would draw most heavily on the American model, notwithstanding their denomination's historic links with Scotland and the continuing importance of sentimental religious attachments to that country.

This set of relationships provided the context within which Canadian Presbyterian women became involved in foreign missions. Well before male church leaders formally sought their participation in the enterprise in 1875, many Presbyterian churchwomen had become familiar with the British and American missionary literature that explained the rationale for 'woman's work for woman' and celebrated the movement's most beloved heroines. A few had entered into correspondence with women in Scottish missionary societies and had undertaken to support their activities. When the time came for the creation of their own large missionary organizations, however, and for actual overseas involvement, the patterns established by their counterparts in the United States were generally the ones they adopted.

ౢౢౢౢౢౢ

The missionary movement's best-known historian, Kenneth Scott Latourette, referred to the nineteenth century as 'the Great Century' of
Christian missions. The era of modern, or European, missions had effectively begun with Portuguese Roman Catholic activity in India in the 1500s.
It was followed during the next three centuries by further Roman Catholic,
and Protestant, initiatives, many of them associated with trade or coloniza-
tion in lands occupied by 'primitive' peoples. Notwithstanding the efforts of
such diverse groups as Spanish Franciscans, French Jesuits, New England
Puritans, and chaplains of the Dutch East Indies Company, secular goals
and the spiritual needs of transplanted Europeans predominated, and
missions to the native peoples for long remained more striking for their
drama than for their size or successes. Yet as the end of the eighteenth
century approached, a new missionary zeal possessed Europeans, and
British Protestants in particular. Despite past setbacks, they now resolved
to carry the gospel not just to indigenous peoples but to all non-Christians,
including those whose religious beliefs were ancient, complex, and
sophisticated.[2]

The person generally regarded as the pioneer in this new era of missions
was the Englishman William Carey. A village shoemaker turned Baptist
preacher, Carey in 1793 began the journey that would culminate in his
lifelong mission to India and in the formation in Britain of both denominational and interdenominational missionary societies.[3] That British trading
companies and many government officials responded to such activity with
outright hostility did not deter those committed to it. Rather, it made them
inspired lobbyists who worked vigorously to win government sanction and
support for their cause. The evangelical Clapham Sect, and particularly
such notable individual members as Charles Grant and William Wilber-
force, won an important concession when Parliament in 1813 forced the
East India Company to allow missionary activity in its territories. And in
the 1830s utilitarian and evangelical strands of thought came together in a
new social liberalism that successfully opened India to a variety of Western
reform efforts.[4] The other significant change in this period involved missionary personnel. In the decades following Carey's departure, English
missionaries had tended to be eager but not very well-educated members
of the working-class elite. By mid-century, however, the participation of
members of higher social strata was becoming more common, and English
societies were emulating their Scottish counterparts by sending out workers

with a high level of education. At this stage, as missions historian Max Warren has observed, 'Missions had become respectable.'[5]

The first missionary societies in the United States had been chiefly concerned with carrying the gospel to North American Indians and to settlers on the frontier. By 1800, however, the overseas activities of British evangelicals had caught the imagination of American Protestants. During the first decade of the nineteenth century, a group of 'awakened' Congregational theological students in New England decided to participate directly in foreign missions. The result was the formation in 1810 of the American Board of Commissioners for Foreign Missions (ABCFM) and the subsequent departure of a missionary party to India. For some years, Presbyterian and Dutch Reformed churches joined Congregationalists in conducting their foreign missionary activities through the ABCFM. But by the time of the Civil War, these and other denominations had developed their own missionary organizations and were funding their own personnel. A period of disruption and stagnation in the movement, caused in part by the Civil War, was followed by an unprecedented burst of missionary activity. For approximately four decades after 1880 – the decades of high imperialism – foreign missions occupied a prominent place on the national agenda as well as within the churches. An ecumenical missionary conference in New York in 1900 attracted more than 170,000 people, among them President McKinley, who opened the conference, and former President Harrison, who presided over several sessions.[6]

Historians have looked to a number of factors to account for the Great Century. In his *History of Christian Missions,* Stephen Neill stressed the importance of the British evangelical revival in creating the climate that gave rise to the nineteenth-century zeal for missionary endeavour. In North America, and later in Britain, scholars agree, that zeal was given a powerful impetus in the early 1800s by the Second Great Awakening and the millennial expectations associated with it. As tens of thousands of Protestant men and women discovered a new immediacy in their faith, Jesus' last commandment – to preach the gospel to all the world – came to be seen as a real and urgent Christian responsibility, one whose neglect meant certain perdition for countless millions of unreached souls.[7] The highly publicized missionary adventures of David Livingstone around mid-century and the revivals conducted in Britain and North America in the 1870s and 1880s by the American lay evangelist Dwight L. Moody gave fresh life and excitement to the movement. The millennial concerns that preoccupied many conservatives were an important part of Moody's message. Yet his was a broad and eclectic theology, appealing to Christians of all types. His support for missions attracted theological liberals as well as conservatives, and members of social and intellectual elites as well as men and women whose backgrounds more closely resembled his own. His appeal to upper-class Christians was most graphically demonstrated in the 1880s when, in the wake of his tour of Oxford and Cambridge universities, seven young men from the latter institution – the celebrated 'Cambridge Seven' – responded positively to his call for foreign mission volunteers and thereby inspired numerous other college students on both sides of the Atlantic.[8]

The same decade saw the organization of the Student Volunteer Movement for Foreign Missions (SVM) with its ambitious and controversial pledge, 'the evangelization of the world in this generation.' The remarkable power of the SVM, in one missions historian's view, lay in its ability to combine '[a] highly individualized and personalized sense of missionary obligation or duty ... with the conviction that God in his providence had now prepared all things for success.'[9] Beyond this, however, in the SVM and in the foreign mission movement generally, millennial concerns were being joined near the end of the century by humanitarian impulses and a more liberal theology: by a desire to express Christian love as well as duty, to make missions the vehicle for ameliorative social reforms, and to have Christianity go before the world as 'a way of living rather than a dogma.'[10] In the United States, these liberal and conservative strands in Protestant evangelicalism would eventually unravel into sharply polarized factions. But in the early decades of the twentieth century, as Robert Handy has noted, 'all but the extremists' continued to work together for such causes as foreign missions, and leading missionary bureaucrats, such as the Presbyterian Robert E. Speer and the Methodist John R. Mott, were able, despite doctrinal differences, to co-operate in the interest of their common endeavour.[11]

ે∾ ે∾ ે∾

The evolution of missionary patterns and motivation in the nineteenth century was accompanied and affected by another change, one that missions historians have been slower to document: the emergence of women as active participants in the movement and their eventual numerical dominance.[12] The feminization of the foreign missionary enterprise constituted the most remarkable element in a nineteenth-century break with a Reformation tradition that had given Protestant women little share in the life and work of the church. Even before the end of the century, the most striking outcomes of the feminization process would become apparent: in the tradition-bound societies of the East, female missionaries would be among the most effective agents of what would later be called cultural imperialism, while with the women who supported them at the home base in many sending countries, they would effectively undermine Pauline injunctions on women's role in the church.

Such developments could not have been anticipated at the beginning of the 1800s, for Anglo-Saxon women at first took little direct part in foreign missionary activity. With few exceptions, the only women who went to mission fields were those who did so as spouses. They were, to use Stephen Neill's distinction, missionaries' wives rather than missionary wives, and the outcomes of their involuntary involvement were sometimes tragic. Thus, William Carey's first wife, Dorothy, impoverished, illiterate, and expecting her fourth child, accompanied her husband to India in 1793 only in response to prolonged pressure. Soon after her arrival she became insane, and while her husband taught, translated, and preached the gospel, she remained shut away until her death in 1807. Some decades later, in Africa, Mary Moffatt Livingstone, the wife of David Livingstone, showed a similar lack of enthusiasm for the missionary cause. When she became ill following the death of a new-born infant, Livingstone packed her and their remaining children off to England in order to be free to explore the continent unencumbered. Not long after rejoining him several years later, she too died under tragic circumstances.[13]

Well before Mary Livingstone's death, however, a new pattern had emerged. As foreign missions came to occupy a prominent place in evangelical Protestant agendas, missions-minded women sought husbands who would take them to heathen lands, and male missionaries sought helpmates who would support them in their work.[14] In the course of the nineteenth century, hundreds of missionary wives became actively and willingly involved in the cause, and, as a different pattern became acceptable, hundreds of single women made missions their full-time, lifelong career. Meanwhile, at home, far greater numbers of women became involved in a volunteer capacity on behalf of the cause.

British women were the first to serve in foreign fields, both as missionary wives and as unmarried career missionaries, and the first to establish their own organizations for sponsoring female personnel. Their initiatives served as important models for an early generation of female missionary enthusiasts in the United States. By the last decades of the nineteenth century, however, American women had outgrown and overtaken their British mentors. They had become involved in the movement in significantly larger numbers, and they had greatly expanded the meaning and scope of women's missionary work.[15] Their zeal and prominence were logical outcomes of a pattern of religious volunteerism that had begun almost a century earlier.

ટ૭ ટ૭ ટ૭

In 1817 the General Assembly of the Presbyterian Church in the U.S.A. declared: 'It is among the distinguished glories of the commencement of the nineteenth century, that PIOUS FEMALES are more extensively associated and more actively useful in promoting evangelical and benevolent objects, than in any former period of the world.'[16] Protestant ministers in the United States had long been accustomed to presiding over congregations in which women predominated, but as this statement makes clear, the existence of women's religiously oriented volunteer organizations was a relatively new – and evidently welcome – phenomenon. The earliest such associations were often interdenominational in character. Boston women set important precedents with the Boston Female Society for Missionary Purposes and the Boston Female Asylum for orphan girls, both organized in 1800. Following another Boston precedent, local 'cent societies' for missionary fund raising came into existence, as did prayer societies, 'educational' societies to provide funds and clothing for needy seminarians, Bible and tract societies, and various organizations for meeting the spiritual and physical needs of the urban poor. Women also became involved in the new activity of Sunday school teaching and, more controversially, in work to rescue and rehabilitate prostitutes. The extent and intensity of their involvement in religious affairs led visiting author and feminist Harriet Martineau to observe in the 1830s that, with American women, religion seemed to serve as a kind of occupation. It was an assessment with which future historians of the period would find ample room for agreement.[17]

Missionary work was, from the first, a central focus in women's organized religious activity. Women met to give, sew, and pray for the cause. A century or more later when they came to write the history of their organizations, various societies would refer to ministers who had opposed these early gatherings on the grounds that there was 'no telling' what women might pray for if left to themselves. In reality, however, despite some cases of reluctance and opposition, clerical support and approval for local associations of missions-minded women seem to have been widespread, for as officers of the ABCFM put it in their fourth annual report, women could take a 'lively interest [in missions] without overstepping the limits which a sense of propriety had imposed on female exertion.' Their gatherings, moreover, remained largely local in scope, while the money they raised was usually spent by the all-male 'general' mission boards to which they were subordinate.[18]

Though it was in work among North American Indians that American women first functioned in missionary roles, and under conditions that were often as hazardous as those across the oceans, these exploits failed to arouse the interest of local churchwomen in the way that foreign work did. Especially after the ABCFM had dispatched its first missionaries to India in 1812, overseas missions captured the imagination and won the support of American women at all levels. The first bequest to the ABCFM reportedly came from a domestic servant who left $345.83 to the cause; the first large legacy – $30,000.00 – also came from a woman.[19]

Overseas missionary wives played a vital role in sustaining the interest of such women and giving it a focus. They 'vicariously represented the women at home,' R. Pierce Beaver has written, 'working out in practice their concern for the salvation of mankind and especially their heartfelt burden of responsibility for the liberation of women in Eastern lands and primitive societies.'[20] While missionary wives' primary duty was to sustain their husbands physically and emotionally and create in foreign lands an example of Christian family life that would serve as a model for the 'heathen,' they were also expected to follow the emerging British example and take an active part in the work, to the extent that their personal circumstances permitted. A farewell sermon preached to two of the departing missionary wives in 1812 thus advised:

It will be your business, my dear children, to teach these women, to whom your husbands can have but little, or no access. Go, then, and do all in your power, to enlighten their minds, and bring them to the knowledge of the truth. Go, and if possible, raise their character to the dignity of rational beings, and to the rank of christians in a christian land.[21]

The justification for sanctioning women's direct involvement in missionary work, as this statement indicates, was the belief that in Eastern societies women were generally denied contact with all males save those of their own immediate family. If they were to hear the gospel, therefore, it would have to be from members of their own sex.

From the first years of their involvement, women such as Ann Judson, first of the three wives of Baptist pioneer Adoniram Judson, wrote numerous letters back to the United States describing their lives and work. These were published in missionary journals, and with the additional publicity generated by eulogistic biographies, songs, and poems, they made their authors celebrated figures in the United States and beyond. Like their counterparts from other countries, American missionary wives were not officially recognized by sending agencies as full-fledged missionaries. But in contrast to the situation that apparently prevailed in Britain, they became, in R. Pierce Beaver's words, 'personalities in their own right,' the examples of their lives held before the young as models for inspiration and emulation. Even those who died without actually having done any missionary work, like the celebrated nineteen-year-old bride Harriet Newell, who succumbed en route to her field, were regarded as having made a significant contribution to the cause. Indeed, they ranked among the movement's most beloved martyrs.[22]

It was because the work of teaching women and children and visiting them in their homes was greater than could be overtaken by missionary wives with family duties that a rationale was reluctantly developed by sending agencies in the half century before the Civil War for employing unmarried missionary women. In 1825 a well-known Presbyterian minister, Dr Ashbel Green of Princeton Seminary, had suggested that single women could usefully serve abroad if properly supervised and directed by men. A British precedent had already been set by the time Miss Cynthia Farrar was appointed by the ABCFM two years later as the first unmarried American woman to be sent overseas in the capacity of assistant missionary. In 1860, when it celebrated its semi-centennial, the ABCFM – still the largest of the American foreign mission agencies – had sent some thirty unmarried women abroad.[23] Calls from the field; propaganda by furlough missionaries; the influence of hagiographic biographies; and the fervent support given the cause by Mount Holyoke Female Seminary, the so-called Protestant nunnery founded by Mary Lyon in 1837, had all played a part in arousing women to the possibility of a missionary vocation. Yet as the second half-century began, the number of single women involved in missions remained relatively small. When Rufus Anderson resigned in 1866 after forty-three years as the highly respected foreign secretary of the ABCFM, he was still uninclined to encourage single women to enter foreign missions, believing that the disadvantages in such a course outweighed the benefits.[24] Other sending agencies remained similarly reluctant to dispatch single women or allow them independence of action on the field.

While Anderson's successor was to take a more positive attitude towards the role of single women in foreign missions, it was the large-scale organizing of regional and national women's mission boards that led, in the last third of the century, to the enormous increase in the number of career women missionaries in foreign fields and in the amount of money being expended on their work. The denominations' male-controlled general missionary societies had for years resisted the formation of such boards, so that the only one in existence prior to the Civil War was the Woman's Union Missionary Society, organized on an interdenominational basis in 1861 by a ubiquitous New York philanthropist, Mrs T.C. Doremus. In the decade after the war, however, regional or national women's societies were formed in rapid succession in all the major Protestant churches to sponsor women's foreign missionary work among women and children. Returned missionary wives or missionary aspirants were often active in organizing the new societies. A few, like the Woman's Foreign Missionary Society of the Methodist Episcopal Church (North), operated independently of their churches' general mission boards. Others, despite the power they eventually came to wield, were constituted as auxiliaries. This was the case in the largest Presbyterian denomination, the Presbyterian Church in the U.S.A., where seven regional women's foreign mission boards came into existence, beginning with the Woman's Foreign Missionary Society of the Presbyterian Church of Philadelphia in 1870.[25] Looking back on the flurry of organizing activity that took place during this period, one clerical supporter of missions wrote in 1890: 'Within less than a decade [there] occurred the most extensive and rapid organization of the religious activities of Christian women that ecclesiastical history records.' Another missions enthusiast and participant would later refer to the 1870s as the 'Church Woman's Decade.'[26]

What accounted for the sudden acceleration of women's missionary activity? Increased leisure time, higher education, access to the teaching profession, participation in the abolition movement, familiarity with the British example – all these were cited by contemporaries or have since been identified by scholars as having played a causal role. But for many of those most directly involved, the crucial factor was seen to be the organizational and administrative experience that American women had gained during the course of the Civil War. One participant in the Woman's Congress of Missions at the Chicago World's Fair, for instance, spoke of the war as 'a training school' that had 'providentially' prepared women for missionary work. Helen Barrett Montgomery, a leading home-base activist in the latter part of the period, referred to the Civil War experience as 'a baptism of power' for American women.[27]

Modern historians of the missionary movement agree that the Civil War played a pivotal role by giving women a taste for the satisfactions that came with 'a larger sphere of usefulness' and by inspiring them with the confidence to undertake complex ventures for the evangelization of their sex.[28] It seems unlikely, however, that such large-scale women's denominational organizations could have developed if church leaders, and especially those on the general mission boards, had maintained their former opposition. The smaller memberships and more limited agendas of the women's foreign missionary organizations that developed in the South, where male opposition was more deeply entrenched, lend support to this view.[29] By the 1870s, male leaders in northern Protestantism had generally come to recognize women's abilities as fund raisers and publicists for missions. Especially if they could be persuaded to form auxiliaries rather than independent organizations, to confine their overseas work to women and children, and to refrain from drawing funds away from the general mission boards, women's missionary enthusiasm could safely and usefully be encouraged.

It was this view that led the General Assembly of the Presbyterian Church in the U.S.A. in 1874 to urge its ministers to encourage the formation of women's missionary circles in their congregations. Aware of the utility of women's involvement, the church's home missions administrators sought, in the course of the same decade, to channel some of their enthusiasm into a national women's organization for home missions. The move brought men and women of the home and foreign missions constituencies into open and sometimes bitter conflict, but it also testified to the value that missions-minded leaders in one conservative denomination had come to place on women's participation.[30]

As a result of the proliferation of regional and national women's mission boards in the years after the Civil War, hundreds of thousands of American women from all levels of society were drawn into the foreign missionary movement. Monthly periodicals, published by all the major women's boards, sustained members' ardour and kept them informed about the need for and the efficacy of women's work for women. Their enthusiastic givings permitted a rapid increase in overseas personnel. By 1880, missionary wives and unmarried women workers already outnumbered their male colleagues in the fields. This numerical growth was accompanied by a dramatic increase in the scope of women's work. Besides following their British counterparts into house-to-house evangelization and elementary school teaching, American women missionaries pioneered and remained leaders in providing higher female education and medical mission services.[31] They also became involved in itinerant evangelism, orphanage and relief work, industrial training, the publication of instructional materials, the teaching and examination of native Christian agents, the nurture of adult female converts, and a wide range of other activities. Their methods were eclectic and their goals ambitious. With their sisters in the home churches they had set themselves to the task of redemptive social house-keeping on a worldwide scale.[32]

ક્ર ક્ર ક્ર

American women's participation in the foreign missionary movement had a significant impact on the religious and cultural life of their own country and on social transformations in the non-European world. It also had an important influence on parallel developments in Canada. By the time that Methodists, Presbyterians, and Anglicans, the three largest Canadian Protestant denominations, became formally committed to overseas missionary activity in the 1870s and 1880s, they were already familiar with the specific patterns for women's involvement established by their American co-religionists. They were equally conversant with the rationales that justified such involvement and established its limits. Making such adaptations as were necessary to meet their own circumstances and traditions, they unhesitatingly drew on these precedents. The constitutions and practices of the women's missionary societies established by their denominational counterparts in the United States became important models for Canadian Protestants' own women's work.[33]

2

Home-base bureaucrats

Although I had received gracious permission to be present, it was with no small degree of trepidation that I took a somewhat retired seat among the ladies who had come from all parts of the Province and who filled the spacious St. James Square Church last week on the occasion of the[ir] annual parliament on Foreign Missions ... In all honesty it must be said that the spectacle was an impressive one. These ladies were not of the Mrs. Jellaby [*sic*] type.

Roy Malcolm, reporting in *The Presbyterian,* 14 May 1904

'These ladies' were the women who had attended the recently concluded twenty-eighth annual meeting of the WFMS – the Woman's Foreign Missionary Society, Western Division, of the Presbyterian Church in Canada. Mrs Jellyby was an unkempt Englishwoman whose far-fetched schemes for the transportation of the London poor and the conversion of the natives of Borriobola-gha had resulted in the neglect of her children and the emasculation of Mr Jellyby. A character in Charles Dickens's *Bleak House,* she was a familiar stereotype even to those who had not read the novel.

The men who comprised the Foreign Missions Committee, Western Division (FMC), of the newly created Presbyterian Church in Canada had obviously been confident that they would not be calling such a monster into existence when at their first meeting following union in 1875 they had authorized convenor William McLaren to investigate the possibility of establishing a woman's foreign missionary society such as already existed in several branches of American Presbyterianism.[1] The FMC members' confidence proved to be well founded. The organization that resulted from their motion eschewed grandiose schemes and remained in a strictly auxiliary relationship to the committee that had called it into being. And yet, over the years, the WFMS came to exercise a degree of influence that belied its purportedly modest goals and subordinate status. Accepting, and even exploiting, their lack of formal authority, the women who managed the WFMS were able to make it a significant force in the church's foreign missionary endeavours and an enriching factor in their own lives. It was only towards the end of the period, when they attempted to resist pressures for an alteration in the society's mandate, that they experienced an unequivocal defeat. Their experience demonstrated the possibilities for female empowerment in a mainstream religious institution, and the limitations.

ॐ॰ ॐ॰ ॐ॰

Unlike Methodists and Anglicans, Canadian Presbyterians began their missionary work overseas and only later turned their attention to their own country. Since foreign work was begun from the Maritime colonies and largely reflected individual initiatives or associations with Scottish missionary societies, the pattern is not as surprising as it might otherwise seem. Overseas involvement started in 1846 when the small Secession Synod of Nova Scotia decided to accept as a foreign missionary a young minister named John Geddie, who had repeatedly offered himself for such service. Geddie and his wife, Charlotte, were sent to the island of Aneityum in the New Hebrides. Their mission took root and prospered, but a second, established in 1857 on neighbouring Erromanga by George Gordon of Prince Edward Island and his English-born wife, ended with their murder by hostile inhabitants. A similar fate overtook James Gordon in 1872 when he attempted to revive his brother's mission. Meanwhile, in 1868, John Morton of Nova Scotia had established a mission among Trinidad's East Indian population, while in the same year another Nova Scotian, Charles M. Grant, had begun work in Madras, India, under the auspices of a Scottish missionary society. Six years later he was joined by Phillipina Johns, a missionary sponsored by St Matthew's Church, Halifax, where Charles Grant's brother, George Monro Grant, was then the minister. A former Halifax school principal, Miss Johns conducted evangelistic and orphanage work only briefly before a fatal illness drove her home.[2]

The awakening of Presbyterians in the Canadas to their foreign missionary responsibilities owed much to the 1854 visit of Alexander Duff, a Scottish missionary who had won international renown for his effective use of English-medium higher education as a tool for gaining access to cultured Bengali families. Though Duff's efforts to have Canadians establish their own permanent mission in India proved unsuccessful in the short run, he effectively conveyed his vision of the British Empire as God's means for Christianizing India. In the wake of his visit, missionary givings rose dramatically, and the Free Church, the largest Presbyterian body, established its own committee on foreign missions. For its part, the continuing Church of Scotland contributed Sunday school funds to the parent church's Indian Orphanage and Juvenile Mission Scheme, an effort nurtured and sustained largely through the efforts of a young Kingston writer, Agnes Maule Machar.[3] Despite these indications of interest, almost twenty years were to pass before Presbyterians in Canada's central provinces sent their own missionaries abroad, and then China rather than India was to be the first recipient country. In 1872, acting largely on his own initiative, a young minister named George Leslie Mackay established a mission in North Formosa for the Canada Presbyterian Church and thus began the colourful career that would for long make him the church's most celebrated missionary. A year later, two professionally trained schoolteachers, Marion Fairweather and Margaret Rodger, became the church's first women missionaries and its India pioneers. Employed and paid by their own church, they were directed to undertake service with an American Presbyterian agency in North India in order to acquire information and expertise that could later be used in an independent Canadian mission.[4]

The various branches of Canadian Presbyterianism had thus acquired significant overseas responsibilities by the time they united in 1875. At its First General Assembly, the Presbyterian Church in Canada resolved to maintain and expand these holdings, however distant their locations and however fragile the footholds. The Eastern Division of the Foreign Missions Committee, with headquarters in Halifax, would be responsible for the missionary activities initiated by Maritime Presbyterians in Trinidad and the New Hebrides, while, from Toronto, the much larger Foreign Missions Committee, Western Division, acting for Quebec, Ontario, and Manitoba, would develop work in China, India, and the Canadian Northwest. The decision was not universally popular. Some Presbyterians questioned the wisdom of accepting extensive foreign responsibilities at a time when home missions work and missions to the Indians posed major challenges in the new Dominion. Their views, however, were of little consequence, for by the last quarter of the century, as one missions historian has observed, participation in foreign missions had come to be seen as 'an identifying mark of mainstream American Protestantism,' and Canadian Presbyterianism's most influential leaders were loath to be left behind.[5]

A healthy flow of offers for overseas service would not begin until the late 1880s, but by 1877 deputations of foreign missions spokesmen were being sent to various congregations with a view to 'evoking increased liberality' in foreign missionary givings.[6] From Montreal, the editor of the *Presbyterian Record,* the church's official connexional organ, undertook to make missionary intelligence a staple element in the monthly's pages. Ephraim Scott, who succeeded James Croil as editor in 1892, vied with his counterparts on other Presbyterian journals for the freshest news from the missionary fronts, though since several of these publications were weeklies he was not infrequently scooped. Through the pages of the *Record* Presbyterians were admonished to study and discuss mission news, 'until the names of our missionaries and the stations they occupy become as familiar as household words,' and were warned that the health and vigour of their church depended on its commitment to the missionary cause.[7]

Not surprisingly, some of the denomination's leading laymen and ministers became involved in foreign missions committee work. During its early years the Foreign Missions Committee, Western Division, included such eminent Toronto laymen as John Harvie of the Northern Railway; educator and author Archibald MacMurchy; lawyer, businessman, and sometime mayor W.B. McMurrich; and another lawyer-businessman, William Mortimer Clark, who would later succeed Oliver Mowat as Lieutenant-Governor of Ontario. Prominent among clerical members over the years were the principals or leading professors from the church's colleges: Donald Mac-Vicar of Montreal, George Monro Grant and John B. Mowat of Queen's, William McLaren and Alfred Gandier of Knox, A.B. Baird and Thomas Hart of Manitoba. A core of members, including Grant and McLaren and Toronto lawyer Hamilton Cassels, demonstrated their interest by serving for decades on the committee. Grant and McLaren symbolized, respectively, the liberal and the conservative strands of clerical thought that were represented within it. From 1892, when the General Assembly belatedly acknowledged that the press of foreign missions business required a full-time secretary, the Reverend Robert Peter MacKay became the FMC's best-known figure and its authoritative voice for those overseas. Combining the denomination's liberal and conservative tendencies within his own complex personality, the widowed MacKay made foreign missions his passionate, lifelong interest, and until church union in 1925 played a key role in determining the course of his church's foreign missions policy.[8]

Over the years, the FMC would adopt various expedients to promote the cause of foreign missions, many of them based on American precedents or undertaken in co-operation with American agencies. Its support for the Student Volunteer Movement for Foreign Missions, the Young People's Missionary Movement, and the Laymen's Missionary Movement illustrated this pattern. But in terms of both immediate and long-range consequences, no step was more important for the church's foreign missionary enterprise than the FMC's 1875 decision to emulate its American Presbyterian counterparts by enlisting the support of women.

ફ⊌ ફ⊌ ફ⊌

In Protestant Canada, as John Webster Grant has observed, women 'have always been the chief instigators of enthusiasm for missions.'[9] Presbyterian women strongly exemplified this pattern. Well before the church officially encouraged them to organize in the 1870s, they had demonstrated the abundance of their missionary zeal. In Princetown, Prince Edward Island, in 1825, a group of women had expressed their concern about the unchurched regions of their colony by forming 'The Female Society for Propagating the Gospel and other religious purposes.' Later, as letters had begun to reach them from the Geddies in faraway Aneityum, the Islanders had joined other Maritime women in praying for the Geddies' work and in sewing garments 'to make the naked savages presentable for church or school.' In Montreal, in 1864, some Presbyterian women had formed the Ladies' Auxiliary Association to assist in the Church of Scotland's conversion work among French Canadians; some had also joined a local branch of the New York-based Woman's Union Missionary Society. During the same decade, a few prominent Ontario ministers' wives had begun to establish local groups of women to support the overseas work of a Scottish mission board.[10] Finally, as noted, three Presbyterian women had themselves undertaken missionary careers in India prior to church union. Yet as in other Canadian Protestant denominations, it was only following the creation of male-sanctioned, supra-local women's missionary organizations that home-base work on behalf of foreign missions could be undertaken and sustained on a large scale and that significant numbers of career women missionaries could be put in the field.

In 1876, the year that saw the first meeting of the WFMS in Toronto, a departing Maritime missionary, the Reverend J. Fraser Campbell, spearheaded the organization of a similar society in Halifax to function as an auxiliary to the Eastern Division Foreign Missions Committee. Six years later, the Montreal Ladies' Auxiliary Association formally broadened its mandate to include home and foreign missionary work as well as missions to French Canadians. By 1883, therefore, there were three major women's organizations within Canadian Presbyterianism engaged in foreign missions.[11] During the years that followed, the Maritime and Montreal societies would jealously guard their regional autonomy and the opportunities for leadership that such autonomy provided in the face of discreet efforts at empire building by their sister organization in Toronto. The Maritime women, in particular, would play a vigorous and disproportionately large role in their region's missionary efforts. But given the more limited Presbyterian populations on which they could draw, neither the Halifax-based society nor the one in Montreal could hope to keep pace with the growth and accomplishments of the WFMS.

ૐ ૐ ૐ

By the terms of its constitution, the WFMS undertook 'to aid the Foreign Missionary [sic] Committee ... by promoting its work among the women and children of heathen lands.' For the furtherance of this goal, auxiliaries were to be organized at the congregational and presbytery levels, supplemented, where possible, by mission bands of 'young ladies.' (Mission bands in which both girls and boys were enrolled would come later.) The society's headquarters were to be located in Toronto, as were its key personnel, who were to direct its business through a board of thirty-two (later thirty-six) managers, meeting monthly or oftener. A smaller executive committee, comprised of the society's officers and four other board members, was authorized to transact necessary business between regular meetings of the board. While delegates from the auxiliaries had an opportunity to vote on the proposed slate of officers and to respond to major policy questions on the occasion of the annual meeting, the centralized nature of WFMS decision making was made manifest from the beginning. One of the most important provisions in the society's constitution promoted this tendency by requiring that all money raised for foreign missions at the auxiliary level be sent to the board for dispersal. A clause allowing auxiliaries that had raised sufficient funds 'the privilege of designating a missionary whom they would wish to support' was quietly dropped in the 1880s. Meanwhile, societies that had organized independently in Hamilton and Kingston were encouraged to surrender their autonomy and become presbyterial auxiliaries of the WFMS.[12]

The direction of the WFMS by a small group of prominent Toronto women also reflected their close marital and family links with members of the FMC. Marjory McLaren, the wife of William McLaren, the FMC's first convenor, served as WFMS president from 1876 until 1881 and again from 1897 until 1899. Like her husband, she remained an influential figure in foreign missions policy making until her death near the end of the period. Her successor in the presidency in 1881, a widow, Catherine Ewart, was a sister-in-law of Ontario premier Oliver Mowat whose brother was an FMC member. Like their counterparts on the FMC, WFMS board and executive members frequently retained their positions for many years. When they died or resigned from office, their daughters or other close female relatives moved into, or upward through, the ranks of the hierarchy, thereby perpetuating a kind of family compact within the church's foreign missions bureaucracy. A daughter of Catherine Ewart, Mrs J. Emily Steele, became WFMS president in 1911, for instance; another daughter also served on the board. Marjory (Mrs Archibald) MacMurchy served on the executive from 1876 until her death in 1889, chiefly as recording secretary. Later, two of her daughters, Bessie and Helen MacMurchy, followed her into WFMS activism, the former holding a variety of executive positions and serving for many years.[13]

Their close personal connections with FMC members and with other prominent Presbyterian leaders ensured that the tone and tactics adopted by WFMS executives would be moderate. But even if no such links had existed, the history of the denomination would have pointed to a conservative approach, for in contrast to Methodism and Quakerism and some of the small Holiness sects, Presbyterianism had no readily usable tradition of female leadership in religious roles. Both Calvin and Knox had interpreted scripture in ways that stressed woman's subservience in the order of creation, and various church assemblies had reaffirmed Pauline injunctions against women's speaking or preaching in mixed assemblies.[14]

Given this context, Presbyterian women readily accepted their society's auxiliary status and the constraints placed on their organizational activities. The WFMS was to have special responsibility for funding and promoting the work of women missionaries, but it was to avoid all measures that would interfere with the church's 'larger' work for missions. The money that members gave to their organization was thus expected to be a 'special gift,' over and above the family's regular givings to missions. Moreover, the selection of women missionaries, their stationing, and the terms of their service were to be the responsibility of the FMC. In its *Fifth Annual Report* the Board of Management declared itself eminently satisfied with this state of affairs:

The position of this Society, as an auxiliary to the Foreign Mission Committee of our Church, affords us an excellent opportunity for doing work of a congenial kind. We are happily free from much responsibility which would be unavoidable in an independent organization. There is nothing to do which ought to bring us before the public, or which will interfere with the priceless possession 'of a meek and quiet spirit;' no selecting or superintending of missionaries; no puzzling questions to settle; but the simple duty of raising money sufficient to meet certain expenses for which we have become responsible.[15]

While statements of this kind suggested a becoming modesty and undoubtedly served to reassure those Presbyterians with lingering doubts about the soundness of women's organized church activities, they were inspired in part by a well-founded sense of what was politic. Moreover, they masked the organization's potential for enlarging women's sphere in the church. Professions of humility notwithstanding, the society's leaders set about their work with vigour and intelligence and soon demonstrated that they interpreted 'the simple duty of raising money' in a fashion that gave them wide scope for activity.

A first task, clearly, was to expand the organization from its Toronto base by increasing the number of auxiliaries. When it issued its *First Annual Report* in 1877, the WFMS could report 18 auxiliaries and 3 mission bands. Ten years later these figures had risen to a gratifying 251 auxiliaries and 74 mission bands.[16] While the co-operation of the local minister was obviously essential in this building process, WFMS leaders recognized that they could not count on the clergy to develop the necessary enthusiasm and lay the groundwork at the congregational level. Particularly in the early years, therefore, representatives went out from Toronto to explain the need for, and the mechanics of, a woman's foreign missionary auxiliary. (Later, as presbyterial societies were organized, their presidents sometimes took on this task in the congregations within their bounds.) Southern Ontario, not surprisingly, was the site of the first auxiliaries, but as early as 1884 in Winnipeg, gateway to the Northwest, Presbyterian women, some of them recently arrived from Toronto and Halifax, laid the base of what was to become a strong regional centre for overseas missionary enthusiasm. Though they would never achieve their goal of every churchwoman in an auxiliary and an auxiliary in every congregation, the society's leaders built a large constituency over the life of the organization, with more than 36,000 members, located in every province from Quebec to the Pacific coast.[17] The majority of this number appear to have been married, middle-aged, and middle class.[18]

Publicizing the work of the church's women missionaries and missionary wives began almost at once, for such a strategy was viewed both as a means of increasing memberships and financial contributions and of awakening in single women a desire for a missionary career. The WFMS availed itself of frequent opportunities to promote its cause through the regular Presbyterian press (here, too, family connections were helpful), but it also moved promptly to establish its own media. Annual reports, published from 1877, undoubtedly found their way into the hands of the most active members, but the society's leaders recognized that what was needed was a monthly periodical, similar to those published by their sister societies in the United States, to take the missionary message into every member's home. An informal newsletter, circulated locally on the initiative of one board member, gave way in 1884 to the *Monthly Letter Leaflet,* which in turn was succeeded in 1897 by *Foreign Missionary Tidings.* An illustrated publication with relevant didactic fiction as well as news of women's home-base and overseas missionary activities, the new magazine was able to attract a substantial readership. By the end of the period more than 27,000 monthly copies were being issued, a figure, its editor claimed, that exceeded the circulation of any comparable publication in Britain or the United States.[19]

Over time, WFMS promotional materials also included maps of mission fields, manuals for those contemplating a missionary career, and a wide range of imported and locally produced books and pamphlets on specific fields and topics. Together with the monthly periodical, such materials provided the auxiliaries with themes and guidelines for their monthly meetings and gave them a sense of being part of a large and progressive movement. For some members, moreover, the mission libraries that the more vigorous auxiliaries and presbyterial societies were able to build up out of WFMS-supplied materials provided perhaps the chief source of reading material in a culturally arid existence. While much of this matter was too brief or didactic to be attractive for its own sake, books such as Dr Susie Carson Rijnhart's *With the Tibetans in Tent and Temple* provided fascinating reading even for the non-dutiful. One widely known textbook, *Western Women in Eastern Lands,* by American publicist Helen Barrett Montgomery, was even available in 'an edition deluxe' for 'the hosts of women who must have something especially attractive to enlist them in the consideration of missions.'[20]

In the central matter of fund raising, the WFMS was an early and unqualified success. Annual and life memberships, mite boxes, and the use of a monthly envelope to promote systematic giving served throughout most of the period as the chief means of acquiring revenue. Unlike the FMC, which faced chronic deficits as work in the field expanded faster than the resources of the General Fund, the WFMS could usually respond affirmatively to requests that it finance new projects and, adopting a pay-as-you-go philosophy, avoided the need to carry deficits forward from one year to the next.

Claiming receipts of just over $1,100 after its first year of existence, the society reported an income of more than $100,000 in 1913–14, its last fiscal year.[21] While these sums constituted from one-third to one-half of total foreign mission givings in the Western Division in any given year, they in fact underrepresented the women's contribution, since, as WFMS spokeswomen were fond of pointing out, a substantial portion of what went into the General Fund from regular congregational givings came from female church members.[22]

The expanding financial capabilities of the society were demonstrated in the growth of its responsibilities. The mission established by the church in Central India in 1877 remained by far the most important field for women's work and the site of its most extensive and costly infrastructure,[23] but other missions also came to absorb its money and attention. Responding to requests from missionaries in the Canadian West in the early 1880s, the society began assisting with educational needs and sending clothing to destitute Indians. From this modest beginning it went on to provide vast quantities of clothing, quilts, and other supplies; schools and boarding facilities for native children; and teaching personnel of both sexes. By 1902, virtually all the church's Indian work in British Columbia and more than half that in Manitoba and the Northwest was being funded by the WFMS.[24] Such activity was obviously something of an anomaly for a 'foreign' missionary society. Foreign Secretary Elizabeth Harvie thus felt compelled to remind readers of the society's *Eighth Annual Report* that, despite its location, Indian work was 'in reality ... work among the heathen.' In the early years of the twentieth century a similar rationale would lead the society into small-scale missionary activity among Chinese and Jewish immigrants in Canada.[25]

In the 1880s, the WFMS had also begun supporting women's work in the church's new field in North Honan, China. For a time, the Woman's Missionary Society in Montreal (successor to the Ladies' Auxiliary Association) bore a part of the cost of this work by paying the salary of a medical missionary. The arrangement, however, caused ongoing friction between the two societies and came to an end in the early twentieth century after the Montreal executive succeeded in getting the FMC to assign it workers in a field where the WFMS did not 'hold sway' – a new mission in Macao, South China, the general area from which many members of Montreal's Chinese community had come.[26] Though the church's mission in North Formosa was more than a decade older than that in North Honan, the WFMS had no workers there until 1905, for throughout his career the mission's domineering founder, George Leslie Mackay, had made it abundantly clear that while he wanted access to WMFS funds, he did not want women missionaries. His attitude was undoubtedly related to the fact that in 1878 he had married a Chinese woman, whom he subsequently put in charge of evangelistic work among women.[27] Near the end of the period, the WFMS became involved in a third East Asian field. It assumed partial responsibility for women's work in northern Korea when the financially hard-pressed Maritime Presbyterians appealed to the church's Western Division for help in meeting the many opportunities said to be opening up in that hopeful country.[28] By 1914, as a result of these accretions of responsibility, the society had thus committed itself to the support of by far the largest share of the church's women's work abroad and to a significant part of its 'foreign' work in Canada.

Its efforts did not go unrecognized. In an 1885 article in the *Knox College Monthly,* WFMS member Mary R. Gordon reflected that when the organization had first been formed, many ministers, perhaps the majority, had 'seemed somewhat shy in countenancing the work.' Now, except in 'the more retired parts of the country,' their attitude was generally positive.[29] If anything, Mrs Gordon was understating the case; whatever lingering doubts back-country clergy may have entertained about the appropriateness of this new sphere for women, FMC spokesmen and many of the denomination's male journalists vied for superlatives in describing its value. In doing so, they focused on several facets of the society's role and influence.

Interest in foreign missions was generally strongest, supporters declared, in precisely those regions where WFMS auxiliaries existed. Writing in 1889, Mary Gordon's minister son Charles W. Gordon, who would later become familiar to North Americans as the novelist Ralph Connor, described women's missionary societies as the most important agents in the missionary movement of the preceding half-century. Within his own denomination, he wrote, the WFMS had played a vital role by educating the entire church about the nature and needs of the foreign missionary enterprise. FMC Secretary R.P. MacKay agreed. At the end of the century, in his draft contribution to a small history of the foreign missionary work of the Presbyterian and Reformed churches of North America, he maintained that no other church agency had contributed as much to the diffusion of missionary intelligence at the congregational level.[30] Gordon and MacKay were scarcely disinterested observers, of course. Yet even those who took a somewhat jaundiced view of the church's participation in the foreign missionary enterprise were forced to agree with their assessment.

Encomiums were particularly likely to be delivered on the occasion of the WFMS annual meeting. Within a decade of the society's founding, hundreds of delegates were coming together for these spring gatherings and remaining in conference for several days. While the daily sessions were closed to most outsiders, an evening public meeting, featuring glowing summaries of the work by FMC leaders and by missionary speakers fresh from the field, came to be a regular and popular part of the program. In 1898, Cooke's Church in Toronto, with seating for some 2,500, was filled to capacity for this event.[31] A year later, J.A. Macdonald, an ordained Presbyterian journalist who would later become editor of the Toronto *Globe,* declared that '[f]rom some points of view,' the WFMS annual meeting had become 'the greatest convention of missionary workers in Canada.'[32] The worship sessions at these meetings were routinely noted and praised. But the devotional aspect obviously did not seem to male commentators quite so remarkable as the meetings' orderly, businesslike aspects. Observing WFMS leaders' ability to transact a large quantity of business with a minimum of confusion and delay, listening to their review of the previous year's accomplishments, and noting their plans for the future, enthusiasts like Macdonald and Gordon were prompted to speak of the society's 'almost perfect organization,' and to commend its methods of work to the church as a whole.[33]

Given their own perennial budgeting problems, FMC executives were particularly grateful for the financial accomplishments of the WFMS. Nor was this merely a matter of the society's raising large sums of money. R.P. MacKay, and later his associate A.E. Armstrong, readily defended the WFMS board's policy of insisting that all money raised at the auxiliary level be transmitted to headquarters for dispersal. Local decision making about missionary objects played havoc with attempts to plan rationally for all aspects of the work, they repeatedly pointed out. It also created a problem that bedevilled the FMC itself, that of complying with requests from contributors – Sunday schools, young people's societies, etc. – for information about 'their' orphan, Bible woman, student, or other protégé. The WFMS, MacKay observed, by making members feel personally responsible for woman's work as a whole, and by promoting regular giving by large numbers of churchwomen, strove to stimulate the enthusiasm associated with special-object giving without being burdened with its disadvantages.[34]

Finally, it became conventional to praise the WFMS for what was called 'the reflex influence' of foreign mission work. By this was meant its capacity to enrich the spiritual quality of women's lives by turning their minds from frivolous activities and narrow concerns to the needs of their benighted heathen sisters. This elevating influence, in turn, enthusiasts maintained, broadened the horizons and raised the spiritual standards of the homes, churches, and communities in which such women lived. As the youthful editor of the missions-oriented *Knox College Monthly,* J.A. Macdonald was in the forefront of those who spoke in this fashion. Writing in 1887, he declared that the value of the WFMS transcended its ability to save heathen women:

If the [Woman's] Foreign Missionary Society ... caused never a single ray of rosy sunlight to enter the darkened zenanas of the East, but only to shine into the homes of the West; if it saved women not from the curse of heathenism, but only from the blight of Christian lands; if it did no more than this – which it has done – if it only saved its own girls from being empty, selfish, shallow things, if it only enriched its own women and made them noble and earnest and heroic, it would not have worked in vain.

Carried away by his own rhetoric and by imagery borrowed from Ruskin, Macdonald contrasted 'giddy creatures ... calling themselves queens' and women 'warped and hardened, made cruel by selfishness and thoughtless-ness and pride' with those who, redeemed by loving service to their benighted foreign sisters, had been made 'queens indeed and given a power "purer than the air of heaven and stronger than the seas of earth." '[35] Not all writers on this subject were as given to hyperbole as Macdonald. Nevertheless, even more than some of the more exotic aspects of the foreign missionary movement, the subject of the reflex influence of women's participation seemed to lend itself to extravagant claims, a tendency that undoubtedly reflected the influence of American missionary literature and WFMS members' own enthusiastic testimony on this feature of their work.[36]

By almost any measure, contemporaries agreed, the WFMS was a success-ful organization. Ironically, its very success proved to be a two-edged sword, giving rise to criticism and jealousy as well as praise. Not surprisingly, the key issue behind much of the grumbling was money. As WFMS revenues steadily climbed, complaints emanated from a number of sources: from ordained missionaries in overseas fields, ambitious on behalf of their own special projects and frustrated by the society's apparent insistence on committing its resources exclusively to woman's work; from hard-pressed administrators in the Eastern Division, covetously eying its bank balance as they faced the fact that their region's historic missionary reach now exceeded its financial grasp; and especially from Western Division church members dismayed by chronic deficits in the FMC's General Fund and convinced that the problem lay in an excess of WFMS zeal.[37] The executives of the WFMS had more money than they knew what to do with, the refrain ran; their fund raising was undermining the 'real' work of the church; their insistence on financing only women missionaries' activities was skewing priorities in the field and giving to female workers an inordinate amount of responsibility. The last of these concerns was particularly interesting in that it reflected a misunderstanding that was shared even by some rank-and-file WFMS members. In reality, WFMS money *was* used at times to help fund work conducted by male missionaries and their wives, particularly educational work. And in most foreign fields estimates for men's work remained substantially larger than for women's. The concern perhaps mirrored a fear that institutional missionary work was gaining ascendancy over the spiritual side as a result of the increasing presence of women.[38]

To some critics, more concerned about hierarchical relationships at the home front than financial disbursements in the fields, it appeared that the WFMS board had forgotten its society's auxiliary status and was 'assuming the authority of a Court of the Church.' Even the WFMS's sister society in Montreal, the Woman's Missionary Society, periodically lodged private grievances: the WFMS took credit for its accomplishments, it maintained, treated it shabbily at joint meetings, invaded its territory, and tried to reduce its status to that of a branch presbyterial.[39]

In an attempt to deal with criticisms of its operations, and of women's work in the fields, the WFMS in 1895 took the unusual step of publishing a four-page circular in its own defence, *Answers to Erroneous Statements Concerning the W.F.M.S.* Neither this nor subsequent efforts could silence the most frequently voiced complaints, however, for the problems that lay behind them did not go away. Moreover, while FMC executives publicly repudiated popular criticisms of the society, asserting that its funds were all fully and wisely committed and that its relationship to the committee remained that of a loyal auxiliary, they privately endeavoured to have the society divert some of its money into undertakings that would reduce financial pressure on the General Fund.[40] And, as will be shown below, the FMC moved quickly to check autonomist tendencies among WFMS executives.

A major source of criticism came from those who, while admiring its successes, felt that the WFMS should abandon its exclusive focus on foreign needs and work on behalf of home missions as well. As early as 1883, letters began to appear in the denominational press suggesting that the romance of foreign missions had blinded Presbyterian women to duties nearer at hand. The letters attested to the frustration experienced by members of the Home Missions Committee (HMC) in the last quarter of the nineteenth century as widespread enthusiasm for foreign work helped to deprive them of the funds and personnel necessary to meet their committee's obligations. Under the circumstances, it was not surprising that they turned to the General Assembly in 1889 to ask for help in gaining access to the fund-raising capacities of the WFMS. In the short run, however, with the FMC's self-interested support, the society was able to resist such pressures.[41]

The growth and success of the WFMS inevitably led it into a more complex relationship with the FMC. From the perspective of the latter, the challenge was how to make use of the time, money, and evident talent in the women's organization without relinquishing to it any of its own authority. For its part, the WFMS board tried to increase the scope of its activities and share in many aspects of decision making without, in most cases, seeking formal responsibility for its actions. In these circumstances, the two organizations were generally able to reach an accommodation and agree on the desirabil-ity of separate spheres in foreign mission work. Nevertheless, an examina-tion of the working out of that accommodation is instructive for what it reveals about the evolution of a large organization of women linked in a subordinate relationship to a male committee whose ultimate goals it shared, and yet developing, over the years, an increasing awareness of its own importance and a desire to pursue its own priorities.

In the early years, the FMC was more inclined to inform its auxiliary after the fact about decisions it had taken with respect to women's work than to consult with it in advance about appropriate courses of action. The society was not at first even provided with annual estimates of how its money was to be spent. Nor was it made privy to vital decisions affecting women missionaries. Thus, when India missionaries Marion Fairweather, in 1880, and Mary McGregor, in 1888, were dismissed from service by the FMC following staff conflicts in the field, the WFMS board apparently received only the same terse explanation as the rest of the Presbyterian public, despite the fact that the dropping of these high-profile missionaries created embarrassing difficulties. Possibly some board members chafed under such treatment from the very beginning, but they did not record their dissatisfac-tion through any official channel.

By the early 1890s, however, there were some signs of change. As reve-nues increased, and as WFMS leaders developed confidence in their ability and became knowledgeable about various facets of women's work in their own and other jurisdictions, they began to make a number of suggestions in regard to their overseas workers. They urged the FMC to allow more adequate outfit and furlough allowances to women missionaries, ques-tioned inequitable retirement allowances, and called for improved housing for their India workers, particularly in view of frequent reports of health breakdowns in the field.[42] In seeking these changes, they were not acting solely on the basis of sentiment and sisterly sympathy. While their approach to money matters at times bordered on parsimony, they had come to believe that there were some areas of mission work in which cheapness was false economy. They were therefore prepared to make whatever provisions were necessary to ensure the efficiency and well-being of their workers in the field and unwilling to leave such matters entirely to the judgment of their superiors on the FMC.

The most significant change in the role of the WFMS in this period came in the important matter of selecting missionaries. In view of staff conflicts and other personnel problems in its fields in the early years, the FMC had good reason to accept the society's assistance in this task. Moreover, in the United States, the Presbyterian Church (North) had set an early and important precedent by having its women's boards play a major role in recruiting and selecting women workers.[43] Even before 1891 when the FMC formally agreed to assign the society responsibility for screening female missionary applicants, WFMS board members had occasionally undertaken this role on an ad hoc basis. Now, to carry out their new task more effectively, they prepared a manual and questions for prospective candidates.[44] Where possible, they interviewed applicants at an early stage in order to determine their fitness for foreign mission work and make appropriate recommendations. (Applicants who lived far from Toronto often had their preliminary interview with local WFMS leaders, a regional FMC member, or their minister.) When the time came for a candidate to meet the FMC, the WFMS board's foreign secretary generally accompanied her to the interview and attempted to ease the strain of the encounter. While the FMC was under no obligation to act on WFMS recommendations, in practice it usually did so, especially as it learned that board members were apt to raise awkward questions about the rejection of candidates whom they had approved, and that in other cases, when the board hesitated to recommend particular applicants, it was usually with good reason.[45]

Its enlarged role in the selection of candidates led the WFMS to its most ambitious project of the decade, a training centre for women seeking overseas missionary service. An arrangement for providing the religious aspects of such training, initiated by William McLaren and Dr William Gregg in 1877, had fallen into abeyance when the women involved left for their mission fields, and subsequent provisions had been of an ad hoc character.[46] When WFMS board member Mrs Campbell first raised the subject of a formal course of training for female missionary candidates in the spring of 1891, she spoke only of arranging for 'definite theological training ... in our various church colleges.' By the end of the year, however, the board was also advocating foreign language preparation and a home where women candidates could reside and receive supplementary Bible training.[47] While some members of the FMC's executive promptly gave their unofficial approval to the idea of providing systematic religious training for intending women missionaries, the committee officially advised delay on the WFMS plan and instead offered to investigate the possibility of making use of existing facilities. It had in mind the Moody Bible Institute in Chicago or one of the three new religious training schools being opened in Toronto in the first half of the decade.[48] Of these – Methodist and Church of England deaconess-training centres and the Toronto Bible Training School – R.P. MacKay particularly favoured the latter, an interdenominational and millenarian institution on whose board of directors he served.

The WFMS board dutifully agreed to consider these alternatives. But since its own preference was for training that imparted 'the distinctive views of the Presbyterian Church' and for an institution in which it could exercise close personal surveillance over candidates through a supervisor of its own choosing,[49] it was inevitable that only a facility of its own would prove satisfactory. Its position was undoubtedly strengthened by an 1894 article in the *Knox College Monthly* that identified the lack of a training institution for female missionary candidates as one of the few gaps in the WFMS's impressive list of accomplishments.[50] Aided by such support, the board waited out, or overcame, the reservations of the committee and of those within its own organization who questioned the need for a distinctively Presbyterian institution. In October 1897, the Ewart Missionary Training Home, named for the society's late president, a leading advocate and benefactor of the project, was officially opened in Toronto. Its affairs managed by a committee comprised of three FMC and four WFMS board members, the home symbolized the persistence with which the organization pursued its goals as well as its increasing part in the church's foreign missionary enterprise.[51]

Besides responding positively to the board's desire for an active role in screening and preparing female missionary candidates, the FMC showed an increasing tendency in the years after 1890 to consult with it about other matters in which it had a direct interest: staffing changes, building plans, annual estimates, regulations for the various mission fields in which it sponsored workers. There was no constitutional change spelling out the new relationship. But it gradually came to be taken for granted by both groups that the society's role involved something more than merely bankrolling decisions already taken by the FMC. Thus, when in 1912, in a routine business letter, R.P. MacKay informed the mission treasurer in Indore that a copy of the annual estimates would be forwarded as soon as they had been approved by the WFMS,[52] he was reflecting practice that had changed considerably since the days when the board had been informed about such decisions after the fact.

Moreover, while WFMS approval was usually forthcoming, it was not inevitable. On occasion, the board proved adept at using its power of the purse, or even its auxiliary status, to express its disapproval of courses proposed or sanctioned by the FMC. In 1898, for instance, the board declined to accede to the committee's suggestion that it fund an ordained missionary's primary schools in India. It had done so during the previous year to relieve financial pressure on the General Fund. However, the FMC had subsequently ignored its petition to restore a joint mission council in India in which both sexes had briefly had equal roles, and the WFMS now declared itself unwilling to meet any estimates not considered and passed by the new Women's Council. Two years earlier, when convenor Hamilton Cassels had sought to have the WFMS pay a portion of the FMC's operating costs, the board had also proven resistant. The society's mandate was to raise and expend funds on women's work for women and children, it had pointed out; such a step as Cassels proposed would violate that mandate and displease the general membership. Furthermore, with respect to such expenses as travel costs, the members of the board absorbed these personally, and they thought the committee might well do likewise.[53]

If a general pattern of increased consultation had emerged by the beginning of the twentieth century, giving the WFMS board a significantly larger role in policy making, it was nevertheless true that the FMC was anxious to maintain both the public image and the formal letter of its authority. Having called the WFMS into being as an auxiliary organization, the FMC was determined not to let the society develop into a parallel missionary body. The FMC's attitude was well illustrated in 1892 in connection with the society's new draft manual for women missionaries. At an FMC executive meeting, R.P. MacKay, then newly appointed as the committee's permanent secretary, reported that in going over the manual he and Professor McLaren had found that 'in two or three places authority was assumed by the [WFMS] Board instead of being stated as belonging to the [Foreign Missions] Committee,' and that its authors had indicated a higher outfit allowance than that fixed by the FMC. Alerted to this irregularity, the executive agreed that the manual should be altered 'so as to make it conform to the [Foreign Missions] Committee's regulations and authority' and that an increase in the outfit allowance would be considered only if the board provided an appropriate rationale. Having demonstrated its authority to its own satisfaction, the committee had no difficulty in agreeing to the proposed increase a month later![54]

As the only member of the FMC who made work for foreign missions his full-time career, and as the official with responsibility for interpreting and implementing the church's foreign missions policy on a day-to-day basis, MacKay was particularly anxious to resist any accretions of power by the WFMS, however small they might appear. He was also careful to dispel any misconceptions that could encourage such a trend. In 1894, therefore, when ordained missionary Harvey Grant wrote from North Honan to suggest that the WFMS sanction the building of a girls' school in his field, MacKay promptly informed him that the society had no authority to make any such decision. While no harm had been caused by the misunderstanding in this case, MacKay told Grant, 'you can see whereunto it might grow, if there were any disposition on the part of the W.F.M.S. to be aggressive, which there is not.'[55]

So long as the lines of authority were preserved, MacKay was quite willing to solicit advice from the women's organization and even to adopt some of its careful administrative practices.[56] Beyond the benefits that such an approach could produce in his own daily work, he shrewdly recognized the need to make concessions on occasion in order to ensure the WFMS board's continued enthusiasm for the foreign missions cause. His approach contrasted sharply with that of the Reverend William Moore, the rigid Ottawa Orangeman who served as FMC convenor from 1897 to 1902. In Moore's view, the price of women's support for foreign missions was too high if it involved any sharing of decision making. Thus, in 1900, when the willingness of the Montreal Woman's Missionary Society to fund a new medical missionary in North Honan seemed to hinge on that society's being able to regard her as 'their very own,' Moore expressed concern. The FMC, he told MacKay, should refuse to enter into any arrangements that would

impair the completeness of our control of the missionaries ... I would rather do without their money than accept it upon any terms which would open the way to the transfer of our women's work to the W.F.M. Society. Whatever we do for Montreal we must do for the larger Society. I think you feel as strongly upon this point as I do.[57]

MacKay was far more pragmatic than Moore, and certainly less forthright, but he did feel as strongly as his colleague about the importance of remaining in charge. At the end of the period, in correspondence on two quite separate matters, he made that abundantly clear. In 1913, forwarding to the Conference of Foreign Mission Boards of North America the FMC's income-based share of conference maintenance funds, he pointed out that the sum did not include a proportion for the income of the WFMS. While the conference could ask the WFMS to contribute such a sum, MacKay agreed, he foresaw a difficulty: 'This would mean that they would want to be represented at the Conference, and while I know that the policy of the Conference admits of that, yet I am not quite sure that it is the best thing.'[58] By the time he wrote these words MacKay had become one of Protestant North America's leading missionary bureaucrats – he had himself been made president of the Conference of Foreign Mission Boards in 1912. With men like the American Presbyterian Robert Speer and the SVM's John Mott, he played a prominent role in the periodic conferences at which broad questions of missionary policy were discussed. However valuable women's work for missions at the home base might be, especially in terms of fund raising and promotion, it did not seem to him desirable to encourage women's participation at the rarefied levels at which the directions of the movement were determined. A few months earlier, writing to WFMS President Mrs J. Emily Steele in regard to the society's new regulations for women missionaries, he had drawn her attention to the board's failure to acknowledge the ultimate authority of the FMC and in characteristic fashion described that failure as both accidental and deliberate:

[T]here is such complete elimination of all reference to the F.M.C. that the lady candidate would not know that either she or the W.F.M.S. have or are expected to have any relation to the F.M.C. The Board is all in all.

That seems to me to look in the direction of independence, and yet I know that such is not your desire. It is the policy that prevails in the Methodist Church, but is not according to the genius of Presbyterianism.

However, I do not discuss that, but simply draw attention to the fact. I read it with the former manual in hand, and the changes are so marked as to suggest that they are not accidental.[59]

Even in the last years of the period, then, any signs of incipient 'aggressiveness' on the part of the WFMS board were quickly nipped in the bud. In reality, however, there were few occasions on which R.P. MacKay and his fellow officers felt obliged to take such action. When in 1900 Mrs Marjory McLaren contrasted the strife between male and female missionaries in Central India with 'the universal harmony and co-operation that ...

[has] always existed between the FMC and the Board,'[60] she was overdrawing the difference, but only somewhat. Such feminist tendencies as some board members harboured were more than offset by a pragmatic recognition of the fact that an overt show of interest in power and independence could be fatal to the future of their organization and that the WFMS as constituted already provided a highly satisfactory outlet for the extra-domestic ambitions of well-connected churchwomen like themselves.[61] Even if they did not exercise formal authority, they knew that their society was a vital and influential force in the church's foreign missionary endeavours. As the agency responsible for generating much of the money and public interest expended on foreign missions, it could scarcely be otherwise.

The time and effort that WFMS board members invested in their society attested to the satisfactions they derived from it. Throughout its existence, the secretary-treasurer of publications was the only salaried officer,[62] though as Toronto journalist Marjory MacMurchy pointed out in her 1916 profile of Canadian women's organizations, the senior officers in such large societies in effect took on full-time occupations, with the president assuming duties 'as complicated ... as any business man would care to handle.' As MacMurchy undoubtedly knew, her late mother, as WFMS foreign secretary, had remained in touch with society business even while on vacation. And Emily Steele's election to the presidency in 1911 had prompted her to change her residence from Dundas, Ontario, to Toronto.[63] Suggestions from within the organization near the end of the period that the terms of executive positions be limited as a way of opening them up to a wider range of members were resisted by those long in office. The management of the society's affairs had grown so complicated, the latter contended, that considerable time and experience were required to understand and administer them. There was undoubtedly some merit in this claim, for with the growth of the society's work, the relatively straightforward organization of 1876 had been transformed by the creation of a welter of new positions and special committees and by a need for more frequent meetings. Yet such arguments could not wholly mask the reluctance of incumbents to relinquish the authority they exercised. Journalist MacMurchy may well have had the WFMS in mind when she deplored a tendency among the officers of some women's organizations to hoard rather than share their power.[64]

The rewards of high office and the leisure to pursue them were, of course, available to only a few. Moreover, the importance of these positions was directly related to the size and vigour of the organization over which the leadership presided. This, in turn, depended on sustaining churchwomen's interest at the local level.

What *did* the WFMS offer to women within their own congregations? Though they varied a good deal from place to place, and over time, the regular auxiliary meetings in communities like Neepawa, Smiths Falls, and Carleton Place offered certain unchanging attractions: the opportunity to come together in a good cause, to enjoy a sense of sisterhood, and to turn for a time from mundane household responsibilities to the exotic challenges of a faraway world. Especially in rural areas, the monthly missionary meeting was often one of the few outings available in a narrow social existence, and many women made extraordinary efforts to attend.[65] 'The meeting' was also a source of local leadership opportunities and intellectual stimulus. Such duties as serving on an executive, preparing a paper on an assigned missionary topic, reading appropriate scriptural passages, and leading a group in prayer might well prove daunting to the congregation's most timid and least educated women, but they undoubtedly appealed to those desiring an outlet for skills and ambitions unused at home. Organizing special events such as the annual autumn thankoffering meeting gave such women additional opportunities to exercise their talents and, briefly, to make the larger community their stage. Not surprisingly, auxiliary and presbytery minutes recorded the same small core of names year after year as executive officers and activists.[66]

These attractions notwithstanding, the enthusiasm and interest of the grass roots could not be taken for granted, as the women at Toronto headquarters well knew. By corresponding and visiting with local workers, providing them with the materials around which stimulating meetings could be structured, and making them feel that they were a vital part of an important and successful organization, board members strove to prevent interest from waning. And while they knew that they themselves were the nerve centre of the organization, they discreetly chose to play down that aspect in their public utterances and instead stressed the importance of the auxiliaries and mission bands as 'the bone and sinew' of the society.[67]

To speak of the WFMS as a volunteer organization that served, at all levels, as an outlet for personal ambitions and social and intellectual needs is not to deny its members' spiritual commitment to the foreign missionary task. Presbyterian churchwomen in fact showed an extraordinary single-mindedness about that task and about their own role in fulfilling it. In the vivid imagery of their missionary literature, millions of Eastern women cried, 'Come over and help us,' and as Christian wives and mothers they felt compelled to do all that their circumstances allowed to meet that appeal. As the years passed, their leaders continued to maintain that in foreign fields there existed a unique need for their support, a need for female personnel unparalleled in Canada, where no religious or cultural barriers existed to deny the ministry of ordained churchmen to spiritually hungry women. In the early days of the society's existence, Presbyterian leaders as eminent as George Monro Grant had assured churchwomen that mission work in Canada could make no equivalent claim on their energies, and nothing, in their view, had happened to change that situation.

This unwavering focus on their foreign responsibilities, together with a probably somewhat exaggerated sense of the constraints placed on them by their society's subordinate relationship to the FMC, led board members to decide in 1894 that the WFMS should not be affiliated with the newly established National Council of Women of Canada. The council's decision not to open its meetings with public prayer provided further reason to remain aloof. Even a personal appeal to the WFMS president, Catherine Ewart, by the council president, Lady Aberdeen – the wife of the governor-general and a fellow Presbyterian – could not move the board from its position. The heads of other women's missionary societies also declined to affiliate their organizations with the council. Nevertheless, the Presbyterian board's position seems to have been unusually rigid: in 1895 it declined to send a delegate or even formal greetings to the council's annual meeting.[68] The same single-mindedness accounted for its unwillingness to send delegates to annual meetings of the Woman's Christian Temperance Union and other benevolent but non-missionary organizations that asked for these tokens of recognition and support.[69] Declaring their fullest sympathy for the goals of such organizations (and in many cases participating in them as individuals), WFMS leaders nevertheless affirmed that concerns such as temperance were outside their society's mandate and must not be allowed to interfere with its work in fulfilling the Great Commission.

The only sisterly networks in which they regularly participated were those linking them with other women's missionary societies. To these they sent delegates, or greetings, on the occasion of annual meetings and with them joined in 'unions of prayer' or occasional petitions to government for their common missionary goals.[70] Outside Canada, their ties were largely confined to other Presbyterian women's foreign missionary societies. In 1893 they decided even to forgo participation in the Woman's Congress of Missions at the Columbian Exposition in Chicago in view of the fact that a decision had been made to keep the exposition open on Sundays. Two years later, they voted to withdraw from the international association of women's missionary societies headed by the American Congregationalist

Abbie B. Child, citing as the reason their desire to confine their links to those available through the pan-Presbyterian Council.[71] Denominational narrowness and economic considerations obviously entered into these decisions (some of Child's proposals threatened to be costly). But above all such decisions reflected the board's desire to limit its official contacts to those that would be most directly relevant to its own foreign mission concerns.

WFMS leaders were undoubtedly sincere in affirming their belief in the primacy of foreign missionary work. At the same time, such an emphasis dovetailed with their determination to preserve the constitutional integrity of an organization whose distinctive focus and rationale had brought them unprecedented influence and prestige. By the turn of the century such determination was necessary, for as the church and the nation responded to the twin challenges of large-scale immigration and Western development, the WFMS came under renewed pressure to alter its mandate and take on responsibility for home as well as foreign missions. The same pressures had been applied to some of the larger societies in the United States in the last third of the nineteenth century. Generally, they had resisted with vigour, for as Patricia Hill has noted, having discovered 'the power they could wield by carving out a special, albeit subordinate, task ... [t]he women's foreign missionary societies clearly felt they had much to lose by being lumped into a single organization with home missions.' Familiar with the experience of their American counterparts, WFMS leaders responded in a similar fashion.[72] For them, however, the challenge from home missions was even greater, for in Canada it fuelled a growing desire, particularly among members in the Western provinces, for a restructuring of the organization that would decentralize its management. Ultimately, these pressures proved irresistible. Nevertheless, an examination of the battle waged by senior WFMS executives to preserve the status quo demonstrates just how important a place the society had come to occupy in their lives.

Lobbying to have the WFMS include home mission work in its responsibilities had begun, as noted, during the first decade of the organization's existence. Faced with expanding costs and challenges at the very time when the foreign missionary movement was capturing the imagination of missions-minded Presbyterians, home missions officials in the 1880s had first sought the creation of a woman's home missionary society to assist them in their work and then the broadening of the WFMS mandate to include home responsibilities.[73] But both in passionate letters from anonymous members and in the more dignified official response of its Board of Management, the society had made clear its determination not to be distracted from its 'special work.'[74] Supported in this position by the FMC, it had been left largely undisturbed to pursue its overseas responsibilities until the last years of the century, when such pressures were renewed.

Fighting the seductive appeal of foreign missions had become, by the 1890s, a major concern of Western missions superintendent James Robertson. Stressing the vast potential for good and evil in the Canadian West, Robertson skilfully linked home missions with patriotism and Presbyterian self-interest. In what was to become a much-used argument, he also insisted that those devoted to foreign missions could best serve their cause by building up strong churches in the homeland.[75] Aroused by his efforts, the General Assembly in 1895 signalled a new interest in home missions by electing him moderator, and the denomination's journalists took up the cause. The *Presbyterian Record*'s Ephraim Scott, despite his ongoing commitment to foreign involvement, began to editorialize on home mission work as 'The Greatest Need' and to promote its claims with increasing frequency. In the *Westminster,* J.A. Macdonald deplored what he saw as a lack of effective leadership within the HMC and called on that body to develop new and effective policies to meet the great challenge in the Canadian West.[76]

Within this context, the immediate factor leading to renewed pressure on the WFMS was a much-publicized appeal for women's help from ordained missionaries in the Klondike gold field. It began in January 1898 with a letter from R.D. Dickey calling for 'trained nurses with the love of Christ in their hearts' to help deal with the distressing physical and spiritual condition of some of the men in the field. In her address to the annual meeting in May of that year, WFMS President Marjory McLaren explained that while such work as Dickey proposed was not their society's 'province,' it could well command the sympathies of individual members. By the time she spoke it was already clear just how strong those sympathies were. In March, several members of her board had participated in a meeting in Toronto, sponsored by the HMC, the outcome of which was the formation of a special committee to raise funds for sending Presbyterian nurses to the Klondike. An appeal to the group from Lady Aberdeen to instead join her in sending out nurses under the newly established Victorian Order of Nurses was declined, since the object was to sponsor workers who could proselytize as well as provide medical care.[77]

In the wake of the establishment of the new committee, which came to be known as the Atlin Nurse Committee after the place to which its first two nurses were dispatched, agitation to have Presbyterian women become more extensively involved in home missions work grew significantly. In an overture to the 1901 General Assembly less than a year before his death, the last in a series of such efforts, Western missions Superintendent Robertson called for an amendment to the WFMS constitution to allow home as well as foreign work.[78] An editorial in the *Presbyterian Record* in support of the overture contained several of the elements commonly used in the campaign to woo WFMS women from their exclusive foreign focus. It began by citing the tremendous success of the Woman's Board of Home Missions in the Presbyterian Church, U.S.A., whose revenue in the preceding year had exceeded a quarter of a million dollars, and went on to suggest that, given the recent influx of immigrants with their 'ignorance both secular and spiritual,' much good could be accomplished if churchwomen were to apply the same noble efforts to this new challenge in their own country as they now directed abroad. Work among immigrant women and girls was essential, it argued, if the motherhood of the nation was not to be permanently debased. A vivid warning was then issued to Presbyterian mothers about another, more immediate, danger in the Canadian West:

Many of your own sons are going to the Northwest. That trinity of ill, the saloon, the house of ill-fame and the gambling hell awaits them in almost every mining town and camp all over the great West. The work that seeks to counteract these ills should appeal to mothers as almost no other work can do. You would give your lives for your sons. Why not in some special manner, by some special organization, give a small part of your lives for them in this way? ... The first great commission, while it looked to all the world, had its 'beginning at Jerusalem.' May Canadians and Canadian Christian women in their Christian work not have to look back some time from clearer vision and regret the keeping of our own National vineyard.[79]

At the *Westminster*, both J.A. Macdonald and his successor, the Reverend Robert Haddow, were more inclined than Scott to use praise rather than veiled reproach in their part of the campaign to nudge the society into home missions work, but their point of view was no less clear: home missions work would benefit and foreign missions work would not be hurt by WFMS involvement in both fields.[80]

Senior executive members, and particularly Mrs Mary Shortreed, the society's president from 1899, employed a variety of strategies to resist such pressures. In articles prepared for the Presbyterian press in 1902, they attempted to counter the criticism that the WFMS was an unpatriotic organization by reminding readers of its preponderant role in missions to the Indians of the Prairies and British Columbia. By educating and evangelizing the aboriginal people, they indignantly pointed out, they were surely doing their part to ensure the well-being of migrants to the Canadian West. In the same year, in a form letter to ministers and auxiliary presidents in the Toronto Presbytery, where the existence of the Atlin Nurse Committee was serving as a focal point for home missions enthusiasts, Mrs Shortreed rehearsed her executive's objections to a broadening of the society's mandate: the work it supported abroad was unique, she insisted, in being a work that *only* women could do; taking on home missions responsibilities would inevitably reduce the society's ability to support its extensive overseas commitments by dividing and diverting its resources; such a step, moreover, would increase the already regrettable tendency for male Presbyterians to leave ever more of the denomination's responsibilities to women.[81] Shortreed was clearly not indifferent to home mission needs – she had herself been a charter-member of the Atlin committee – but she was determined that such needs be kept in perspective and prevented from impairing the integrity and effectiveness of the WFMS.

Sustained once again by the FMC, which recognized the financial threat to its overall endeavour in proposals to broaden the society's mandate, Shortreed and her associates held their ground. But a determination to have churchwomen share in the burgeoning work of home missions had grown among Presbyterians of both sexes. The Eastern Division Woman's Foreign Missionary Society was already contributing informally to such work, and one of its members had openly attacked the WFMS for allegedly hoarding large sums of money in the bank while ignoring the needs of the West. Within the WFMS itself, a small group, weary of what it saw as the intransigence of the old guard, reportedly asked to be formed into a separate society. The result was the creation in Toronto in June 1903 of the Women's Home Missionary Society (WHMS), an organization auxiliary to the HMC and, like the small Atlin Nurse Committee from which it had grown, committed to assisting the HMC in providing Presbyterian religious and social services to the thousands of immigrants and migrants flocking to the Canadian West.[82]

The creation of the WHMS did not end the pressure on the WFMS, or the tensions within it. Despite claims that the new society complemented rather than competed with the older one, a spirit of rivalry developed between the two organizations, particularly in small communities with limited financial and membership resources. In larger centres, in theory, the WHMS could draw on a pool of still-unorganized churchwomen for members; in practice, it often drew on the WFMS membership as well. (R.P. MacKay would later speak of the WHMS as having sown 'disaffection' in WFMS territory in order to gain adherents.) In the West, some ministers were now decidedly hostile to a foreign missions focus, while many auxiliary and presbyterial societies were openly resentful of the tight control exercised over the society by the remote and inbred Toronto board and anxious for the freedom to do home as well as foreign missions work.[83]

In an effort to shore up its position, the board in 1904 hired a full-time field secretary, former India missionary Maggie Jamieson. While she was also expected to promote a missionary interest among young people, Miss Jamieson's main task was to visit congregations in the West in order to revivify existing auxiliaries and organize new ones. Within a year, the challenge of her job was made even greater when the WHMS appointed a worker to a similar position. In 1906, in a further effort at fence mending, the WFMS held its annual meeting in Winnipeg and thus made it possible for a large number of Western delegates to attend. Yet by the end of the year, the WHMS field secretary was reporting – probably without much exaggeration – near unanimity in the West in favour of a united women's missionary society, and an overture calling on the General Assembly to impose such a union had only been defeated when the venerable William McLaren had spoken against it. Its author, R.G. MacBeth, a Manitoba lawyer turned Ontario minister, was the most persistent and outspoken advocate of this cause. In the wake of the defeat of his overture, he headed a General Assembly committee which recommended that in future the approval of the (all-male) church session be required as a condition for forming any new congregational organization.[84] The object, clearly, was to prevent the formation of new WFMS auxiliaries.

Given these developments and a small but worrisome drop in its general membership figures, the WFMS board was forced to consider some compromises. Meetings were held in 1907 with WHMS board members to discuss possible forms of co-operation.[85] In 1909, pressed by the FMC, which in turn was responding to Western unrest, the WFMS board prepared a draft of a new constitution that would reduce its own authority by creating provincial boards and, where necessary, allow local associations of women to pursue both home and foreign mission work.[86] Despite these concessions, it was reportedly 'of one mind' in believing that the foreign part of the work should continue to be conducted 'along distinct lines' and that co-operative societies with the WHMS should be accepted only as a last resort.[87]

By 1910, it was clear that the proposed compromises would not solve the problems facing the WFMS board. Reviewing the nature and sources of

Western resentment at a January meeting at which the draft constitution was discussed, board member Mrs Falconer observed, 'The Central Board is bound to make jealousy in the West; we have either given too much or not enough.' On the basis of her field work in the region, Maggie Jamieson agreed. '[T]he West will be satisfied for a time,' she reported, 'but the small Executive will always be a stumbling block.'[88] Meanwhile, other pressures were pushing the society inexorably in the direction of union. Ministers and their wives, harassed by the demands of a bevy of church organizations, were said to be well disposed towards union.[89] Within the church hierarchy, there was a growing belief that the denomination should emulate trends in the business world by rationalizing its operations. Five separate departments of missionary work in Canada were brought together under a new Home Missions Board. The move towards a central budgeting plan, designed to eliminate competition for funds among the various schemes of the church, was another important step in this direction. Though the plan did not cover fund raising for women's missionary work, it signified the general direction in which the church wished to move.[90] The high-profile Laymen's Missionary Movement, introduced into Canada in 1907, provided an appropriate model by endorsing home and foreign missions as two sides of the same coin in the evangelization of the world. In the Maritimes, the Eastern Division Woman's Foreign Missionary Society had set an even more relevant example in 1905 by officially adding home missions work to its mandate. Even the ongoing discussions of interdenominational church union were brought to bear in the campaign. R.G. MacBeth, himself a strong anti-unionist, was quick to argue that those working for the large project of union with Methodists and Congregationalists should surely support this smaller merger within their own denomination.[91]

Most important, by the spring of 1910 even the FMC had abandoned its support for the status quo. Home missions advocates, most notably MacBeth, had long urged the FMC to stop deferring to the wishes of the strong-minded women on the WFMS board and instead insist on their uniting with their home missions counterparts. The board's refusal to amalgamate, MacBeth now declared, amounted to nothing less than a sabotaging of the church's best interests.[92] With the death in 1909 of the FMC's William McLaren, the board had been deprived of its strongest ally in resisting MacBeth's pressure tactics. At the same time, with the advent of the new budget plan, the FMC appeared to have lost much of its financial incentive for prolonging the society's separate existence. R.P. MacKay, one of the key spokesmen for the plan and a strong advocate of church union, stoutly defended the board's record and motives in the face of overt and implied criticism, but he could not, logically, continue to support its resistance to union.

At an April 1910 conference, MacKay and other members of his executive asked the board to give 'sympathetic consideration' to a plan for amalgamating with the WHMS.[93] When it failed to do so at its annual meeting the following month, reporting instead that it interpreted presbyterial societies' views on the draft constitution as indicating a desire 'to retain the foreign work as at present conducted,'[94] pressure from the FMC was quietly but firmly increased. Forced, finally, to recognize that the committee's request amounted to an order, WFMS leaders dutifully made plans to meet with WHMS representatives in order to work out a basis for union. President Mary Shortreed urged her associates on the Board of Management to fall in loyally with the proposed changes, bearing in mind that the work before them was all God's work. Her message was seriously undermined by her own action in resigning from office in 1911, but her successor, Mrs J. Emily Steele, took both a more pragmatic and a more sympathetic approach to the impending new order.[95]

Still, it was clear that the WFMS board had not been converted to the idea of amalgamation. Negotiations with WHMS representatives to devise the constitution for a united society bogged down on a number of issues. The WHMS proposal to allow local auxiliaries the right to determine the missionary objects on which their funds should be spent, together with its willingness to support work that was not exclusively women's work, seemed to WFMS negotiators to jeopardize both the economic security and the philosophical basis of their existing overseas obligations. It appeared that the new society could become a mere fund-raising arm for the general work of the church. The question of a name for the united organizations was also a stumbling block.[96] Impatient with the delays in ironing out these differences, the FMC in 1912 itself presented the WFMS with a draft basis for union. Further evidence of its new hard-line approach came later in the same year when it arranged to transfer all missionary work among Canadian Indians to the HMC without even consulting the WFMS.[97] Even at this stage, some board members wanted to continue their resistance, but they were counselled against doing so by their president. It was, she affirmed, the board's duty ... to fall in as far as possible with the basis proposed by the F.M.C.' At the June 1913 annual meeting, the same recommendation was officially made to the society's general membership.[98]

A year later, the formal merger took place. Following their thirty-eighth and final annual meeting, WFMS delegates joined their home missions counterparts in Knox Church, Toronto, where both societies had come into being, and united to form the Women's Missionary Society of the Presbyterian Church in Canada, Western Division. Representatives of the Montreal Woman's Missionary Society also participated in the union meeting, for after years of pursuing small-scale but determinedly separate missionary effort, they, too, had been persuaded by the FMC to become part of the new organization.[99] A major organizational change had taken place, but one thing remained constant: the Women's Missionary Society was to exist in an auxiliary relationship to the Home and Foreign Mission boards, as its constituent groups had done.

From the perspective of those who had led the WFMS there were several causes for satisfaction in the structure and management of the new organization. Though newly created provincial boards were given 'special care' for the work within their bounds, a central executive board with headquarters in Toronto would continue to have the major role (in conjunction with the men's Home and Foreign Mission boards) in hiring overseas missionaries, planning for new work, and preparing annual estimates. Mrs Emily Steele became president of the Women's Missionary Society, and many of her former colleagues on the WFMS board became part of her new executive. Mrs Janet MacGillivray, former editor of *Foreign Missionary Tidings,* obtained the important post of senior editor of the society's new publication. Even the WFMS motto, 'The World for Christ,' was to be retained as the motto of the new organization.[100] Yet neither these successes nor the show of unanimity and brave talk about new opportunities at the Knox Church meeting could mask the fact that the leaders of the WFMS had been coerced into union. As R.G. MacBeth had pointed out in 1906, the tide in Canadian Presbyterianism had become 'Home Missions strong.'[101] Caught by that tide, and by their church's anxious search for order, the WFMS board had been unable to prevail.

ẻ❧ ẻ❧ ẻ❧

One WFMS member who must surely have rejoiced at the unification of Presbyterian women's work for missions was Lucy Maud Montgomery. 'I think these missionary society meetings will be the death of me,' she had confided to her journal in 1912. 'We have three societies here – Woman's Foreign, Home Missions and Mission Band. And I have to attend all three every month.' A year earlier, the famous Prince Edward Island novelist had married the Reverend Ewan Macdonald and moved with him to Leaskdale, Ontario, where she was expected to fulfil all the usual roles of a dutiful minister's wife. The surfeit-of-societies difficulty was compounded for Montgomery by the fact that while she 'believe[d] in Missions,' she found missionary meetings 'deadly dull.' Some women really enjoyed them, she conceded, and had 'a sort of *flair* for them'; for herself, she saw no prospect of their ever being anything but 'unpleasant duties.'[102]

The women at WFMS headquarters would probably have been horrified at the frankness of Montgomery's confession, but they might not have found it surprising. After all, as a busy author she was not in need of diversion, and the meetings she attended in the hamlet of Leaskdale were hardly momentous events. For themselves, the situation was very different. Like Montgomery, they had energy and talents that were not wholly absorbed by homemaking, but theirs were abilities of a different order and they required a different outlet. Living in Toronto, and closely connected by personal ties to their church's male foreign mission leaders, they had been well positioned to take advantage of the administrative opportunities that had opened up in the late nineteenth century in connection with women's work for missions. Their task had involved elements of building up a business, and the challenge of a spiritual crusade. It was a task for which they had developed a '*flair*,' and they had found it anything but dull.

Thus, in 1914, while Montgomery heaved a sigh of relief, they could look back with a mixture of nostalgia and pride on a record of significant accomplishments. For some thirty-eight years their organization had arguably been the single most important agency in publicizing their church's foreign missionary cause. They had operated a sizable publishing and promotional endeavour, and they had moved to professionalize the selection and training of women missionaries. Insisting that their chief obligation was to those living 'in darkness' in foreign lands, they had nevertheless broadened their mandate to include work among Canadian Indians and two non-Christian immigrant groups. With a total income of more than one and a half million dollars over the life of their organization,[103] they had been able to build an impressive infrastructure of schools, hospitals, and other facilities and to sponsor by far the majority of the single women who had become Presbyterian foreign missionaries. Their investments of money and effort had not yielded the rich harvest of souls for which they had always laboured; but there had been other, more personal, benefits. In seeking to liberate their 'heathen sisters,' they had made considerable progress in enlarging their own sphere.

3

The context of a calling

When they became their church's pioneer women missionaries in the autumn of 1873, Marion Fairweather and Margaret Rodger were professionally trained schoolteachers, just past their mid-twenties. Canadian-born, of Scottish background, they came from church-going Presbyterian families of respectable middle-class status: Fairweather's father had been a shopkeeper in Bowmanville, Ontario; Rodger came from a large farm family near Lachute, Quebec. While living in Montreal to attend normal school, both had belonged to a church that was, even then, strongly missions oriented. Probably, too, they had found their way to meetings of that city's branch of the Woman's Union Missionary Society. Following the completion of their normal school training, they had returned to their home communities. The sojourn in Montreal thus appears to have been their only experience of living on their own before they began the long journey to India.[1]

In many ways, Fairweather and Rodger were to prove remarkably typical of the more than one hundred single women who followed them to the church's foreign mission fields in the years before the First World War. The similarity in missionaries' backgrounds reflected both the pool of volunteers on which the church was able to draw and the winnowing process in which its foreign missions administrators engaged. An analysis of the women's backgrounds and training thus reveals a good deal about the outlook and values that guided these officials as well as about the women missionaries themselves. By looking at the social and religious context in which the women came to maturity, and at their own statements about their sense of calling, it is also possible to suggest some of the factors that led them to become foreign missionaries. Their motivation emerges as a complex phenomenon, one in which secular and spiritual elements were subtly intertwined.

ટ⊛ ટ⊛ ટ⊛

In 1882, following his world tour of Protestant mission fields, U.S. missions bureaucrat William F. Bainbridge published a book in which he expressed strong views about the appropriate age for beginning women missionaries. '[T]hose who go out single from the christian women of the home lands to lift up their degraded sisters in heathendom, should not go out too young,' he urged. 'Better err on the side of maturity and experience.'[2] An examination of age data on the Presbyterian church's women missionaries suggests that, on balance, its officials concurred with his view.

Between them, the Eastern and Western divisions appointed women who were as young as twenty years of age and as old as forty-seven in the year their service began. The average age, however, was 29.4 years.[3] Within the Western Division, the policy was to seek candidates who were well into their twenties but not more than thirty. While no explicit rationale was provided for the minimum age, it was probably meant to deter youthful enthusiasts and to provide adequate time for educational preparation. The upper limit was based on candidates' presumed difficulty in acquiring a new language after age thirty.[4] Faced with the fact that a number of attractive candidates fell outside these upper and lower age limits, both the Foreign Missions Committee and the Woman's Foreign Missionary Society tended, in practice, to take a flexible approach to the age question. Thus, in 1888, two twenty-two-year-old schoolteacher volunteers who had completed part of the course of study at the Women's Medical College, Kingston, were asked to leave immediately for Central India to meet an urgent request for educational workers. While one of the two, Jean Sinclair, went on to a long and successful career in school and evangelistic work, the other, Elizabeth Scott, was sent home for health reasons within three years. Shortly thereafter, she married an Anglican missionary and settled in western Canada and was thus lost to her own church, if not to the larger cause.[5] Two years prior to Scott's return, another relatively young volunteer, twenty-four-year-old Amy (Amelia) Harris, had been sent to India to take charge of the girls' boarding school. Harris was unusually gifted, academically, and her family was prominent in the foreign missions bureaucracy. Moreover, her appointment to the headship of the school was seen as a way of ending a controversy in the mission. To those in authority, these factors seemed to outweigh the disadvantages of her youth and inexperience. Following her illness and death in 1892, however, WFMS leaders concluded that she had perhaps been too young for so much responsibility in so unfamiliar a setting.[6]

At the other end of the age scale, an initial reluctance to accept candidates who were markedly over age was frequently overcome when such women had impressive educational and occupational backgrounds and came highly recommended. This was the case with Janet White, a thirty-seven-year-old Dundee-born schoolteacher from the Northwest who had lived in India as a child. Well travelled, and highly regarded by those in Scotland and Canada who knew her work, such a candidate could be expected to pass relatively easily through the general adjustment and language acquisition processes. Following her appointment in 1893, White served in India for twenty-seven years, winning honours from the imperial government for public service to that country.[7] Of four other missionaries who went out to India before 1896 and who were thirty years of age or older when they received their appointments, three, like White, went on to long and highly successful careers. These successes made home-base officials increasingly well disposed towards the candidacies of older women, and in the period that followed, the average age of beginning missionaries rose noticeably.[8]

Older candidates were particularly likely to prove acceptable when they were available at reduced cost to the church, or had previous experience in missionary work. Such circumstances – and dogged determination – eventually resulted in Korean appointments for Maritimers Louise and Elizabeth McCully, at ages thirty-six and forty-seven, respectively. From the time they were children in Truro, Nova Scotia, the two sisters had reportedly dreamed of a missionary career. At one stage, they had even organized a small home mission to serve those unreached by their town's churches. Louise McCully's original plan, to join her fiancé, Korea pioneer W.J.M. MacKenzie, was cut short by his death, but in 1900 she became the church's first woman missionary in Korea following three years' service in China under another missionary agency. Perennially short of funds, Eastern Division officials were understandably reluctant to sponsor her older sister, but in 1909 Elizabeth, too, obtained an appointment when a group of local foreign missions enthusiasts agreed to be responsible for her salary. While waiting for her posting, Elizabeth McCully had unflaggingly supported the cause, writing a biography of MacKenzie, producing annual missionary calendars to raise money for women's work in Korea, and participating in the activities of the local WFMS auxiliary.[9]

In summary, during the years between 1876 and 1914, the church's foreign missions officials refused to be constrained by their own guidelines on age. Some youthful appointments were accordingly made. Over time, however, officials leaned in the opposite direction as they discovered that women of maturity and experience – and perhaps with fewer other options – were likely to have more staying power than their younger colleagues.

Available data indicate that the missionaries came from slightly larger than average families and that most were born in Canada.[10] Not surprisingly, the national background of many appears to have been Scottish. Though only five women are known to have been born in Scotland, at least twenty-three had fathers who were born there. Other missionaries or their families came from England or Ireland. None appear to have had national origins outside Great Britain.

Within Canada, Presbyterian women missionaries came predominantly from rural communities or small urban centres, though a large number had spent time working or studying in such cities as Halifax, Montreal, and Toronto. All provinces from Prince Edward Island to Alberta were represented on the church's foreign fields, with Ontario producing by far the largest number of workers. The Maritime missionaries came predominantly from Nova Scotia, where Presbyterians had long formed the largest Protestant denomination. The advance of Presbyterianism to the same status in the Canadian West by 1901 was reflected in the vocations of a small but significant group of women missionaries from Manitoba in the later part of the period. Within these three provinces, certain regions were particularly productive of missionaries and missionary aspirants of both sexes. In Ontario, the rough triangle formed by Hamilton, London, and Owen Sound constituted particularly fertile missionary territory; the area defined by Kingston, Brockville, and Almonte was another. The majority of the Nova Scotians came from Colchester and Pictou counties, while the Manitobans' homes were in several small communties in the southwest corner of the province. Some of these areas were, of course, especially strong Presbyterian enclaves. Other possible reasons for regional patterns in vocations will be explored later, but it is worth noting here that a significant number of the missionary-producing counties in Ontario and Nova Scotia were among those identified in a 1913 study as particularly hard hit by rural depopulation. The outward-bound missionaries were part of a larger phenomenon.[11]

Irrespective of where their home communities had been, Presbyterian women missionaries tended to come from respectable but modest middle-class backgrounds. Fathers' occupations are known for more than half.[12] Somewhat surprisingly, only eight have been identified as ministers' daughters. Several did have fathers who were prominent in professional, business, or political circles, but such family backgrounds were far from common. Even among the eminent clergy and laymen who invested substantial amounts of time and money in foreign missions, there were few whose daughters became career missionaries (though occasionally, like R.P. MacKay's daughter, Margaret, they became missionary wives). The availability of a greater range of options for the daughters of the largely urban Presbyterian elite and a reluctance to sacrifice them to the supposed rigours of the foreign field may help to explain this pattern. Whatever its causes, it is in striking contrast to the close and numerous linkages that existed between leading WFMS executives and the church's best-known clerics and laymen. Women missionaries were much more likely to be farmers' daughters. Almost half the Western Division workers are known to have belonged to this category. Most others had fathers who were small businessmen or tradesmen. No daughters of urban labourers have been identified among the missionaries.

Other factors, in addition to fathers' occupations, are indicative of the missionaries' modest origins. As teenagers or young women several had had to interrupt or delay their schooling in order to take on the role of family housekeeper, or to earn money for fees and living expenses. Later, when they had decided on a foreign missionary career, many obtained assistance from the WFMS or borrowed from other sources to meet the expenses of preparatory training. Few could afford to pay the cost of their own missionary outfit and transportation to the field, or go out as 'honorary' (unpaid) missionaries, though administrators and publicists tried to encourage such practices by giving them wide notice. Finally, despite the modest salaries they earned in the field, some women evidently sent financial aid to their families in Canada from time to time.[13]

If the missionaries did not generally come from families that were socially or economically prominent, they constituted something of an elite themselves in terms of their own attainments. Some 70 per cent of the ninety-three women sponsored by the Western Division during this period had been employed as teachers prior to their appointment. Teaching, of course, was not so much a prestigious profession as one of the few generally available to Canadian women in the last half of the nineteenth century. Among the missionaries, however, a comparatively large number – almost 59 per cent – are known to have attended normal school. (By contrast, in Ontario in 1895 only 40 per cent of the province's teachers had normal school training; the figure was even lower when city and town schools were excluded.)[14] While most such missionaries had been engaged in public school teaching, some had taught in high schools, colleges, and commercial institutions. A few had been head teachers or principals. Teaching was by far the most common paid occupation of the women who became career missionaries. Others had been engaged in such activities as nursing, office work, dressmaking, domestic service, settlement work, and church work.[15]

At least five professionally trained teachers were among the fifteen Western Division women who completed medical courses and became medical missionaries. The majority began their medical studies with missionary careers specifically in view.[16] Perhaps fearful that they might be lost to another sending agency if they studied outside the country, the FMC insisted from the beginning that medical women expecting to go out under its sponsorship must take their training in Canada. Its attitude was probably an important factor in the establishment in 1883 of the Women's Medical College, affiliated with Queen's College in Kingston, Ontario. The principal of Queen's, George Monro Grant, who actively supported the creation of the Women's Medical College, was a leading advocate of the appointment of female medical missionaries within the FMC.[17] All the medical women appointed during this period attended either this institution or its Toronto counterpart, affiliated with Trinity College and the University of Toronto. Following graduation, many spent a brief period acquiring postgraduate training or practical hospital experience, generally at one of several women's hospitals in the United States, before going abroad.

The educational background of other Western Division missionaries was diverse: ten had professional nurse's training; eleven had BAS; three had MAS. Among the nurses were several who had undertaken their studies specifically with the mission field in view. At least another ten missionaries had incomplete medical or undergraduate education. Others had received professional training in such areas as music, domestic science, and commercial subjects, with the first of these being particularly valuable from the perspective of hiring officials. Overall, by the time they were appointed, the majority of the Western Division missionaries had received a level of education that was well beyond the norm for contemporary Canadian women.[18]

Among Eastern Division missionaries, the situation with regard to qualifications was somewhat more complex. For its northern Korea field, opened in 1898, the Eastern Division Foreign Missions Committee was evidently anxious, to the extent that its finances allowed, to make use of well-trained professional women in a variety of missionary roles. Thus, by the end of the period, its small Korea staff included a doctor, a nurse, several teachers, and women with appropriate training for full-time jobs in direct evangelism. However, in Trinidad, where the division operated a mission to indentured

East Indian labourers, women's full-time missionary work was much more narrowly conceived. From 1876, when Annie Blackadder was sent to the island as the church's first woman worker, women missionaries were almost exclusively appointed to do elementary-level teaching and were hired on short-term, usually five-year, contracts. Even these appointments were curtailed at the turn of the century when mission-trained East Indians became available as teachers. The only Canadian woman appointed to the mission staff between 1900 and 1914 was Marion Outhit, a Dalhousie University MA graduate hired in 1912 as head of the new girls' high school.[19] With the exception of Outhit, who left the island after four years, the Trinidad missionaries appear to have been hired with markedly less training and work experience than their counterparts in other fields. They were also somewhat younger. Their low salaries,[20] their frequent designation in official records as 'lady teachers' or 'missionary assistants,' the scant attention paid to their work in contemporary reports, and the paucity of biographical data available on them reflect the lack of importance that was attached to their role.[21]

The higher priority that Western Division administrators placed on hiring mature, professionally trained women for their various overseas missions was evident in their selection procedures. In the early years, a number of volunteers with little or no professional training were accepted. Later, however, as more adequately qualified candidates presented themselves, both the FMC and the WFMS Board of Management were reluctant to hire such women. Applicants and inquirers who presented little or no evidence of relevant work experience or professional training were apt to be given indefinite responses, told that other candidates had precedence, redirected to other forms of church work, or advised to get preparatory training. Unenthusiastic responses were especially likely if, in a letter or a personal interview, poorly prepared candidates did not offset their limitations by making a strongly favourable impression on hiring personnel.[22] The FMC's position was perhaps made clearest in its reply to a young woman who offered for India in 1890 and who proposed to take short-term, informal medical training as preparation. '[A]ny ladies who desire to engage in India missions,' she was told, 'would need to give proof of special aptitude in teaching or in scholarship or in medical work.' The WFMS board took essentially the same position, affirming in 1891 in response to an inquiry that training as a teacher or a medical missionary was *absolutely* necessary.'[23]

Obviously, home-base officials did not always insist on such credentials. Nor did their concern for professional qualifications lead them to minimize the importance of spiritual commitment and denominational orthodoxy. Thus, despite their enthusiasm for appointing medical missionaries, FMC and WFMS officials agreed in 1896 that Dr Kate McKay of New Glasgow, Nova Scotia, ought not to be hired, notwithstanding good testimonials about her medical work, since she was not a church communicant and lacked experience in Christian work.[24] Yet though purity of faith and a demonstrated zeal for Christian service undoubtedly remained prerequisites, the clearly established policy of Western Division administrators was that these qualities were not in themselves sufficient. A pamphlet on desirable qualifications in female foreign missionaries prepared by the WFMS in 1892 aptly reflected the situation: it began by emphasizing the importance of a sense of calling and of a Christ-like personal witness; significantly, however, the first item on its accompanying list of questions for candidates enquired about the place and extent of their education.[25] In practice, moreover, it was the latter aspect that proved to be the chief stumbling block for many would-be missionaries: unsuccessful candidates provided at least as much evidence of personal piety in their application data as women accepted for service.

The policy of encouraging only well-educated volunteers created few staffing difficulties for the Western Division during the late 1880s and the 1890s when enthusiasm for a foreign missionary career was high. Yet even in the last years of the period when the supply of suitable candidates of both sexes was proving wholly inadequate to meet existing needs in the fields, administrators did not respond to the dilemma by accepting all offers or making appeals that emphasized spiritual fitness alone. However much some of them might admire the zeal and dedication of the so-called 'faith' missions, whose policy was to accept volunteers with little or no advanced education and to require of them only an ardent commitment to evangelism and a willingness to adopt a near-native standard of living, they were never seriously tempted to adopt a similar policy for their own fields. Instead, faced with a shortage of acceptable volunteers, administrators appealed more vigorously to their colleges, and called on the heads of Presbyterian foreign mission boards outside the country to forward the names of qualified candidates whom they themselves would not be able to employ.[26]

In attempting to put only well-qualified candidates into their foreign fields, Canadian Presbyterian officials were seeking to emulate the standards of their Scottish and American counterparts. Such standards, in turn, were in keeping with the widespread view that the peoples of Asia, and most particularly India, as the possessors of ancient and complex religious and cultural traditions, required missionary strategies and personnel more sophisticated than those thought adequate for Christianizing African or North American peoples.[27] George Monro Grant's *The Religions of the World in Relation to Christianity,* with its relatively enlightened approach to the world's main religions, was not published until 1894, but well before that time missions-minded Presbyterians were at least superficially aware of the religious complexities of the East and of the innovative strategies that would be required for effective proselytization. Writing from Central India during that mission's first years, Marion Fairweather repeatedly stressed the need for intelligent, well-educated men and women to meet the challenge of 'the subtle Hindoo' and warned officials against sending what she called 'half-way people.'[28] The same officials would later recall Fairweather following internal troubles in the mission, but their appointment practices remained generally consistent with her advice.

The view that overseas missionary service was more challenging, physically and intellectually, than comparable work in Canada prompted both the WFMS and the FMC to recommend for their Canadian Indian missions, or for deaconess work, applicants considered unsuitable for their foreign fields. The practice was particularly evident in the late 1880s and in the 1890s. Applicants rejected for overseas service on grounds of being over age, inadequately educated, or in questionable health were told almost routinely that, if they wished, their names could be passed along to the FMC official responsible for hiring Northwest personnel. (The only education required of women teachers in the latter field, R.P. MacKay told an inquirer in 1902, was 'the ordinary public school certificate.')[29] Corresponding attempts were made to prevent well-qualified volunteers from being inadvertently 'thrown away' on the Northwest.[30] Occasionally, highly regarded women were drafted from deaconess work. Thus, in 1911, MacKay's associate secretary, A.E. Armstrong, asked to have musician Leah Dinwoody released from her job as deaconess with Erskine Church, Toronto, for 'the larger and more pressing work of one or other of our foreign fields.' A year later, MacKay declined to bring University of Toronto graduate Agnes Dickson home from South China and find her church work in Canada, as her aged parents had requested. 'The work [in China] is infinitely larger and more interesting and hopeful,' MacKay wrote, and calling her back to Canada 'would simply blight Miss Dickson's future.'[31]

Given foreign missions officials' concern about missionaries' secular education and their views about the special and sophisticated needs of their Asian fields, there is at least a seeming paradox in their lack of emphasis on the systematic religious training of women candidates. Prior to the establishment of the Ewart Missionary Training Home in Toronto in 1897, the FMC had provided religious instruction for women candidates only on an occasional and ad hoc basis. The training home, moreover, had come about only through the persistence of the WFMS board. And even after the FMC had approved the draft regulations drawn up by the board and itself prepared a course of study, it reserved the right to waive the six-month-minimum-residency requirement on which board members wanted to insist.[32]

Not surprisingly, formal religious instruction did not become a significant element in women missionaries' backgrounds even with the opening of the home. Only about one-quarter of the Western Division missionaries appointed after 1897 took the full two-year course of study offered at Ewart before going abroad; almost half seem to have spent no time at all there prior to their departure. Acknowledging would-be missionaries' reluctance to attend the home, R.P. MacKay in 1913 attributed the phenomenon to financial factors.[33] For some women, the $3.00 (later $3.50) weekly charge for room and board was undoubtedly a major obstacle. Significantly, however, it was candidates who already had some advanced academic or professional education who often appeared most reluctant about attending. Some of them seemed insulted at the idea of an enforced period of residency, or suggested that their time would be better spent out in the field learning the language, views that were endorsed by ministers writing on their behalf.[34] Such attitudes reflected a prevailing scepticism about the value of the Ewart curriculum, and perhaps resentment of the home's role as a vetting agency for prospective missionaries.

The Ewart curriculum combined a program of Christian studies with instruction in such practical subjects as home nursing, sanitation, bookkeeping, and elocution; students also did field work in city missions. Teaching was normally provided on a voluntary basis by Knox College faculty and by missions sympathizers with expertise in non-theological subjects. A few of the former tried teaching Ewart students and male theological candidates in the same classes and giving them the same examinations, but the experiment was abandoned in 1908 when the two professors then involved declared that separate classes were after all more advantageous. The Knox faculty's generally conservative teaching was reinforced by the compulsory Bible studies conducted by the home's resident superintendent.[35] After 1908, when Ewart became formally responsible for training deaconesses as well as missionaries, some changes were introduced into the curriculum to meet the distinctive needs of the two groups. Overall, however, the program of study remained more noteworthy for breadth than for academic rigour until after the end of this period.[36]

When they had first conceived the idea of a training centre for their own missionary candidates, WFMS board members had emphasized that the investigative function of such an institution would be more important than the educational one.[37] A pamphlet on the Ewart home published about 1907 described its objects as, first, the training of missionary candidates, and, second, the provision of an 'opportunity of judging by kind and careful oversight as to the physical, mental and spiritual fitness of candidates to enter upon the trials and responsibilities of foreign missionary life.' Despite the sequence in which these objects were listed, the second seems to have remained more important to the WFMS board. It was also the aspect that the FMC seemed most willing to support. While the WFMS was unsuccessful in its periodic attempts to insist on an extended minimum-residency requirement, FMC members on the home's Joint Board of Management agreed that prospective missionaries should be required to spend at least a few weeks there. In 1909, the FMC members also agreed that the superintendent should continue to furnish private reports on residents' conduct and character, despite the resentment that this practice had evidently aroused in the past.[38] Faced with the awkward task of responding to well-educated missionary candidates reluctant to attend the home, R.P. MacKay played down the need for them to spend a long period of time there and instead argued, albeit rather feebly, that even a short stay gave 'the ladies of the home' an opportunity to get to know their prospective workers and thus to establish harmonious relations and prevent unsuitable appointments.[39]

Foreign missions officials' apparently casual attitude towards the religious education of prospective women missionaries reflected two related factors: their knowledge of candidates' personal religious backgrounds, and their expectations about their future work in the fields. Women who volunteered for foreign missionary service, they realized, typically came from homes where religious instruction was provided and where one or both parents were actively involved in church work, often in leadership roles. Besides being church communicants, they themselves had routinely been Sunday school teachers or mission band leaders and prominent members of one or more religiously oriented organizations. In these positions, they had sometimes demonstrated outstanding leadership and speaking skills. Quebec high school principal Esther Smith was one such candidate. Her minister, writing on her behalf, described her weekly talks to his

Sunday school and Bible study classes as ones that the whole congregation frequently stayed to hear. Some women had initiated religious work on their own. Several schoolteacher applicants, for instance, had started Sunday schools or Christian Endeavour societies in the rural communities where they were teaching; one, finding her district without the services of a minister, began doing regular evangelistic work among the parents of her pupils.[40] A few candidates had experience in full-time religious work as Bible women, deaconesses, or settlement workers. (Bible women were occasionally employed by urban churches to call on the poor and unchurched; the position appears to have evolved into that of deaconess even before such an order was officially established in 1908.) In brief, by the time female missionary candidates sought appointments, they had generally had years of experience both in getting and giving religious instruction.

This background was considered adequate for the roles they were expected to play in overseas mission fields. Officials' views regarding these roles were based largely on their knowledge of older societies' foreign missions endeavours and took shape with India particularly in mind. It was not these officials' intention that their women missionaries would take part in complex theological debates with well-educated, disputatious non-Christian men, or engage in advanced scriptural exegesis. Leaving such tasks for their ordained colleagues, the women were to work among a largely illiterate female population, employing whatever skills proved most useful in 'breaking down ... the barriers of heathendom.'[41] Medical work, teaching, sewing, and music – these, and a friendly, sympathetic personality, were the keys that would give them access to high-caste girls and women in seclusion, and to their poorer sisters in bazaars and farm fields. The barriers surmounted, they could go on to introduce the most elementary and appealing aspects of the Christian faith. For that task, and even for training their Indian evangelistic assistants, the level of Christian knowledge required of them would not be beyond that routinely provided in the home and church in the course of a proper Presbyterian upbringing.

Foreign missions administrators were thus more concerned to ensure that their women candidates had had such an upbringing, and that they possessed the personalities and professional skills that would commend them to 'the heathen,' than that they had been exposed in a training school to the rudiments of such subjects as 'Christian Evidences' and 'Church History.' A personal zeal for evangelism was obviously also a prerequisite. But, again, evidence of such zeal was to be found in the women's backgrounds rather than in formal religious training. Writing to India missionary

Norman Russell in 1894 in reference to a newly appointed missionary, R.P. MacKay effectively made this point: 'I think you are going to have in Miss Campbell a valuable worker – the Lord has been using her to the conversion of souls in her own neighbourhood and there is no certificate like that.'[42] Given such an emphasis, it was hardly surprising that it was the investigative rather than the tutorial function of the Ewart home that MacKay was most ready to defend.

How closely did women missionaries' backgrounds resemble those of male missionaries and missionary wives? Biographical data on the men and married women who were in India during this period may be taken as indicative for comparative purposes, especially since, with the exception of Trinidad, the church did not seem to have a policy of fitting particular missionary backgrounds to particular overseas fields.

Predictably, in the matter of education male missionaries had generally received more extensive preparation, both academically and theologically. Most of those who were ministers (a quarter were laymen)[43] had taken university degrees before beginning their three years of theological training. For the latter, the majority had attended either Knox College in Toronto or Manitoba College in Winnipeg, with Knox having a slight edge. Knox was widely regarded as a citadel of Presbyterian orthodoxy. Even so, the missionaries who studied there had probably had a somewhat greater exposure to new currents of religious thought than their female counterparts by the time they reached the foreign field. The Knox faculty at the turn of the century included John E. McFayden, a leading exponent of the higher criticism. (McFayden had received a frustrating lesson in the unwisdom of introducing his Ewart students to the new teaching in 1899 when the first superintendent of the Ewart home, a minister's widow named Anna Ross, had expressed concern to the home's Board of Management that he was exposing her 'girls' to unsound theology.)[44] By the end of the period, as well, many Knox men, fresh from the University of Toronto and from courses in such relatively new fields as psychology, had been exposed to ideas that R.P. MacKay characterized as the 'rankest radicalism' and that he suspected of contributing to a decline in missionary vocations.[45]

Male missionaries, moreover, had had a broader range of experience by the time they left Canada. The ministers as well as the laymen had frequently been employed in business, on the railroads, or in other lines of work unrelated to evangelism. In addition, most had spent one or more summers, and sometimes a period of years, working in home mission fields. Such work often brought them into contact with people and social conditions markedly different from anything in their previous experience. By contrast, the educational and work experiences of female foreign mission volunteers had generally kept them closer to home. The case of schoolteacher Bella Ptolemy was probably fairly typical: writing to MacKay prior to her departure for India in 1895, Ptolemy expressed the poignant hope that she would be sailing in the company of other missionaries, 'for I have never travelled further than one day's journey at a time.'[46]

In other respects, however, the male missionaries had a great deal in common with their female counterparts. Like the latter, they were in their late twenties or early thirties when they left Canada, and they had strikingly similar geographic and socio-economic origins. The sense of superiority they felt towards 'lady missionaries' on the basis of their sex and advanced education and (usually) ordained status was probably offset to some degree by an awareness of these shared and rather ordinary origins.

The women who went out to India as missionary wives or fiancées were younger as a group than those appointed as career missionaries – 26.9 was the average age – and somewhat more likely to have come from cities and towns.[47] In the early years most of them probably had little in the way of advanced academic or professional education. In time, however, this changed. Male candidates frequently became engaged, or married, while seeking appointments, and they became increasingly conscious of the need for selecting partners who would make appropriate missionary wives. Experienced missionaries and missionary manuals repeatedly warned of the importance of caution in this regard.[48] The women chosen, in turn, knew that they would be expected to play an active missionary role to the extent that their circumstances permitted. They therefore understood that they were accepting a way of life as well as a husband and that such factors as their age, health, and level of education were matters of more than passing interest to the FMC. Indeed, such factors could help or hinder their partner's chances of getting an appointment. The application of the Reverend John Cook was a case in point. Cook had already been turned down by an American mission board when he applied to the FMC in 1910. He was not impressive intellectually and he had what one referee called a 'watery personality,' but he *was* earnest, and he was engaged to Ruth Bremner, a student volunteer with professional training in music whom referees enthusiastically endorsed. Both points evidently counted in his favour when the FMC considered his case and decided to give him an appointment.[49] Would-be missionary wives knew, then, that it behooved them to equip themselves as thoroughly as possible for the life that lay ahead. By the latter part of the period their ranks in India included three teachers with university degrees as well as a doctor, two nurses, and women with special training in music and evangelism. In this respect, as well as in terms of their social and economic backgrounds, they resembled the single women.

Missionary wives, male missionaries, and single women missionaries thus had remarkably similar origins. Undoubtedly, too, certain common experiences in the backgrounds of all three groups had predisposed them towards the life they were undertaking. Nevertheless, as contemporaries recognized, the decision to become a foreign missionary was a significantly different and more daring one for a single woman than it was for either her male counterpart or his wife.

ࢽ࢙ ࢽ࢙ ࢽ࢙

What prompted single women to become foreign missionaries? In an article entitled 'The Woman for the Foreign Field,' published in the *Knox College Monthly* in 1890, an unidentified writer acknowledged that a number of factors, not all of them spiritual and selfless, could enter into the decision:

Dear Christian sisters, whose thoughts are turning towards the foreign field ... Think long and deeply over the matter ... Beware of being carried away by romantic or emotional feelings, let there be no lurking desire to get rid of duty which lies at hand, because it is irksome or dull ... The soul's unrest and love of change must have no part in this matter ... The hope of gaining a comfortable livelihood must not be allowed to weigh with you. If it is a livelihood that is wanted, the intellectual qualifications and professional enthusiasms needed to ensure success in the mission field, will earn you that in your own land, with far less weariness of the flesh and far more of the good things of this life.

The writer went on, however, to express her [?] confidence that the hypothetical young woman she was addressing would be led, finally, by a true missionary spirit and would be prepared to go 'even unto the ends of the earth to serve her Lord.'[50] Despite its hyperbole and inspirational purpose, this article was probably substantially accurate in reflecting prevailing aspects of motivation: it acknowledged the personal and worldly considerations that could enter into the decision, while emphasizing the strong sense of Christian vocation that generally lay at its core.

The foreign missionary movement became important in Canada at a time when English-Canadian women were gaining access to higher academic and professional education. It was an education for which there were not corresponding employment opportunities. Professional teacher training was the first such avenue to open. While there were plenty of teaching jobs available, especially for professionally trained applicants, rates of pay were very low – indeed, they were declining relative to male teachers' salaries – and chances for advancement were few. For the early women graduates of medical schools, prospects were also poor. Hospital facilities in which women could practise and develop their skills were often denied to them. Male colleagues were frequently hostile and the general public sceptical. If the early graduates of the country's universities faced no such wall of resentment, it was nonetheless clear that there were few job opportunities commensurate with their new status.[51] Finally, both for well-educated women and for those with little or no advanced training, there was the further constraint of the widely accepted social norm that, except in unusual circumstances, it was the 'sacred' duty of an unwed daughter to remain at home and care for aged parents or unmarried siblings.[52] Given this context, it was not surprising that women who had not found (or perhaps not wanted) marriage partners should have looked for broader horizons.

Through their overseas missionary endeavours, the Protestant evangelical churches were providing a vehicle through which new career avenues could justifiably and respectably be explored. Throughout North America, foreign missions advocates of both sexes were eager to emphasize the acceptable new roles that were available. Typical of their approach were several articles in the Reverend B.F. Austin's *Woman; Her Character, Culture and Calling,* an 1890 work that was designed to serve as both a tribute and an inspiration to the much discussed 'new woman.' The contributors of the articles, Canadians and Americans representing different Protestant denominations, joined Austin himself in enlarging on the opportunities that existed for women to exercise their professional and administrative talents in missionary work. The very disabilities under which Eastern women laboured, they explained, created unparalleled opportunities for their Western sisters. At the same time, because they were Western ers, women missionaries could live and move about in perfect safety in these lands.[53]

Within their own publications, Canadian Presbyterians conveyed the same message, stressing that the mission field – as opposed to the pulpit – was a place where talented, godly women could acceptably exercise their gifts. The point was perhaps made most effectively by the *Knox College Monthly*'s J.A. Macdonald in 1888 following the designation of a trained nurse for the church's new mission field in North Honan:

This appointment ... illustrates the prominence that must be given to woman's work in the evangelization of the world. Here is a sphere less injurious to true womanhood than many into which women are clamouring for admission, more in harmony with her better nature and God's evident designs, in which her own long pent-up energies and powers may find full scope to her own advantage and the immeasurable blessing of humanity.[54]

Seeking new rights and roles for their own sake clearly remained unacceptable. Being a new woman for the extension of the Kingdom, however, was a matter for commendation and celebration. Women anxious for enlarged roles *and* public approbation could scarcely remain insensitive to the opportunities available.

The precise nature of the new roles and opportunities, as well as basic information about the geography and climate of the church's mission fields, was made widely known through its periodicals. The princely states of Central India, site of the church's first and most important field for women's work, appeared to be particularly rich in opportunities. There, local princes and other educated Indian men were beginning to seek some of the benefits of Westernization for their wives and daughters. Despite their continuing opposition to aggressive Christian proselytizing, they generally accepted the educational and medical services that women missionaries offered. Indeed, they often actively sought such services, offering land and other incentives to attract mission workers to their districts. Even zenana visiting – calling on high-caste Hindu, and Muslim, women in the secluded quarters of their homes – was reportedly encouraged, since, despite its evangelistic purpose, it gave reform-minded Indians free and private access to women missionaries' skills. Because Hindus and Muslims believed in segregating the sexes, male missionaries could have no direct part in most of these forms of work. In such a setting, it followed, Canadian women would have far greater opportunities for autonomy in their work than existed in their own country. In their reports, both the missionaries themselves and their WFMS publicists took care to let this aspect come through.[55]

By the end of the period, a network of schools, dispensaries, hospitals, widows' homes, and orphanages had been established in Central India, and the work had grown to include a variety of unanticipated but interesting and rewarding tasks. For reasons that reflected indigenous conditions or home-base officials' priorities, none of the other missions had developed quite such an elaborate infrastructure for women's work. As a result, the missionaries who served in those fields had a somewhat more limited range of job opportunities. Nevertheless, as their reports made clear, in whatever capacity they were employed, as Western women in Eastern societies they enjoyed a gratifying level of prestige and an unaccustomed authority.

Women, moreover, could undertake such careers without consigning themselves irrevocably to spinsterhood or to life in a foreign land. While the decision to become a foreign missionary was normally viewed as a permanent one by all parties concerned, there was a good deal of flexibility in the arrangements that existed, for, especially given its abhorrence of 'Romanism,' the church was unwilling to extract a commitment similar to that required of women entering Catholic orders. Thus, missionaries who became ill in the field or experienced other personal difficulties were brought home and permitted to return to private life. Furthermore, more than a quarter of the women who went out during this period married. Some found partners among their fellow workers, or among men in other missions. Harriet Sutherland, the nurse so proudly dispatched to North Honan in 1888, was lost to her church through the latter route within a year of her arrival in China, becoming the wife of a recently bereaved American missionary and stepmother to his several children. In India, several missionaries married British soldiers who were stationed in their districts.[56] Far from being 'an environment where eligible males were rare,' as American missions historian Valentin Rabe has claimed, the mission field was often a more likely place for an older woman to find a partner than her own home community.[57] Indeed, in some circles, an unsubtle brand of humour developed about this aspect of its attraction (such as the story of four American women in central China nicknamed 'Hunt, Search, Seek, and Rob'). Following his world tour of mission fields in 1882, the American William F. Bainbridge felt called upon to affirm that it was 'a cruel libel upon the young unmarried missionary women to declare that they have gone to foreign lands to watch their matrimonial chances there.'[58] He was probably right. In all likelihood, few women set out for the foreign field with the conscious hope of finding a husband, or on a casual whim. In case any were inclined to do so, however, the WFMS drew up a contract for outgoing missionaries to sign; it required them to refund a portion of their salary, as well as travel and outfit expenses, if for reasons other than a breakdown in health they did not remain in service for a stated minimum period. In practice, the society exercised a good deal of discretion about applying its penalties to the full, especially in cases where one of its workers was marrying a fellow missionary, since, as the fiancés concerned and the FMC were fond of pointing out, such women would still be serving the cause, though in another sphere of usefulness.[59]

The church's foreign fields, then, provided women with attractive career opportunities without extracting a lifetime commitment. They also offered the added attractions of an exotic setting and the chance to lead an adventurous life in a good cause. Because so few other avenues for an unconventional life were open to them, women may have been particularly susceptible to these attractions. Commenting on the latter aspect of their appeal in the United States in the years before 1860, historian Barbara Welter noted that '[m]ission boards ... were firm in ruling out "adventuring" as a satisfactory motive.'[60] While the Canadian Presbyterians who promoted their church's foreign mission enterprise in this period were presumably no more anxious than their earlier American counterparts to dispatch mere adventurers, they recognized that sheltered Victorian women, no matter how intense their evangelistic zeal, were unlikely to take up the work unless they had some taste for excitement and for unfamiliar horizons. They therefore joined other mission agencies and the popular press in acknowledging and even accentuating these aspects. By the mid-1880s this approach had done its work: overseas missions had captured the imagination of supporters and would-be participants in a way that the evangelization of the homeland simply could not match.[61]

It is clear both from their reports of the initial outward journey and from enthusiastic accounts of extensive holiday and furlough travels that, for a number of women, the opportunity for foreign travel was an attractive aspect of a missionary career. The author of a booklet about India veteran Maggie MacKellar noted the aptness for her subject of a popular saying, 'Only millionaires and missionaries can travel.' Taking care to emphasize that the spiritual primacy of MacKellar's motivation was beyond question, the author went on to speak of her 'inherited' love of travel (MacKellar's father had been a Hebridean seaman) and to note some of the places she had visited on her own time and money.[62] Home-base officials sometimes published the travel pieces written by these sojourning missionaries, particularly during the early years. There was a certain risk that in doing so they might alienate prospective financial supporters by creating the impression that their overseas workers were merely having a good time. But given the inherent interest of such copy, it was a risk worth taking, especially since the authors usually included references to visits to other missions, denunciations of 'heathen monuments,' and other 'relevant' content.[63]

The chief object of interest for the would-be missionary was, of course, the mission field itself. For some, its allure seemed to increase in direct proportion to its remoteness and inpenetrability. This was evidently the case for Dr Susie Carson Rijnhart, a Methodist-born school inspector's daughter from Strathroy, Ontario, who described her experiences in 1901 in a remarkable book called *With the Tibetans in Tent and Temple*. Operating largely as free-lance missionaries, Rijnhart and her Dutch husband, Petrus, bypassed the millions of unreached souls in more accessible fields and attempted to penetrate the mountain fastness of Tibet, despite that country's well-known hostility to outsiders. In the course of the attempt, their infant son died, their guides deserted, and Petrus mysteriously disappeared while trying to get help from nomads. Dr Rijnhart herself barely succeeded in making her way out to China. Yet following a trip to North America to publish and lecture, she returned to the East to resume her missionary career.[64]

Rijnhart's experiences were undoubtedly well known to Presbyterian women: the WFMS promoted her book in its own press, notwithstanding her patently impractical approach to the missionary task, since it provided a compellingly attractive tale of missionary adventure. Meanwhile, the society's own missionaries wrote of experiences that, while less dramatic than Rijnhart's, were nonetheless colourful and exciting and (perhaps more important in the long run in terms of their impact on impressionable young readers) accessible in the course of everyday mission duties. Some women became particularly adept at working local colour into correspondence intended for publication. India missionary Mary Dougan was such a writer. One of her reports, written in 1895 and subsequently printed in the *Monthly Letter Leaflet*, seemed in fact to epitomize what 'the romance of missions' was all about. At the beginning of the year, Dougan and medical missionary Margaret O'Hara had joined an ordained colleague in the city of Dhar to investigate the possibility of establishing a mission station there. '[T]he Maharajah invited us to be his guests for a few days,' Dougan wrote:

Two fine tents were pitched for us in the most beautiful garden I have seen in India. Bananas, papyias [sic], pomolas, peaches, oranges, lemons are growing in rich abundance and the dark green of cypress and palm is brightened by roses and tropical plants ...

On Monday last we were called to the palace ... A royal carriage came for us early in the afternoon and for an hour we had the privilege of singing the glad new tidings before His Highness, the Rani, and the young Prince ... Before her own exit the Rani presented us each with a brooch of silver. Afterwards the Prince ... sprinkled us with perfume and strung garlands round our necks.[65]

Mary Leach was another India missionary who was highly skilled at writing colourful reports. A 1907 description of a dinner party at which she and some other missionaries had been the special guests of well-to-do Indians was so richly detailed and evocative that the *Presbyterian Record*'s Ephraim Scott devoted more than a page to it, though, as Leach herself acknowledged, it was difficult to see what either the dinner party or a subsequent follow-up visit had done for the missionary cause.[66]

Reports such as those penned by Dougan and Leach conjured up a world where one was treated with deference by prominent Indians, freed from mundane household duties through the use of domestic servants, and exposed to a rich variety of new scenes and experiences. While the writers generally took pains to suggest that their experiences were marred for them by the black shadow of heathenism, the vicarious excitement of reading about such an apparently glamorous life was probably not greatly lessened by their caution.

If the missionaries in East Asia did not usually have quite such gratifying personal experiences to report, it was nonetheless clear that they were living in a world where the ferment of societies in transition brought its own drama and excitement. This was particularly true of the church's mission in North Honan, China. The dangers experienced by the North Honan missionaries during their flight from the Boxer uprising of 1900 resulted within the church in a greatly increased interest in that field. With the defeat of the Boxers and the new openness to outside influences that followed, the entire foreign missionary enterprise increasingly focused on China. Service there thus provided women with an opportunity to become actors on the world's most important missionary stage. The attractiveness of this field was reflected in the increasing number of China appointments after the turn of the century.[67]

In 1908, in her classic novel, *Anne of Green Gables,* Lucy Maud Montgomery alluded to another important aspect of the romantic appeal of foreign missions: the allure of eventually becoming part of the church's pantheon of missionary heroes. In the course of discussing an upcoming school literature assignment with Marilla, the imaginative Anne observes:

Mustn't it be splendid to be remarkable and have compositions written about you after you're dead? Oh, I would dearly love to be remarkable. I think when I grow up I'll be a trained nurse and go with the Red Crosses to the field of battle as a messenger of mercy. That is, if I don't go out as a foreign missionary. That would be very romantic ...[68]

Anne's role models reflected the kind of literature that girls of her era were encouraged to read. Books and articles about missionary heroes were an important part of their literary fare. Recalling her upbringing by a Methodist mother who was fervently interested in missions, a real-life contemporary of Anne's, the feminist Alice Chown, wrote in 1921, 'We were forbidden to read Hans Andersen, but our imagination was fed by heroic tales of real life pursued for high purposes.'[69]

Presbyterian foreign missions publicists were keenly aware of how valuable heroic missionary literature could be in stimulating young people's interest in overseas work. In the early years, when they had few established missionary celebrities of their own, stories of the Geddies and the Gordons were supplemented in the church press by frequent sketches of such legendary figures as Carey of India and Livingstone of Africa. By the first decade of the twentieth century, Canadian publicists were able to produce two books dealing with their own heroes, *Reapers in Many Fields* (1904) and *Missionary Pathfinders* (1907), both intended for the same audience, Presbyterian young people's societies. While these and later biographical studies prepared for the young people's market focused chiefly on male workers, the women's missionary societies in both the Eastern and Western divisions were able through the pages of their periodicals to celebrate the exploits of their own missionary heroines. They also continued to promote a large body of literature produced by other agencies in order to familiarize their constituency with the lives and accomplishments of internationally renowned missions-minded women.[70]

Throughout the period, the church's most celebrated missionary heroes continued to be its martyrs, those who, in some broad sense, could be said to have died for the cause. At first glance, this approach seems somewhat surprising, for, especially as they gained experience in the movement, both FMC and WFMS officials liked to think that they had moved beyond sentiment and that they were conducting their enterprise in a practical and scientific spirit. Nor were examples of such a spirit lacking in their recruitment and field-administration policies. By 1890, for instance, they had implemented standardized procedures for checking on the fitness of missionary applicants and detecting those with a propensity for martyrdom. Though the questions in their application forms still left room for a good deal of subjectivity on the part of candidates and their physicians, they nonetheless indicated the direction in which the officials wanted to move. Ongoing efforts were also made to maintain the health of workers already in the field.[71] The church's foreign missions officials were caught, however, in the cross-currents of the romantic missionary spirit in which they themselves had been nourished and the businesslike attitudes towards which they were striving. Thus, when death or disaster did occur in the field, they were tempted – and urged – to employ the familiar metaphors of martyrdom, especially since the romanticization of missionary deaths did seem to bring results.

The way in which WFMS executives and their workers in the field publicized the death of India missionary Amy Harris in 1892 provides a good illustration of this pattern. WFMS members were told that their 'sainted missionary' had sacrificed her own frail health for the good of the cause and were given moving details of her last days on board ship as a futile effort was made to bring her home.[72] Extravagant tributes were printed in the *Monthly Letter Leaflet*, among them one from former co-worker Dr Maggie MacKellar, who had accompanied her on her final journey. MacKellar concluded her tribute by speaking of the 'good seed' her young colleague had begun to sow and by calling on others to take up her work: 'Will not the young women of our Church come forward gladly to fill her place? She is our first maiden missionary who has died in the work. Will not ten, at least, at this time lay themselves on God's mission altar and say, "Lord, here am I, send me." '[73] In the wake of Harris's death, the number of women volunteering for overseas missionary service showed a slight increase over figures for the two preceding years. Notable among them was the late missionary's schoolteacher cousin, who had allowed herself to be persuaded that Harris's vocation should become her own.[74]

Two years later when missionary wife Christina Malcolm and medical missionary Lucinda Graham died within days of each other in North Honan, the latter, like Harris, having barely begun a promising career, the editor of the *Canada Presbyterian* made it clear that he did not lag behind the WFMS in perceiving motivational value in such losses. 'Our Church is becoming more and more enriched by such treasures laid up in Heaven,' he told R.P. MacKay, 'and I doubt not that the example of those who have laid down their lives for Christ will stimulate many others to say, "Here am I, Lord, send me." '[75] If MacKay suspected that this approach to missionary recruitment might be undermining efforts to implement scientific selection procedures, he could not afford to say so publicly, for much of the foreign missions constituency – including many of the missionaries themselves – remained convinced that the 'blood of the martyrs' was still the most effective seed for a church's missionary efforts.[76]

Foreign missions administrators tried to increase the appeal of missionary work not only by emphasizing its exotic and adventurous aspects and romanticizing its personnel but also by minimizing its less attractive features. This did not mean that difficulties went unpublicized. Indeed, the problems faced by missionaries in coping with natural hardships and local opposition were the staple elements in mission reports. More mundane topics such as financial problems and housing shortages were also publicly discussed, especially in the annual reports of the FMC and the WFMS. But the truly unedifying features of mission life – the acrimony of mission politics; the petty jealousies; the ongoing frustrations over real or imagined inequities – these were another matter. Such things were reported to home-base officials in often astonishing detail and discussed at length in private committee meetings, but great care was taken to try to ensure that they did not become subjects for harmful gossip in the larger church community. Even privately owned Presbyterian periodicals generally co-operated in this effort. The positive and inspirational aspects of the church's work in the fields should be accentuated, they seemed to agree, while occurrences likely to undermine recruitment and fund-raising efforts should be left for the consideration of those in charge.[77]

Inevitably, especially if they had friends or relatives in the mission fields, single women occasionally learned of problems there that the church had been loath to publicize. But female missionary aspirants did not have access to a regular – and often discouraging – foreign missions grapevine as many theological students and ministers evidently did. The case of the young Alfred Gandier, the future principal of Knox College, provides a striking example. Asked to go to Central India in 1892, Gandier declined to do so. In view of the ongoing staff conflicts there, he wrote, it would be 'a kind of hopeless task.'[78] Largely shielded from any detailed knowledge of such problems as those to which Gandier had referred by their physical and social distance from the circles in which they were threshed out, single women were perhaps especially vulnerable to the romantic allure of missions.

The romantic images associated with foreign missionary work undoubtedly contributed to the increased status and attention conferred on those accepted for overseas service. These aspects, in turn, added to its appeal. The rewards in one's own country could be enjoyed only briefly, of course: during the period prior to departure and while home on furlough. Nevertheless, the activities that took place during these intervals could be exhilarating experiences for those at the centre of attention and important sources of inspiration for young people with their own vague dreams of a missionary vocation. For officials, the challenge was to make such activities appealing without running the risk of attracting recruits for the wrong reasons.[79]

The announcement of a successful candidacy could effectively turn an anonymous woman into a local and denominational heroine. *Foreign Mis-*

sionary Tidings often carried her photograph and a biographical sketch; a notice frequently appeared in other church papers as well. She was likely to be the featured guest at several public events in the weeks prior to her departure and to be the object of especially fond farewells from former Sunday school pupils and members of her church groups. The centrepiece in the pre-departure ceremonies was an impressive designation service, normally held in the home church. Members of the FMC and the WFMS board frequently took part, along with local WFMS leaders. Clergy from other denominations might participate, and, especially in smaller centres, the local press was likely to give the occasion front-page coverage. An inscribed Bible and appropriate practical gifts were presented, and, after the early years, the newly designated missionary generally responded with a brief address (a male relative or clergyman spoke on behalf of some of the first women appointed). As the service ended, she took her leave to the accompaniment of an emotional farewell hymn, almost invariably 'God Be with You till We Meet Again.'[80] Near the end of her life, Dr Belle Choné Oliver recalled the powerful impression created on her when, at the age of fifteen, she witnessed such a service in Ingersoll, Ontario, for the departing Dr Maggie MacKellar. While she had been interested in mission work before, it was this occasion, she wrote, that had galvanized her interest and led her to a definite decision to become a medical missionary.[81]

When they came home to Canada on furlough after six or more years of service, missionaries could again enjoy the esteem of their fellow Presbyterians and at the same time deepen others' interest in a foreign missionary career through the favourable attention they attracted. As they travelled from one community to another in the course of deputation work, sometimes donning native garb and exhibiting exotic artifacts, they often aroused a remarkable degree of interest. Indeed, the WFMS officials who acted as their 'booking agents' were sometimes compelled to refuse requests for popular missionaries' visits in order to prevent them from returning to the field more exhausted than when they had come home.[82] In the course of their furloughs, highly regarded missionaries appeared before a variety of audiences. None perhaps was more gratifying than the General Assembly of their church. When Jean Sinclair, a harness-maker's daughter from Madoc, Ontario, was invited to address this august body in 1896, the first woman ever to do so, the event served to demonstrate as few others could have done the prominence that churchwomen could attain through the vehicle of foreign missionary service.[83]

Celebrity status was usually greatest in the home community. There, the attention that briefly attached itself to anyone who had returned 'from away' was augmented by the mystique of a period of foreign service. In 1899 when University of Toronto graduate Rachel Chase returned to Orillia on sick leave from Central India, the interest was so great that a younger sister waggishly devised an unusual means of dealing with inquiries – a placard inside her coat with printed answers to the anticipated questions:

> Yes, my sister from India is home.
> Yes, we were glad to see her.
> No, she is not in bed.
> Yes, she can go out.
> Yes, she will receive callers.
> No, she is not very thin.
> Yes, it is nice for me to have her home.[84]

Abiding by her widowed father's wishes, Chase remained permanently in Canada. If she had returned to India, her home church would probably have staged an elaborate departure service similar to the one that had marked her original leave-taking. She might not have received such impressive gifts as her older colleague Dr Margaret O'Hara, whose Smiths Falls congregation in 1898 gave her a two-seater buggy, a portable organ, and a silver communion service to take back to her station; and she might not have attracted such a large crowd as Formosa pioneer George Leslie Mackay, for whose farewell service officials prepared by booking Woodstock's Methodist church rather than the smaller Presbyterian building. Even so, she would have known that her official leave-taking was a significant and impressive community event as well as a personal milestone.[85]

The regional patterns in missionaries' origins to which reference has already been made were an important outcome of ceremonies such as these – an outcome that local missions-minded clergy were clearly anxious to produce.[86] The favourable attention paid to native sons and daughters on furlough and their own vigorous recruitment efforts contributed, over time, to a significant number of candidacies from the same region. The large number of men and women who volunteered from Oxford County and other parts of southwestern Ontario following the early and much celebrated example of George Leslie Mackay is perhaps the best illustration of this pattern. Flamboyant missionaries like Mackay generated an interest in the movement that crossed denominational lines and fed into the already intense evangelical culture of the communities from which they came. (Southwestern Ontario was also the home of several early Baptist missionaries and of the missionary-widow-turned-evangelist Aimee Semple McPherson.)[87] Even after local missionary heroes had died, their influence lived on indirectly as the workers they themselves had motivated became, in their turn, effective recruiters of a new generation of the region's young people.

Regional or institutional ties among missionaries could develop for other, or additional, reasons. Young women sometimes planned together for a missionary career over a period of years. This was evidently the case with Ontario schoolteachers Jean Dow and Lizzie McWilliams, and with Maritimers Catherine Mair and Edith Sutherland of Dalhousie University. In the latter case, it seems clear, Mair's youthful commitment might well have been abandoned had it not been for the stimulus provided by her friend Edith, who preceded her to Korea as a missionary wife and from there wrote letters sustaining her interest and strengthening her resolve. By the time she was designated, Mair could look forward to the company of six other Dalhousie graduates in the small Korean field.[88]

The part played by family example in the decision to become a missionary is even more striking. During the period, an extensive network of brothers, sisters, cousins, and other relatives found their way into foreign missionary service. They did not necessarily serve in the same field or at the same time. Margaret Rodger went to India from a farm near Lachute, Quebec, in the early 1870s, for example; her cousin Dr William McClure left the region for China about a decade later, while his son, Dr Robert McClure, began work in China in the 1920s.[89] The idea of serving with another family member was obviously an attractive one for many volunteers, however, as the examples of Maggie Jamieson and her brother in India, the McCully sisters in Korea, and the McCalla sisters in China all indicate.[90] Moreover, parents with two or more children engaged in foreign mission work were naturally eager to see them located in the same field. As the FMC became aware of the internal tensions these family networks could create in a mission, they were not always prepared to comply with such requests. Yet given the obvious value of family ties in staffing their mission fields, they were careful to word their refusals as tactfully as possible.[91]

Personal influences were demonstrably important in the decision to become a foreign missionary. It is much more difficult to assess the importance for women of a broad cultural factor commonly thought to have been associated with that decision, that is, the imperialist climate of the late-nineteenth and early-twentieth centuries. Nevertheless, it seems logical to enquire whether Canadian Protestant women participated in foreign missions in part as a means of associating themselves with British imperial enterprise.

While such imperialist rhetoric as that described in Carl Berger's *The Sense of Power* is largely absent from the application data left by the Presbyterian women who aspired to become foreign missionaries in this period, there is no reason to believe that they were immune to its appeal. Certainly, as Canadian Protestants of the late-Victorian era, they were exposed to frequent and extravagant claims about the providential role of the British Empire in the spread of Christianity. Indeed, in 1876, in the first issue of the *Presbyterian Record,* George Monro Grant advanced such a claim in the context of a review of his church's missionary initiatives. Having outlined the pioneer endeavours of Maritime Presbyterians, he went on to speak of India and to endorse the view of his missionary brother in Madras that the conversion of the subcontinent was 'the work given by God in a special sense to the whole British Empire.' The following year, focusing in the same publication on the church's new mission in Indore, Central India, WFMS recording secretary Mrs Marjory MacMurchy was even more specific, depicting the task of evangelization as Canada's distinctive contribution to imperial teamwork. 'England has given the people of Indore an organized army, protection, wise administration of law, and education,' she wrote. 'To Canada is left the distinguished honour of sending the gospel.'[92] Such views as these suggested a way in which even women could share in the work of Empire.

And yet it would be a mistake to associate the missionaries too narrowly with *British* imperialism. They were, of course, proud of their links with the Empire. A number of the women who served in India during this period would rejoice in close associations with civil and military officials and report gratifying instances of honours and recognition from the raj. Nevertheless, once in the field, they quickly became conscious of the fact that British imperial policy did not always coincide with the interests of Christian missionaries. Indeed, in both India and East Asia, it sometimes seemed that in cases of conflict, British officials actually favoured 'the heathen.'[93] At the same time, as missionaries and their home-base supporters well knew, it was American co-operation and precedent that had been instrumental in the establishment of some of the church's most important fields; and American literature and contacts continued to be important, even decisive, influences in shaping Canadian Protestants' understanding of the missionary movement and enlarging the scope of mission work.

As a result of their exposure to these two strands of influence, aspiring missionaries were led to regard the missionary enterprise as a joint Anglo-American responsibility and therefore one to which, as Canadians, they were doubly called to service. The imperialist ethos to which they responded was a broad cultural imperialism, reflecting their belief in the superiority – and the 'peculiar burden' – of the Anglo-Saxon 'race.'[94]

When they volunteered for foreign missionary service, Presbyterian women did not normally refer to career ambitions or romantic dreams, or even to a desire to help shoulder the burdens of empire. They spoke, instead, of a longing to spread a knowledge of Christianity and to witness through Christian service. Often, they expressed their sense of commitment through scriptural imagery or the language of well-known hymns. Schoolteacher Maggie Jamieson of Quebec City, for example, wrote in 1889:

I have consecrated myself to God in the words of Miss Havergal's hymn, 'Take my life and let it be, Consecrated Lord to thee,' and am willing to separate myself from home and all that is dearest of earthly ties to be buried as a grain of seed, in order to tell to the Heathen the wonderful love of a saviour.[95]

Most successful applicants were not quite as given to self-dramatization as Jamieson, but they generally expressed similar sentiments. Many cited Christ's last commandment: 'Go ye into all the world and preach the gospel to every creature,' (Mark 16:15). Others spoke of a desire to 'liberate' their 'heathen sisters' or to employ their talents where they would be of most value. They referred to a conviction that missionary work was God's will for their lives, and they repeatedly emphasized that their candidacy had not been entered into lightly.

Such motives, however stated, cannot be neatly separated from the factors discussed above. A twenty-one-year-old applicant who would later become a successful China missionary acknowledged as much when she wrote in 1891 that, though she had aspired to the work 'from early years,' it was 'probably from motives which required much pruning.'[96] Nevertheless, it would be a serious mistake to interpret the missionaries' formal statements of motivation as no more than rationalizations for romantic fantasies and self-serving ambitions, for to do so would be to ignore the intellectual climate in which church-going Protestant women of the era came to maturity. In such a climate, it was quite natural that those whose spiritual and emotional sensibilities were particularly acute and whose lives were largely without domestic responsibilities should have felt themselves under an obligation to share their faith with the unchurched in distant lands.

The seeds that would ripen into this sense of obligation and ultimately bear fruit in a missionary vocation were often planted in the home. Missions propagandists never tired of reminding their audience of the importance of home nurture in the vocations of past missionary heroes. The case of John Geddie, the church's first overseas missionary, came to be used as a classic example of the value of home influences in Presbyterian missionary lore. As a newborn infant Geddie was said to have been so small and frail that his parents had despaired of his life. When he survived, they secretly dedicated him – their only son – to missionary service, and as he grew older they provided him with as much missionary literature as they could obtain. Despite the many obstacles and detours on their son's path, the end result of their faith and devotion had been a successful mission in the New Hebrides. Parallels to the Geddie story can be found in accounts written by or about several women missionaries of this period. Thus, in a brief biography of another Nova Scotian, Dr Mary Mackay Buchanan, her daughter explained that when Mary had been a small child, her mother had asked God to accept one of her children for the foreign field. Mary, the gifted one, was educated appropriately and in due course sent to India as a medical missionary.[97]

These parental commitments may not have taken place in quite as formal and conscious a fashion as later accounts suggested. In any event, there were probably few men and women who took up missionary work solely because of them. What is clear, however, is that parents who raised their children in a home environment that made missionary work familiar and attractive and that made them sensitive to other signs of a calling appear to have been the norm in missionaries' backgrounds. The letters written by or on behalf of applicants suggest that this was so. Nurse Harriet Thomson, for instance, applying in 1896, wrote of her late mother: '[H]er heart would have rejoiced to send a child to distant lands to tell of the Saviour she loved.' Years later, and in much more prosaic terms, Margaret Brown, recalling the factors that had led her to China in 1913, highlighted the influence of her schoolteacher mother, who had herself cherished missionary ambitions.[98]

Even if they were not raised in homes that actively fostered a missionary spirit, Presbyterian young people were exposed to other influences that did so. Within the local church there existed a network of agencies whose mandate consisted partly or entirely in the cultivation of such a spirit. Each agency had access to appropriate missionary literature to assist it in its work. In Sunday schools and mission bands very young boys and girls learned of the church's work in foreign fields. For a time in the 1890s, thanks to Ephraim Scott's zeal, they even had their own periodical, the *Children's Record,* 'to give missionary information to the young and to cultivate a missionary spirit among them.' Missionaries shared in this task by writing directly to the children in these organizations, thanking them for money or supplies, describing the progress of particular children in mission care, and asking them to think about one day becoming missionaries themselves.[99] At a later stage, in Christian Endeavour groups and other young people's societies (which, in practice, were often more nearly young women's societies), youthful Presbyterians were given further opportunities to become acquainted with their church's overseas work. Here, if meetings were well planned, the world of missions would be dramatized through such devices as magic-lantern shows, missionary role-playing games, and displays of 'heathen' curios.[100] Rounding out this network of congregational agencies was the WFMS auxiliary, where young women received a particularly thorough course of education in the missionary work of their sex.

Inevitably, much of the vigour and missionary enthusiasm in these organizations depended on the local minister. His role in local recruitment efforts could be crucial in other ways as well. Besides preaching strong missionary sermons and holding monthly missionary prayer meetings, he could keep his eye on the devout and eligible women in his congregation and speak to them individually about the possibility that they might have a vocation. While some ministers seem to have gone about this task in an awkward fashion, engaging in crude and futile forms of spiritual impressment, others were notably effective at turning a young woman's interest into a definite, considered commitment. Thus, at St John's Presbyterian Church in Toronto between 1896 and 1909, no fewer than seven women from the Reverend J. McPherson Scott's congregation went to Presbyterian fields overseas, while others found missionary careers with non-Presbyterian boards, or in the Canadian West.[101] Rural and town ministers, with smaller congregations, could scarcely hope to match Scott's record, however great their personal enthusiasm for foreign missions. Collectively, however, these congregations seem to have produced more overseas workers than such big-city 'missionary' churches as St Matthew's in Halifax, Stanley Street in Montreal, St John's in Toronto, and St Stephen's in Winnipeg. In fact, some of the missionaries designated in the latter churches were women who had already decided on a missionary career before coming to the city to study and joining these churches' congregations.

Supplementing the influences of the home and local church were those provided by popular evangelists. The American layman Dwight L. Moody was only the most famous of a large band of travelling revivalists who made Canadian tours during this period. Like Moody and his musical partner, Ira D. Sankey, lesser figures such as the Methodist team of John D. Hunter and Hugh T. Crossley also contributed to the cause, either by their direct advocacy of missionary work or through the spiritual climate they created. They were able, moreover, to visit numerous small communities that could not be included on the itineraries of their more famous colleagues. Presbyterian women in this period seldom referred specifically to revival experiences in applying to do missionary work, perhaps out of a fear that such references would raise questions about the rootedness of their candidacy. Years later, however, they sometimes acknowledged the crucial role of a revival in creating the kind of intense religious experience that had subsequently made them seek a missionary purpose for their lives. As one Presbyterian journalist pointed out in 1886, even those observers who disparaged the revival phenomenon were forced to acknowledge its crucial role in filling the ranks of the church's clergy and missionaries. Certainly, the Presbyterian press gave frequent and generally favourable coverage to the activities of well-known evangelists.[102]

Also operating beyond the congregational level but within an institutional framework and with a specific focus on young people were four international and interdenominational agencies: the Young Men's and Young Women's Christian Association, the Student Volunteer Movement for Foreign Missions, and the Young People's Missionary Movement (YPMM). Best known for its spiritual and social service outreach to urban working-class women, the YWCA had an early and strong commitment to the foreign missionary cause, its college branches serving throughout the period as important vehicles for developing, or heightening, a missionary consciousness among Protestant female students.[103] Growing directly out of the strong foreign missions focus within the YMCA and YWCA, and out of Moody's celebrated Mount Hermon summer conference of 1886, the SVM came to have a uniquely high profile as a student recruitment agency across North American campuses. In 1910, its long-time chairman, John R. Mott, described the SVM as 'the principal agency through whose instrumentality candidates have been obtained for the foreign field.' The data on Canadian Presbyterian missionary women do not support this claim.

Relatively few have been identified as formal svm volunteers, and among this category were several who had already made a firm commitment to the foreign missions cause before beginning their college studies. Maggie MacKellar, for instance, was at Queen's specifically to prepare for missionary work when she joined the svm. Moreover, as contemporary references make clear, there was a good deal of 'leakage' among Presbyterian volunteers; that is, significantly greater numbers were volunteering than actually made their way to a mission field. Nevertheless, the svm does seem to have been an important factor for Presbyterian women by strengthening their identification with the cause. Certainly, the wfms regarded svm publications and activities as useful adjuncts to its own work.[104]

wfms and fmc officials were similarly enthusiastic about the Young People's Missionary Movement, an agency founded in 1902 by representatives of the major North American missionary boards (among them R.P. MacKay) to enlist young people of all denominations in the study of home and foreign missions. While the primary function of the ypmm was to develop home-base support for missions, its organizers expected that like the svm, with which it was closely associated, it would also lead to decisions for overseas service. Besides publishing a wide range of missionary literature, the ypmm worked with the churches to organize summer conferences in such attractive settings as Lake George, New York; Whitby, Ontario; and Knowlton, Quebec.[105] As with svm volunteers, there was a disappointing gap between the number of young people who spoke at these gatherings about becoming foreign missionaries and the number who actually did so. Several women who began their service after 1902 did refer to the role of the conferences in quickening their interest in missions.[106] What needs to be stressed, however, is that generally the young women who attended svm and ypmm conferences had already demonstrated their interest in evangelistic work through congregational and other activities. The conferences merely served to further that interest and sharpen its focus.

With the exception of the wfms and the ys, the institutions and agencies just described worked among prospective candidates of both sexes. Yet the doctrine of separate spheres was a fundamental aspect of the missionary enterprise, and at all levels, from the home outward, a distinctive appeal was made to women. Reference has already been made to the strong emphasis in missionary propaganda on the special opportunities that foreign mission work offered to talented, eligible women. The other side of such propaganda was an emphasis on obligations and responsibilities. Three broad and interwoven themes stand out in this connection: women's peculiar obligation to spread the gospel, given their own blessed status under Christianity; the tremendous spiritual and social needs of their 'heathen sisters'; and the absolute necessity for their participation if non-Christian societies were to be effectively proselytized.

The contention that women had a special obligation to promote Christianity had been associated with North American missionary endeavours from the early eighteen hundreds. The claim rested on popular comparisons of the historic and contemporary lot of women in Christian and non-Christian lands and emphasized that women even more than men had benefited in spiritual and social terms from the witness and teachings of Jesus. No other religion, it was argued, put women and men on a spiritually equal footing, and by the same token no other religion could claim as much from its female adherents.[107]

By the last decade of the century, a few daring American feminists, most notably Elizabeth Cady Stanton and Matilda Joslyn Gage, were challenging this line of argument. Perhaps in response, churchmen sometimes delivered their lectures on the subject in a notably censorious tone. In 1890, in his *Woman; Her Character, Culture and Calling*, B.F. Austin spoke on various aspects of the theme in a chapter ringingly entitled 'What Christ Has Done for Woman, and What Woman Has Done for Christ.' A few years later, however, in a book distributed by the YPMM, the eminent American Presbyterian foreign missions bureaucrat Robert E. Speer pointedly adopted only the first part of the title for his chapter on women and missions. 'I wish I could say something that would make women sensible of what every [Christian] woman owes to Christ,' he wrote. 'Everything that they are that is worth being Christ has made them.' Given that great debt, and the contrasting condition of their heathen sisters, eligible young women should consider bypassing 'the frivolous, commonplace social existence of the town or the city without any great, worthy, consuming, absorbing passion' for a life devoted to foreign missionary service.[108]

Far from resenting this line of argument, missions-minded women adopted it. From its earliest days, the WFMS had made the message its own, using it to encourage both support for its activities at home and participation in its work abroad. Readers of its *Second Annual Report* had thus been told: '[A] grave responsibility is resting upon the privileged women of Christian lands if *they fail* to utilize or wield this *power*, and permit the last command of an ascending Lord ... "Go teach, or make disciples of all nations", – to fall unheeded on their ears.'[109] The doctrine of *noblesse oblige*, applied in the spiritual realm, effectively meant that Christian women had a unique obligation to carry out Christ's last command.

The WFMS typically combined such messages with an emphasis on heathen women's great need. The challenge thrown out to single women to show their gratitude for their own Christian privileges by going off to meet that need could sometimes be quite pointed, as in this statement from Mrs Emily Steele's 1914 presidential address:

Some of you can *go*. You are a strong, well educated Christian young woman without special ties to keep you at home; in fact, some of you have taken situations in order to keep yourself occupied ... Again, some of you have daughters who could go if they were made to realize the tremendous need. Will you help in making this clear to them?[110]

Both the WFMS and its Eastern Division counterpart also used poetry and fiction, much of it reprinted from American periodicals, to contrast the condition of Christian and non-Christian women and thus arouse the consciences of all churchwomen, whatever their circumstances, who were not doing their utmost for the cause. These stanzas from a poem called 'Work in the Zenana,' published in the *Message* in 1909, typify the approach through poetry:

Do you see those dusky faces
Gazing dumbly to the West –
Those dark eyes, so long despairing,
Now aglow with hope's unrest?

They are looking, waiting, longing
For deliverance and light;
Shall we not make haste to help them,
Our poor sisters of the night? ...

It is time; then let us labor
That His Spirit be not grieved;
Let us give to others freely
What we freely have received.[111]

The fiction written for the delivery of this message generally followed a standard formula: it depicted a comfortably off Christian matron whose worldly preoccupations made her indifferent to foreign missions until some particular, epochal event – the generous giving of her maid, perhaps, or a vivid dream of her heathen sisters' pathetic calls for help – broke through her wall of indifference and led her to give her time, her money, or even her daughter to the cause.[112]

Given such appeals, it was not surprising that eligible young women with spiritually sensitive natures should have felt called upon to offer themselves for foreign missionary service; nor that they should have described their sense of vocation in terms of both guilt and gratitude. A young school-teacher named Agnes Hall who applied to become a missionary in 1909 was altogether typical: '[W]henever I am tempted to take up any other line of work I feel as if I would not be doing my duty. Also Jesus has done so much for me.'[113] Once convinced that they had an obligation to participate directly in the world's evangelization, such women could not find release merely by giving money to missions. As a young milliner in southwestern Ontario, Maggie MacKellar tried that, at one point pledging more money than she then possessed, but it did not work. And so, at age twenty-two, she went back to public school to begin the long course of study that would equip her for service as a medical missionary.[114]

The third and most positive theme in the appeals directed specifically to women was the one that emphasized their usefulness in the task of evangelizing Eastern societies. This aspect had of course provided the chief rationale for single women's involvement from the early nineteenth century, when returning missionaries and their wives had reported that because of the custom of segregating women in the East, there was a missionary work among them that only women could do. In the course of the century, however, the emphasis on converting women increased enormously, for it came to be argued that notwithstanding their downtrodden condition, Eastern women were the chief conservators of their societies' religious traditions and that no effective inroads on heathenism could be made unless they were reached. 'Save the women and you save the nation,' J.A. Macdonald declared in a typically fulsome statement of the idea in 1887. 'Neglect the women, and ... your efforts must remain forever vain and impotent because you have neglected the homes and home-life of the people.'[115] The point was clear: female missionaries, by converting wives and mothers, could make *them* the agents for introducing Christian belief and family life to their husbands and children. A Christianized family life, in turn, would free women from such misogynistic customs as purdah, child widowhood, footbinding, and female infanticide and would ultimately result in the transformation of the societies in which they lived.

The increased emphasis on women missionaries' importance also resulted from the realization that, because of the social service strategies they employed, they were often more successful at gaining a foothold than ordained missionaries were. Presbyterian foreign missions promoters placed great confidence in these strategies, particularly when women's medical skills were involved. A saying that appeared from time to time in missionary books and periodicals and that was variously attributed to Indian and Chinese spokesmen reflected their faith: '[W]e dread your women and your doctors, for your doctors are winning our hearts and your women are winning our homes.' Another version declared, 'Only get the *hearts* of our women and you will get the *heads* of the men.'[116] Viewed from this optimistic perspective, women missionaries appeared to be not only desirable but essential agents in scaling the walls of heathendom.

Attempts to induce vocations in eligible women by implanting a sense of obligation and by stressing their utility in missionary work were complementary strategies. Also necessary for maximum effectiveness were appeals that translated the general need for women workers into the particular needs of the church's own fields. Realizing this, foreign missions officials provided their constituency with detailed information and specific requests from each field. Especially when the needs seemed urgent – when a new station was being opened, for example, or when a worker had to be replaced – officials themselves made direct, personal appeals to likely prospects. More typically, however, they relied on the contents of missionaries' published letters and reports to speak to the hearts of potential candidates about the needs of the church's fields. Such materials, because they reflected firsthand experience and were written by workers who were seen to be bearing more than their fair share of the burden for the world's evangelization, were particularly poignant and difficult to resist. This was their effect on thirty-seven-year-old Jean Riddell of Perth, Ontario, in 1892. Riddell told the FMC that she had thought of supporting missions only from the home base until two missionaries, writing from India, had called in the *Monthly Letter Leaflet* for more workers, even those 'with ordinary attainments.' That aspect of their appeal had convinced her that even she had a role to play in the foreign field. (Alas for her faith, the FMC subsequently informed her that in view of her age she could be considered only for an appointment to the Canadian Northwest.)[117]

Foreign missionaries could be even more effective at presenting the needs of their fields when they came home on furlough. Trained by years of experience in various methods of persuasion, they could describe the claims of their stations in concrete and compelling terms and ideally could arouse a sense of responsibility even in those inured to other appeals. Recognizing this fact, foreign missions officials generally welcomed them home and put them to as much deputation work as their health and strength would permit. Furlough missionaries, they knew, epitomized the altruism as well as the romance of a foreign missionary calling and thus could serve as the church's ultimate weapons in attracting new recruits.

ཇ༦ ཇ༦ ཇ༦

The backgrounds of the women missionaries appointed by the Presbyterian Church in Canada in the years before the First World War were remarkably similar in many respects to those of the women identified in Jane Hunter's recent study of American women missionaries in turn-of-the-century China.[118] Well educated and with some work experience behind them, they were the products of farms or small urban centres, and of large families more noteworthy for pious respectability than for elite social status. Like their American counterparts, too, they were women with considerable personal drive, women 'who wanted more for themselves than they saw in conventional alternatives.'[119] A foreign missionary career appeared to offer unique opportunities for power, adventure, and heroic status, and a respectable escape from the restrictions and responsibilities that were often an unmarried woman's lot in late-Victorian and Edwardian Canada.

Such concerns were combined with genuine altruism and a deeply rooted sense of Christian vocation. Bound by the conventions of their evangelical culture and by a desire to make their lives an inspiration to others, the missionaries and their publicists were generally unable to speak of their career choice except in terms of these factors. (Hunter has characterized the kind of language they used as 'the wispy rhetoric of feminine self-sacrifice.')[120] Years later, however, a Presbyterian missionary who began her career just after this period and whose background was similar in many respects to that of the women described here was able to reconstruct her sense of calling in a fashion that acknowledged both its personal and religious aspects.

Dr Florence J. Murray was born in Pictou Landing, Nova Scotia, in 1894, the eldest of six children of a minister father and a schoolteacher mother. At an early age she learned of her father's unrealized desire to be a foreign missionary. She also became aware of how limited the opportunities available to young women were in rural and small-town Canada: 'Growing up in a farming community, the only careers that I knew of open to girls were teaching, nursing and stenography, none of which appealed to me. I wanted to do something different.' Fascinated by the stories of need and adventure told by visiting missionaries, Florence Murray made an informal decision: 'I would go and help in my father's place.' Later, at Prince of

Wales College in Charlottetown, Prince Edward Island, she and her brother heard the stirring appeals of students newly returned from an SVM conference, and each formed a definite resolve to become a foreign missionary. Learning of her intention, her parents 'informed me ... that at my birth they had dedicated me to the Lord and were happy that I had made such a decision.' After studying medicine at Dalhousie University and interning in Boston, Florence Murray worked in Nova Scotia to repay the costs of her education before setting off for Korea.

I went because Korea then had few trained doctors and more diseases than we in the West ... I was young, strong, well trained, and no longer needed in Canada now that the war was over ... Why shouldn't I go? It would be a great adventure.

Furthermore, brought up as I was in an earnest Christian home and with a strong personal faith, I wanted to use my life where it would count most. I wanted to serve others and share my knowledge of God as our loving heavenly Father ...[121]

The 'wispy rhetoric' employed by Murray's predecessors obscured the complex interplay of personal and religious factors that drew them to foreign missionary work. Unlike Murray, they lacked the assurance that they could speak of a desire for self-fulfilment without calling into question the sincerity of their Christian commitment.

4

Women's work in Central India

By 1880 single women missionaries and missionary wives outnumbered male workers on the foreign mission staffs of most North American societies. In the mission established by the Presbyterian Church at Indore, Central India, in 1877, this pattern of female predominance was even more pronounced: single women alone outnumbered men from the first year of the mission's existence. As a result, 'woman's work for woman' became more important in Central India than in any of the church's other fields. An examination of the development of this work in the years before the First World War indicates that at an early stage institutional and social service activities took precedence over evangelism, notwithstanding the missionaries' continuing commitment to the long-range goal of converting India to Christianity.

ৡ৶ ৡ৶ ৡ৶

Central India was the administrative label adopted by the British in the early nineteenth century for a group of princely or native states located in the Malwa plateau region of west-central India. With the weakening of Mughal rule in the subcontinent in the eighteenth century, the region had come under the control of militant Maratha rulers from the south, united in a loose confederacy under the leadership of *Peshwa* Balaji Rao at Poona. Indore had become the special fiefdom of Malhar Rao Holkar, a Maratha military chief who had played a leading role in the conquest of Malwa, while the even larger state of Gwalior had emerged as the special territory of the Sindhia family. By the end of the century, however, with the Maratha confederacy torn by internal divisions and Malwa in administrative chaos, the region was ripe for a British takeover. In 1818, following a series

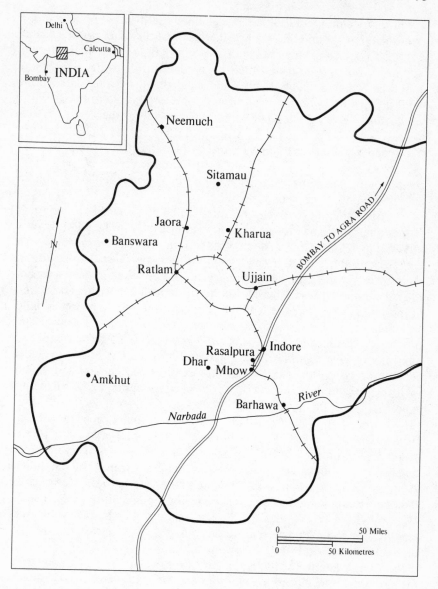

Central India mission stations of the Presbyterian Church in Canada, 1914

of military victories and diplomatic alliances, British paramountcy was confirmed. Holkar and Sindhia and the heads of the other princely states remained responsible for the day-to-day internal administration of their territories, but the ultimate authority of the British in the region was established beyond doubt.[1] Central India was organized into a number of political agencies, with the head of each one responsible to the agent to the governor-general (AGG), who resided at Indore, the capital of the princely state of the same name. After 1854, when an eastern block of land was added to the original Malwa portion of Central India, the size of the agency was greatly increased. The first systematic census of the region, completed in 1881, reported a population of some nine million people in an area of more than 75,000 square miles.[2]

The British found in much of Central India an agreeable climate and rich agricultural land. A hot season, lasting from April until July, was followed by the monsoon. The end of the rains marked the advent of the cool season, which lasted from October until March. Despite this pattern, there were not the extremes of temperature to be found in other parts of the subcontinent. G.R. Aberigh-Mackay, a British historian who resided at Indore in the 1870s, described the climate of the Malwa region as 'mild and equable,' with relatively cool nights even during the hot season. The black 'cotton' soil that covered much of the plateau effectively retained moisture, making several harvests possible each year. In addition to cereal crops, tobacco, cotton, sugar cane, various vegetables, and spices, opium was grown in large quantities both for local consumption and for Britain's export market. The importance of the latter was signified by the fact that the AGG in Aberigh-Mackay's time was also the opium agent for Malwa. Blessed with fertile soil and a favourable climate, Malwa had often been called 'the garden of India.'[3] In 1881 the chief census taker reported, 'Famine is here unknown ... and even a temporary scarcity in Rajputana at once produces a long train of immigrants ... all pressing forward to the opportunities which offer themselves for an agricultural existence in Malwa.'[4] Given this pattern, the drought-induced famine that struck the region at the end of the century was all the more devastating for its unexpectedness.

By the last quarter of the nineteenth century, Indore had emerged as the most important city in Central India, commercially as well as politically. Textile production gradually developed into a significant industry following Maharaja Holkar's establishment of a cotton mill in 1869. Railway and telegraph lines provided a rapid means of communication with external centres such as Bombay as well as with some of the other cities within the agency itself. In addition, Indore was conveniently located for trade and travel on the Bombay-Agra Road and had links to the other metalled roads in the region that served as imperial lines of communication. Finally, in addition to being the centre of British civil administration in Central India, Indore also housed a small number of British troops, supplemented by a much larger contingent in the cantonment at Mhow, some fourteen miles distant. The presence of the military added to the strategic importance of the city and to the availability of Western shops and amenities. One young missionary, arriving in 1889, would report: 'Indore, the houses, and surroundings generally are far beyond my expectations.'[5]

In Indore, and throughout Central India, a variety of linguistic and religious groups were represented. Hindi was the most commonly understood language, but Marathi was spoken by the Maratha rulers and by many of the Brahman officials who had come up from Maharashtra in the eighteenth century to help administer their government. Urdu was in use where Mughal influence had been strongest, while the aboriginal Bhils, whose home was the remote hill region of the southwest corner of Malwa, mixed Hindi and other languages with their own Bhili dialect. Illiteracy was high among all language groups and almost universal among women. Muslims constituted the largest religious minority in Central India, though only one major state, Bhopal, continued to have a Muslim ruler. Parsis and Jains, with much smaller numbers, were disproportionately prominent in urban commercial and intellectual circles. Hinduism, however, was the religious faith of by far the majority of the people, its caste system determining their place in the community and the nature of the rituals that punctuated their lives.[6]

Dwelling predominantly in agricultural villages where a large measure of local self-government and economic self-sufficiency typically prevailed, the inhabitants of Central India were bound by centuries of attachment to the social and religious customs of their own particular communities. There were local festivals, sacred sites, and capricious village goddesses for which even the most careful reading of Indian histories and classic Hindu texts could not have prepared the outsider.[7] There was, accordingly, immense opportunity to misunderstand and give offence. Recognizing this fact, Sir John Malcolm, the first British administrator of the region, had argued that imperial interests would be best served if Christian missionary activity and other outside influences were prevented from disrupting the social fabric of the newly acquired territory. His successors had generally shared his view. This policy, and the region's distance from the major centres in British India, had effectively served to deter missionary activity. With the exception of a few members of an Anglican order, the Cowley Fathers, who adopted a native life style and lived in the region in the early 1870s, no Western missionaries had tried concertedly to evangelize Central India before 1877 when the Canadian Presbyterians arrived in Indore.[8]

ॐ ॐ ॐ

Neither the AGG nor the Maharaja Holkar had invited the Canadians into Central India, and both would remain opposed to their presence until the mid-1880s. What, then, had brought them to the region? The choice of Central India as the location for the Presbyterian church's mission in the subcontinent owed something to mission comity and a good deal to Marion Fairweather. By the time that Fairweather's church was ready to begin work in the subcontinent, a good deal of British India had already been 'claimed' by British, American, and continental European missionary societies.[9] Under a policy of mission comity it was generally understood that Protestant agencies would not initiate work in territory already occupied by other mainstream Protestants. What *was* accepted, and common, was for newcomers to begin work with their denominational kin and then strike out into recommended new territory. This was where Fairweather came in. In 1873 she and Margaret Rodger had been sent to live and work with the American Presbyterians at Allahabad, North India, until their own church could establish a foothold in the country. Following their departure from Canada in the autumn of that year, the two women had received a letter from Foreign Missions Committee Secretary Thomas Lowry indicating that no ordained candidates had yet volunteered for India and explaining what was expected of them under the circumstances. 'As you are our pioneers,' he had written, 'we must be guided very much in our future plans by the information which we may get from you and from other sources respecting the state of affairs in the place to which you have gone.' A taciturn and generally unassertive woman, Margaret Rodger had failed to take advantage of this remarkable opportunity to influence her church's future plans in India. By contrast, Marion Fairweather had responded with alacrity. Early in 1874 she had urged her ordained colleagues at Allahabad to advise the Canadian church about an appropriate location for its proposed mission. Subsequently, she endorsed their advice that Canadian Presbyterians should undertake work in the still-unclaimed territory of Central India, and over the course of the next two years wrote a series of letters describing the needs and advantages of that field. In 1876, the Western Division Foreign Missions Committee of the Presbyterian Church in Canada formally acted on this advice. The Reverend James M. Douglas, a minister in Cobourg, Ontario, was instructed to proceed to Central India as the official founder of its mission.[10]

Fairweather was just as anxious to help shape the policies that would guide the church's new mission as she had been to influence its location. In the months after she had learned of Douglas's appointment, she wrote a series of letters – to Douglas, to the FMC, and to the newly established Woman's Foreign Missionary Society – describing the missionary agencies that she thought should be established in Central India and her own efforts to prepare the ground.[11] Her advice reflected her experience in three American stations, where she had participated in both evangelistic and institutional missionary work. While she recommended advancing on both these fronts and recognized that, in a broad sense, all missionaries were expected to be evangelists, it was the institutional approach that she favoured. Her views alone would not have carried the day. However, they reflected a growing trend in mainstream Protestant missions towards the use of such agencies as schools, dispensaries, hospitals, and orphanages as indirect means for securing conversions.[12] An examination of women's evangelistic and institutional work in Central India reveals the early emergence of this pattern.

ई॰ ई॰ ई॰

Public preaching was the most characteristic form of evangelism for male missionaries in India during much of the nineteenth century. For women, the equivalent was zenana visiting. So important was the zenana to Westerners' conception of the woman missionary's role that in the course of the century the term 'zenana missionary' came to be virtually synonymous with that of woman missionary.[13] Zenana visiting itself, however, referred to a specific missionary task: calling on Muslim and high-caste Hindu women in the zenana quarters of their homes in order to bring them the Christian message that their seclusion prevented male missionaries from delivering. Accompanied if possible by their Bible women – typically, low-caste converts with sufficient training to read portions of scripture in the vernacular – missionaries would endeavour to spend one or two hours per week in such homes and, through a slow and often frustratingly indirect process, reshape the inhabitants' religious beliefs.[14]

When the members of the FMC had called for the creation of a woman's foreign missionary society to support women's work for women in 1875, they had been guided by the assumption that seclusion was a near-universal condition for all but the most wretched of Indian women and that zenana visits constituted a key means for bringing about their conversion. The same perception was evident in early WFMS statements about the work it was supporting in Central India.[15] Yet within a few years of the mission's founding, the majority of WFMS personnel were spending most of their time in other avenues of women's work, and zenana visiting was being relegated to a distinctly secondary role. A number of factors were responsible for this ironic development.

The problem was not lack of access. After some initial resistance to their visits during their first years at Indore, the missionaries found themselves with abundant opportunities to enter private homes. Indeed, within a few years, the complaint that they had more zenana-visiting opportunities than they could possibly keep up with became almost a refrain in their reports. In 1879 the WFMS even reported that the day schools established at Indore had been discontinued for some months 'on account of the rapid increase of Zenana work.'[16] Access to zenanas sometimes developed as a result of invitations from zenana women themselves. Most often, however, the opportunities originated with a husband or father who had had some Western education, and perhaps friendly contacts with a mission, and who was anxious to have his wife or daughters learn to read, speak English, do needlework, or acquire some other 'Western' accomplishment.[17]

While such invitations opened doors for the missionaries, they could not ensure results. Marion Fairweather made this point in 1877 in response to a WFMS enquiry about the relative merits of school and zenana work. Both types of missionary activity were worth pursuing, she maintained, but the former was more valuable, since it caught Indians when they were young and malleable. Moreover, children taught in mission schools could themselves serve as missionary agents by disseminating a knowledge of Christian teaching in their homes. Zenana women, by contrast, accepted the visit of the missionary only as a means of learning a skill, or as a diversion from the seclusion and boredom of their daily lives. They nodded and smiled when she spoke about Jesus, but her words did not sink in. She left, and they returned to their idols. Fairweather's colleagues told of similar experiences: of visiting women who cheerfully listened to the *bhajans* (Indianized hymns) they sang but who employed a variety of delaying tactics to forestall the Bible lesson; of paying repeat calls only to find that the lesson 'learned' on a previous visit had been entirely forgotten.[18]

In those instances where zenana women did start showing an interest in the doctrinal aspects of the missionaries' teaching, relatives frequently intervened and tried to prevent further visits. In 1907 Edith Menzies described this response in two Muslim homes to which she had gained access in the city of Neemuch. She had been invited to the first by its young mistress, who wished to learn how to read, but when, with the latter's permission, she followed up the reading lesson with a hymn, she was confronted by the woman's angry husband. 'Before I realized,' Menzies reported, 'we were in the midst of an argument and soon he was hurling epithets, which were anything but complimentary, at Europeans, their religion and everything about them.' In the second home, she was welcomed by the husband, who had asked her to teach his wife reading and showed no objection when she also taught hymns and Bible verses. However, when the young wife's parents learned that their daughter was being instructed in Christianity, they angrily pointed out that she already had a religion and forbade the missionary to call again.[19] Hampered by a limited formal education, Menzies probably found it particularly difficult to respond effectively to such overt challenges to her attempts to proselytize. (A missionary widow with a common school education, she had been hired only because she was already on the ground and eager for the work following the sudden death of her husband.) Yet even her more highly trained colleagues were little better equipped to defend their own faith and take the offensive in circumstances such as these.

In the early days, invitations to visit and teach in the zenanas of important Indian families were taken as hopeful signs of friendly openings for the gospel. Later, however, missionaries became somewhat more sceptical about such invitations, especially if they sensed that the only likely outcome would be their own exploitation. Jean Sinclair, for instance, was indignant when in 1905 she was invited by the companion of the Maharani of Indore to call on her on a regular basis in order to help her improve her English and learn to play tennis, the harmonium, and billiards. 'I had to disclaim any knowledge of the last-mentioned accomplishment,' Sinclair wrote, 'and discouraged her desire to acquaint herself with it. This woman – a native – gets almost as much salary as I do and she wanted to strengthen her position by acquiring these accomplishments from me.'[20] What had to be weighed, of course, in regard to such invitations, was the possible diplomatic value of complying with the request against the loss of the missionary's time.

Despite the frustrations and slow pace of zenana work, most missionaries, including Sinclair, continued to maintain that it was worthwhile. But even those who sounded most positive about the value and satisfaction to be derived from zenana visiting did not, in fact, devote much of their careers to it. Jessie Duncan was a case in point. In an 1896 letter to FMC Secretary R.P. MacKay she declared that zenana visiting was her favourite work despite the high degree of language skill it required. Four years later, addressing a WFMS annual meeting while home on furlough, she maintained that such work would continue to have a place in women missionaries' agendas so long as so many Indian girls did not attend school, or were removed early to marry. Moreover, she reassured her audience, the need for such subterfuges as sewing lessons was disappearing, and zenana women were increasingly recognizing that if they wanted to learn to read, they would have to accept the Bible as a text.[21] These views notwithstanding, in the years that followed, Duncan became increasingly caught up in school work.

Her experience typified what was happening throughout the mission: as women's educational and medical work developed, it effectively opened new doors for zenana visits, but it also placed additional, and more pressing, demands on the missionaries' time and absorbed new personnel from Canada. In this situation, zenana visiting became the spare-time activity of many missionaries and the chief occupation of few. The latter, moreover, were typically women without much advanced academic or professional training. Bible women and missionary wives were left to take up the slack. But since most Bible women were low caste and lacking in the skills that would commend them to zenana residents, they were generally not welcomed on their own, while the amount of visiting done by missionary wives was limited both by family responsibilities and personal inclination. An 1898 report on zenana work in Indore revealed its increasing marginality: '*All who find it possible to do so* engage in this interesting department of work. Miss White and her Bible woman had access to 32 homes in which 85 women were reached. Miss Grier and Miss Chase also visit a number of homes, *as frequently as other engagements make it possible.*' (Italics added.)[22]

The declining emphasis on zenana work was not lost on R.P. MacKay. In an 1895 letter to Dr Maggie O'Hara he observed that whereas such work used to appear to those at home as 'the chief employment of lady missionaries,' it was now mentioned much less often in letters and reports. Had changed social conditions in India reduced the need for it, he enquired.[23] In her reply, Dr O'Hara echoed Fairweather's earlier judgment about the greater value of working with children; she also referred to the difficulties missionaries experienced in finding trained Bible women to accompany them on their visits. Most striking, however, was her acknowledgment of a phenomenon seldom emphasized in reports of women missionaries' work: the relative unimportance of the zenana in Central India: 'The majority and the large majority of the women in Central India are not zenana women. Some of the high caste women are *purdah*, but the majority of the women go out in the streets as freely as the men do.'[24]

If the majority of Central India's women did not live in strict seclusion – and historical accounts of the region support O'Hara's contention[25] – why did the women missionaries not make that fact clearer to their sponsors in Canada and abandon zenana visiting altogether? One reason may have been related to mission politics. The notion of Eastern women's enforced seclusion had provided the strongest rationale for single women's presence in the mission field. Similarly, it played an important part in their struggles against male attempts to control their work. Given these circumstances, it was perhaps not expedient to be too emphatic about the fact that a significant amount of 'women's work' could be done by men.[26] (Nor would it have been helpful to WFMS leaders, who, as we have seen, used images of Oriental seclusion to help justify their insistence on maintaining an exclusive focus on foreign work.) One must be cautious about pushing this argument too far, however. Whether through choice or compulsion, the zenana *was* a reality for a large number of the society's most respected women,[27] and especially in the early days, it was this class that the missionaries had been most anxious to reach. Moreover, acceptance within the zenanas had provided them with a sure means of establishing their own status as respectable women. Zenana visits continued to be a valuable tool for cultivating good will among the most influential segments of the local population, and there was always the hope that the seeds of faith sown in these settings would somehow take root. Finally, and perhaps most important, even if strict seclusion was not the norm, it was still the case that the zenana ideal prevailed widely, making many women feel most comfortable about talking to the missionaries in the privacy of their own homes.

There were thus several practical reasons for retaining zenana visiting as a branch of women missionaries' work. Nevertheless, over the years it was assigned an increasingly lower place in their priorities. Given the growing demands of their institutional work, on the one hand, and the lack of any solid evidence that zenana evangelism led to conversions, on the other, this was scarcely a surprising development. The absence of any detailed discussion of zenana work in a study book published by the Women's Missionary Society in 1915 was a significant comment on its decline.[28]

Itinerating was both a more enduring and a more popular form of evangelism with the missionaries in Central India. Also called camp work and district or village visiting, it was not exclusively, or even chiefly, women's work, but was rather an attempt by missionaries of both sexes to introduce the rudiments of Christianity to the masses of Indians who lived beyond the immediate reach of the mission stations. In an 1890 article in the *Knox College Monthly,* the Reverend W.A. Wilson, one of the chief enthusiasts of itinerating, spoke of such work as 'the delight of most missionaries in India' and went on to describe some of its characteristic features:

All who are not tied to the Central station, by educational or medical claims, rejoice, when at the close of the rains, they can go into tent and travel from village to village to preach the Gospel to the multitudes to whom it is a new story ... When ... the cool season comes round gladly does the missionary pack a few boxes with tracts and books, necessary food and clothing, and loading them, with his camp furniture, on two or three ox carts, go forth into the regions beyond.[29]

Taking advantage of the short distances that separated villages in many districts of Central India, itinerating missionaries would set up camp in a convenient location and then call on several villages in the course of a day. To attract and hold an audience they employed a variety of techniques. Tracts were distributed to the few who could read – and probably to many who could not. *Bhajans* were sung to the accompaniment of a portable organ, and simple medicine was practised. At evening meetings, held outside the camp or in a nearby town, magic-lantern slides were shown, often to capacity crowds. While the ordained workers typically followed up on such openings with a formal address, women missionaries tried to assemble small groups of village women in the fields where they worked or in the courtyards of their homes and hold their attention with short conversational talks. Especially as they moved beyond their stations into districts where only local dialects were understood, both groups of missionaries depended heavily on Indian assistants to get their message across.[30]

District work appealed to the missionaries for several reasons. In addition to allowing them to work in the open air during the most pleasant season of the year, it gave them the stimulus of new scenes and experiences, or, if they were reworking familiar territory, the possibility of encountering a welcome from those who remembered their previous visit and something of their teaching. Moreover, the unsophisticated villagers they encountered on their tours seemed to many of them more likely prospects for conversion than the town dwellers back at their stations, who had learned, over the years, to challenge their claims about Christianity or to take advantage of their skills without really listening to their message.[31] Often, they knew, it was the novelty of their presence rather than the content of their preaching that gave them an audience. But there were gratifying exceptions. During the 1890s, fruitful work among the aboriginal Bhils was opened up as a result of earlier seasonal tours, and towards the end of the period there were signs of incipient mass movements as missionaries working in the northeastern section of the field established contact with *Ballais* (weavers) and other groups whose depressed social and economic conditions made them ready, even eager, for conversion. As a result of such responses, the missionaries opened new stations in a number of outlying districts and thus were able to establish a more substantial presence in the vast field for which they claimed responsibility.[32]

District work was regarded as a particularly appropriate form of activity for missionary wives. Especially if they did not have small children to care for and were physically fit for the rigours of ox-cart travel and camp life, wives could remain out in the district with their husbands for the entire season, since they generally had no institutional responsibilities to call them back to their stations. Thus, during the 1880s, Mary Forrester Campbell and Margaret Caven Wilson, both childless and both married to men with a strong commitment to evangelism, joined their husbands on extended tours, with the Campbells in 1880 covering a three-hundred-mile area in the course of a season's work.[33] After seventeen years as a single missionary engaged chiefly in educational work, Jean Sinclair turned with enthusiasm to district visiting following her marriage in 1906 to the Reverend James Sutherland MacKay, a kinsman of R.P. MacKay. Her interest reflected a number of factors in addition to a desire to share in her husband's ministry. On a visit to China during her 1903–4 furlough she had been impressed by the amount of direct evangelistic work being done by the missionaries there, and by its apparent effectiveness. Even more important was a growing conviction that the mission's past focus on urban institutional work had been a strategic mistake. More time should have been devoted to 'the plain & pure preaching of the gospel to the masses,' she now declared. 'Agencies are good – but we have shut ourselves up to [*sic*] them & relied on anything except the word.' In 1909, in a letter to R.P. MacKay written while on tour, she conveyed her satisfaction with the directness of district evangelism: 'We spent a day last week at Mandesaur – preached the whole day – Jim in the open bazaars – & I in several houses where I am welcomed & where from 5–30 women gather. We came home utterly exhausted but joyful. There was nothing but hatred and opposition in that city a few years ago.'[34]

Notwithstanding its attractions, district work required patience and endurance. Especially when they were working in new districts, or those remote from centres with European residents, missionaries sometimes encountered villagers who fled from them in fear or hostility. As late as 1910, Jean Sinclair reported going into villages where no European woman had ever been seen. While the novel appearance of a memsahib could create the interest necessary to draw a good crowd, it could also be personally disconcerting. During the first decade of the twentieth century, when outbreaks of plague were a recurring problem in Central India, itinerating missionaries were sometimes accused of deliberately spreading the disease by poisoning wells or burying bottles of germs in farmers' fields.[35] Finally, though there were occasionally the kinds of encouraging responses that led to the opening of new stations, there were other experiences that could momentarily overwhelm the missionaries with a sense of the futility of their task: returning to a district after several years' absence to discover that their teaching had been all but forgotten; trying to instil in a few brief visits the alien Christian concepts of sin and redemption; realizing, as they toured the field, how numerous were the villages that had never yet been visited.[36]

It was not, however, the problems in itinerating but rather their obligations in schools, dispensaries, hospitals, and orphanages that kept most WFMS missionaries from participating extensively in the work. Despite the frustrations, most delighted in it. Dr Maggie O'Hara, for example, wrote in 1904: 'You know, I like the hospital work, I love the work among the orphan girls, but this going about from village to village preaching the gospel and healing the sick seems to me to be, more than anything else, walking in His footsteps.' But as the missionaries' institutional work developed, it could not easily be left to assistants or simply closed down. As an alternative, some missionaries went out to villages near their stations on day trips for combined evangelistic and practical work. Because the doctors were such valuable drawing cards in a touring party, they sometimes joined all or part of a season's tour, especially if they were between postings or just back from furlough. Thus, in 1907, both Dr Elizabeth McMaster and Dr Maggie MacKellar participated in lengthy tours, the former accompanying an ordained missionary's party, the latter travelling with an Indian companion in a light tonga and covering 663 miles in the course of her outing. Two years earlier, however, a report on evangelistic work in Central India had referred to only one WFMS missionary as having participated in a season's tour, and that appeared to be the more typical pattern.[37]

Zenana visiting and itinerating were the most important forms of direct evangelism in which women missionaries engaged, but they were not the only ones. There were also Sunday school classes to be taught, and in

Central India these included large numbers of non-Christian children and adults, as well as Christian children. Some women did outdoor religious work in the *mohullas,* or urban communities, where the poorer occupational and caste groups lived.[38] Neither activity, however, appears to have absorbed a significant proportion of any worker's time.

During the last decade of the period, the women missionaries began to express increasing concern that they were not doing more direct evangelism. In their calls for staff in these years they stressed the need for more full-time evangelistic workers. They were particularly anxious to be in a position to follow up on the home contacts created by their school and hospital work and to go out to the districts where new stations were being established in order to work with enquirers and newly converted women and children.[39] Yet as the supply of new workers repeatedly fell short of the demand, newly arrived personnel continued to be absorbed chiefly into the mission's institutions, and evangelism remained the poor relation in women's missionary work.

३๑ ३๑ ३๑

Among the institutional agencies used in women's work in Central India, schools were the earliest and most numerous. When the first missionaries arrived in Indore in 1877, education for girls was almost non-existent throughout the Central India agency. The WFMS workers therefore had an open field for their efforts. In general, the parents of their pupils were of two sorts: those who regarded a Western-style education as a desirable attainment for their daughters and actively sought the missionaries' services in achieving that goal, and those who could be persuaded to allow their children some rudimentary education in response to persistent pressure, material inducements, or both. While schools for the children of the latter were always the most numerous, and the least controversial within the mission, it was those providing a higher level of education that added most to the mission's status and that excited most interest at home.

The missionaries typically started one or more schools during their first year in a new station. Initially, they often had to struggle against popular indifference or opposition and suffered from their own ignorance of local conditions. Yet at an early stage their educational work began to attract support from Indian officials. This was particularly striking during the first half of the 1880s when the aggressive street preaching of the ordained missionaries provoked strong opposition in Indore. It was opposition that the AGG, Sir Lepel Griffin, was in no hurry to quell, even after missionaries

John Wilkie and J. Fraser Campbell went over his head and sought support from the viceroy's office. The situation showed marked improvement only after November 1885, when the new viceroy, Lord Dufferin, a former Canadian governor-general, visited Indore and spoke informally on the missionaries' behalf with both the AGG and the maharaja.[40] Prior to Lord Dufferin's visit there had evidently been a brief period of hostility to all missionary activity; then, state officials had allowed women's educational work to continue. Mrs Margaret Caven Wilson had stressed the significance of this concession in a letter to the WFMS:

In a city [Indore] where the Prince, and, as a matter of course, nearly all the officials are violently opposed to all kinds of Christian mission work, Miss Rodger, Miss McGregor and Miss Ross have opened, and kept open, five schools, where nearly 200 Hindoo and Mohammedan children receive daily instruction ...[41]

Writing in December 1885, Mary McGregor reported that 'a general in Holkar's army' who had formerly spearheaded opposition to missionary work in Indore had now offered her a building and equipment for her two girls' schools:

At present I am to pay rent; but I have been told that donations will be given for this and all other expenses connected with the school, as it is now looked on as a public benefit.

For the last few months the schools have been much more popular; but now the tide has fully turned, and the enthusiasm is quite as great as the opposition formerly was.[42]

The full turning of the tide undoubtedly owed something to Lord Dufferin's visit.

If women's educational work was increasingly encouraged by local officials, it was not without its problems. Particularly when schools were being opened up in a new area, facilities were often entirely lacking, or lamentably inadequate by Canadian standards. Thus in 1880, five years before the favourable circumstances described above, Mary McGregor's two 'schools' in villages outside Indore had consisted of herself and a few children gathered together under the shade of a banyan tree. Years later in the city of Neemuch, Maggie Jamieson taught in rented quarters that were badly located, inadequately roofed, and foul smelling until a male colleague complained on her behalf and a new building was erected. Village schools were sometimes merely mud huts, with a single door serving as the only source of light and ventilation.[43] When the WFMS Board of Management learned of such conditions, it was generally willing to finance improvements, though in villages where schools operated only on a seasonal basis it was sometimes not feasible to erect new facilities.

By employing Indian assistants to teach all subjects except English and the Bible, a missionary could maintain several schools in different parts of her station. Especially in the early years, however, such assistants were often the cast-offs of other missions, and they frequently had little more schooling than the pupils they taught. In 1890, for instance, one missionary reported that the teacher of her younger pupils could do arithmetic only up to simple addition.[44] Moreover, many of the early helpers were non-Christian. This pattern, which prevailed in many India missions, and in men's schools as well as women's, largely reflected the shortage of even poorly qualified Christian teachers.[45] Aside from the problems created by employing workers who did not share their commitment to the inculcation of Christian values and beliefs, the missionaries had to contend in these circumstances with pressure from home-base officials anxious for them to make their staffs wholly Christian. Soon after the establishment in 1897 of a separate women's mission council, therefore, the WFMS missionaries developed a program for training and examining their own Indian Christian teachers and other native Christian agents. The program enabled them to reduce their reliance on non-Christians, so that by 1900 the council was able to report that 93 per cent of its Indian employees were Christian.[46]

In the vernacular schools that they operated in bazaars and villages, missionaries could sometimes teach girls and boys in the same class, as well as children of different caste and religious backgrounds. Almost invariably, however, the parents of such children were themselves poor and illiterate and unlikely to pay much attention to the missionaries' desire for punctuality and regular attendance. Callers were therefore employed to go to their homes and escort their children to school. As in missions elsewhere in India, clothing, money, food, prizes, and other inducements were also used on a regular basis to encourage attendance. Recalling her early teaching days in a school for the poor, Jessie Duncan candidly wrote, 'Many a time I took a bag of pice [coins] with me, each pice being worth half-a-cent, to distribute them to the children who attended regularly and were making some progress.'[47] In 1899, in a reform-minded mood, the Women's Council declared its opposition to 'the keeping up of schools by any such means ... in our opinion the annual distribution of prizes is all that should be given.' However sound in principle, such an approach was simply not feasible. In 1903, while home on furlough, Jessie Weir candidly told a WFMS board meeting that all but one of the schools in her station had closed and that attendance had fallen off in others 'on account of the children receiving no more rewards for coming to school.' Six years later the council sounded a more realistic note when it recommended that all gifts for school children sent from Canada be reserved for use in the non-Christian day schools as a means of sustaining attendance; in the wholly Christian schools and orphanages, only end-of-term prizes need be given.[48]

Even among those families who were not motivated mainly by inducements, and not so poor that they needed to terminate their children's education in order to have them work, attendance was a perennial problem. Religious festivals emptied classes for days at a time, while the marriages of young girls removed them permanently from the classroom just as they were beginning to make progress. Epidemics could reduce student numbers by the fears they induced as well as by outbreaks of disease. Finally, of course, problems sometimes arose out of the fact that Bible study and Christian teaching were compulsory parts of the curriculum in mission schools. Especially in the early days, the conversion of a pupil, or even the rumour of a conversion, could temporarily cause the wholesale withdrawal of the student population.[49] Some parents reportedly warned their children that the missionaries would take them away, or cast spells on them; others were themselves advised that Christian teaching would undermine their daughters' character and destroy their reputation.[50] By the latter part of the period there were state-sponsored schools in some of the larger centres to which parents could turn if they wanted to remove their children from Christian influences. In other areas, however, those parents who wanted an education for their daughters had little option but to turn to the mission schools, and most were prepared to accept some daily Christian teaching as the price to be paid. That they so readily did so was one indication of how seldom such teaching led to conversions.

The problems associated with day schools and the limits on what missionaries could accomplish with children who were in their care for only a few hours a day prompted several members of the mission staff to declare by the mid-1880s that such institutions should be supplemented by the provision of a girls' boarding school. John Wilkie, the senior ordained missionary in Indore and the most influential advocate of a boarding school, stressed to home-base officials that such an institution was especially desirable as a place to educate the children of Indian Christians, train them as future mission employees, and protect them from 'being bespattered by the filth around them.' Though as a missionary wife she had no official voice in the mission's affairs, Agnes Neilson Wilkie joined her husband and Margaret

Rodger, the proposed head of the school, in making this argument, and in 1886 the WFMS summarized it in its *Tenth Annual Report:* 'By separating these [Christian girls] from home associations, and bringing them up more in harmony with our civilized and Christian ideas, in one generation, as much will be accomplished as could otherwise be done in three or four.' The WFMS noted approvingly that Rodger had already created the nucleus of such a school by taking three needy Christian girls into her own residence.[51]

Notwithstanding the emphasis on the needs of their Christian community, the advocates of a boarding school did not propose to establish such an institution exclusively for Christian girls. Early plans called for separate departments for 'heathen girls, who may be sent by parents and guardians, for the sake of the instruction given' and for the care and training of 'that sorely-tried class, the widows, especially those who have lost their husbands before they had resided with them, and who are too young to have fallen into the grosser forms of sin.'[52] Despite the enthusiasm of advocates in the field and of the WFMS at home, internal mission controversies over the boarding school delayed FMC approval for several years and resulted in Rodger's resignation from the mission staff. In 1889, however, the committee formally approved the project and instructed the Mission Council to prepare and forward construction plans at the earliest possible date.[53]

Designed to accommodate thirty to forty students, the boarding school opened in Indore in December 1891 with only fourteen, so that its headmistress, Jean Sinclair, was able for some time to continue overseeing a Marathi day school. Notwithstanding earlier plans, no widows were brought into the school, and during the first years few if any non-Christians enrolled their daughters.[54] However disappointing these relatively small start-up numbers may have been, they enabled Sinclair to concentrate on developing the academic as well as the religious side of the school's program. By 1895 the two highest classes were studying in English, and the inspector of European schools in the region was reporting favourably on the school's progress. Three years later, increases in the number of girls studying at advanced levels led Sinclair to apply to the University of Calcutta for the right to have her pupils write its matriculation examinations. Subsequently, the influx of a large number of famine orphans with more basic educational needs and the intrigues of mission politics prevented her from taking advantage of the university's agreement. However, in 1909, under Sinclair's successor, the school did obtain high school status, affiliating with the University of Allahabad and becoming the first institution for the higher education of girls in all of Central India.[55]

The boarding school's rapid advance to high school status is particularly striking when compared to the pace of its counterpart at the American Congregationalist mission in Ahmadnagar in the Bombay Presidency. There, the girls' boarding school, established in 1840, did not offer a full high school program until 1914. Moreover, the Canadian Baptists, at work on the east coast of India from the 1870s, were apparently still without a girls' high school in the early 1920s.[56] In part, the different pace reflected different denominational patterns – Presbyterian missionaries were well known for their interest in higher education. But it also reflected local conditions: as in other parts of India, a demand existed within the Indore region for advanced female education in English, but only the Canadian Presbyterian missionaries were in a position to meet it.

With its advanced classes conducted in English, and government examinations at both the middle school and high school levels, the school attracted an increasing number of day students from the Christian and non-Christian communities. By 1914, day pupils outnumbered boarders and represented all local religious groups except Muslims. Parsis, particularly prominent both for their early interest and their marked academic ability, at times outperformed their Christian classmates even on scripture tests. Science classes were made available through the mission college, and, near the end of the period, normal school training was introduced. (In 1917 the Education Department of the United Provinces would increase the value of the latter by agreeing to recognize the school's teaching diplomas.) Extras such as piano and elocution lessons supplemented the regular academic program and increased the school's appeal for parents wanting a Western-style education for their daughters. For a price, even social distinctions were accommodated by the provision of a 'Special table.'[57] The school's popularity was not lost on the AGG, who in 1914 offered the Women's Council land on which to build much-needed new facilities and, somewhat later, the building services of his European engineer.[58] It was a graphic demonstration of the fact that those missionary institutions that commended themselves to local elites were also most likely to win the support of British officials.

The Indore Girls' High School formed the apex of the mission's system of female education. Beginning in the 1890s, however, several women missionaries and missionary wives became involved in teaching beyond this level in men's educational work. Though their numbers remained small, their experience was significant for what it revealed about the gap that could sometimes exist between the rationale for women's missionary work and its actual practice.

The opportunity arose in connection with Indore Christian College, an institution for young men established by John Wilkie in 1887 and affiliated a year later with the University of Calcutta. Wilkie's ordained colleagues were opposed to the college, and he was unable to secure an annual grant-in-aid for its work from British government officials.[59] In these circumstances he had difficulty in obtaining qualified male faculty and therefore turned to the WFMS missionaries. Following the arrival in 1895 of Bella Ptolemy and University of Toronto graduate Rachael Chase, Wilkie recruited the two women to spend part of their time teaching English literature in the college. He also arranged to have Chase and Ptolemy and a third well-qualified teacher, Janet White, assist with his 'Training Classes.' The latter were coeducational normal school and Bible school classes that he organized in 1896 for Indian Christian workers as an adjunct to his college work.[60]

Despite the fact that the new teaching arrangements were contrary to the WFMS policy of funding only women's work for women and children, and, in the case of the training classes, challenged the traditional separation of men and women for educational purposes, they were commended to home-base officials by several prominent women missionaries, including the most influential, Dr Marion Oliver.[61] Oliver's support lent strength to the arguments put forward by Wilkie and his new employees in defence of the innovations. The need for teaching the sexes separately had been exaggerated, they claimed, while the need for properly trained Christian teachers was very great. Moreover, within the college proper, the young male students were responding positively to women's teaching and were acquiring a higher estimation of woman's sphere in the process, while the contact with them was opening up valuable opportunities for doing zenana work in their high-caste homes.[62] Though some of Wilkie's ordained colleagues condemned the new departures in educational work as naive and premature, FMC and WFMS officials gave them their blessing and justified them to the church at home.[63]

The particular arrangements implemented by Wilkie were short-lived: Chase and Ptolemy returned to Canada in ill health in 1899, and Wilkie himself was withdrawn from the mission in 1902. The coeducational training classes were abandoned, leaving the ordained missionaries for many years without any formal arrangements for training male teachers for their schools.[64] The original problem of finding affordable, trained staff for Indore Christian College remained, however. To meet it, Wilkie's successor, the Reverend Robert A. King, turned to the only pool of qualified labour available, the missionary wives.

Even more perhaps than in other India missions, the married women of the Central India mission had thus far concentrated on the chief duty associated with their role: that of creating for the society around them a model of exemplary Christian family life.[65] The exceptions to this pattern had tended to be those women who had come out as single missionaries, women like Mary Forrester Campbell and Mary Mackay Buchanan, the former, childless and somewhat frail; the latter, a mother of several children and also frequently unwell, but involved throughout her life in an intense if informal ministry as a doctor, teacher, and evangelist.[66] When other missionary wives undertook extra-domestic responsibilities, they were most likely to be involved in evangelistic activities, such as zenana visiting, itinerating, and Sunday school teaching, and in such informal but important kinds of missionary work as socializing with converts and entertaining mission visitors. Any institutional work they did was likely to be in one of the vernacular schools, and on a temporary basis, supervising Indian teachers until a WFMS missionary could be appointed, for example, or filling in during her absence. Whatever their work, they were employed on an honorary basis and they were given no official status.

These temporary and voluntary features were understood to apply when King began employing missionary wives to teach in the college. Yet given the demands of the work, they were compelled for the duration of their employment to function more as professionals and less as casual labourers than most previous working wives had done. The arrangement began in 1903 when King's wife, Annie Murray King, a University of Manitoba graduate and former high school teacher, began teaching English literature in the college, 'filling the breach,' as her husband put it, during a temporary staff shortage. In the absence of anyone to replace her, however, Annie King continued teaching until she and her husband returned to Canada in 1912. Lamenting Robert King's departure, a colleague pointed out that the FMC would now have to replace not one but two staff members.[67] Following Annie King's example, several other missionary wives with attractive educational qualifications were drawn into college or boys' high school teaching in the first decades of the twentieth century. With the establishment of Malwa Theological Seminary in 1908, several more taught normal school or Bible classes to the wives of theology students.[68] Given the needs of the mission's institutions, such women were seen to be too valuable to be left exclusively to a career of exemplary domesticity.

To an even greater extent than educational work, women's medical missionary activity commended itself to Indian and British officials in Central

India and captured the imagination of missions supporters in Canada. As missionaries of both sexes wrote from the field to inform home-base officials that women's medical services were an open sesame to new stations and opportunities, FMC and WFMS officials responded with enthusiasm, stressing to volunteers the value of medical training and assisting them, when necessary, to obtain it. For a time in the 1890s more than one-third of all WFMS missionaries in Central India were medical doctors.[69]

As a missionary agency, women's medical work was, of course, relatively new: the first fully qualified female medical missionary to serve in any field, the American Methodist Dr Clara A. Swain, had gone to India only in 1869.[70] But even before they had opened up their own mission in Central India, Canadian Presbyterian foreign missions officials had learned of the potential value of women's medical work from a variety of sources, including Marion Fairweather. In the course of working with the American Presbyterians, Fairweather had come to know their pioneer woman medical missionary, Dr Sara Seward, niece of the late American secretary of state. Fairweather wrote enthusiastically of Seward's accomplishments and of the opportunities medical work offered for gaining access to high-caste families and winning the tolerance and support of native princes. She cautioned, however, that medical missionaries should be fully trained professionals, especially given the damage that could be done to a mission by the mistakes of amateur practitioners. Despite her warning, the early missionaries, both men and women, distributed medicines and performed simple treatments, though they generally had little or no medical training. As in other parts of India, the temptation to try to open doors in this way was simply too great to resist.[71]

Professional medical work officially began in the mission in 1884 with the arrival of Dr Elizabeth Beatty. A farmer's daughter from Lansdowne, Ontario, Beatty was part of the first class to graduate from the Women's Medical College, Kingston, and the first female medical missionary to serve abroad under a Canadian agency. She had undertaken medical studies with mission service specifically in mind and had left for India within months of her graduation. Working initially in an Indore dispensary operated by John Wilkie, she began treating patients with the help of an interpreter while she got on with the study of Hindi. Later, she was able to rent a mud-walled house, the ground floor of which became her dispensary and the upper floor a four-bed hospital.[72]

While many of Dr Beatty's early patients were poor and low caste, she gradually gained access to high-caste women, including the wives and daughters of court officials. Her successful contacts with the latter group had an important bearing on the future growth of the mission. As ordained colleague W.A. Wilson later acknowledged, the early medical work did much 'to quiet the irritation and disarm the opposition manifested by the Indore officials in the earlier days of the mission.' During her voyage from England to India Dr Beatty had formed a friendship with Lady Dufferin on the basis of their common interest in medicine. (At the time of her husband's appointment as viceroy Lady Dufferin had been commissioned by Queen Victoria to establish secular medical facilities for training and treating Indian women.) When the viceregal couple visited Indore in 1885, Dr Beatty and the Wilsons, who had been part of the same outward voyage, were invited to an official dinner in their honour.[73] It is likely that this impressive connection also played a role in increasing Beatty's – and the mission's – acceptability in the eyes of Indore's leading families.

In 1888 the dowager maharani of Indore offered the mission land on which to build a hospital for women.[74] Three years later the hospital was completed. Ill health forced Dr Beatty to return to Canada before she could practise in the new building, but her colleague, Dr Marion Oliver, who had arrived in 1886, presided over its opening. In a speech welcoming the wife of the viceroy to the hospital, Dr Oliver was careful to acknowledge the part that local support had played in the building's completion and to stress that care would be taken to respect local customs:

We cannot omit to inform Your Excellency, that in this work we have been ably seconded by our friends in India. H.H. the Maharajah Holkar has kindly granted us the magnificent site on which the building stands, together with the gift of Rs 750 and the promise of a much needed addition to our grounds in the rear.

The wife of the Minister of His Highness ... several of our Indore merchants and friends have kindly aided in the work of rearing this 'Hospital for Women;' and several of our Central India Princes have likewise promised us their hearty aid.

This Building is in every way complete: private and public wards, dispensing and operating rooms all furnished with every needed appliance. It is conducted on the strictest of purdah system, and caste prejudices are respected.[75]

In 1887, after an official from the state of Dhar had brought a member of his family to Indore for treatment, the Dhar maharaja had invited Dr Beatty to reside and practise at his court. With work already established in Indore, she had not accepted his offer, but when ordained missionary Norman Russell sought to open a station in the state in the following decade the promise of a female medical worker was an important part of his campaign: 'We ... told him [the prime minister], for the missionary propaganda has its diplomacy, that our staff would include a lady doctor to minister to the ills of the women.' In 1895, a medical missionary, Dr Maggie O'Hara, in fact became the pioneer worker at Dhar. The maharaja welcomed her enthusiastically to his state, providing land for a bungalow and a hospital, and money for the dispensary that preceded it.[76]

The advance of women's medical work was also facilitated by the encouragement and help of British officials. Medical aid to Indian women was the form of missionary endeavour that imperial representatives could most safely support without appearing to be partial to proselytizing efforts. Indeed, such work served to strengthen the image of a benevolent raj. As a brigade-surgeon who had befriended some of the Central India staff grandly wrote, it 'tended towards inducing the native to view the Great Sarkar with a more and more trustful and kindly eye.'[77] During the period, imperial agents provided the medical missionaries with various tokens of their approval. These ranged from the professional recognition and co-operation that military medical officers accorded them to visits from touring viceroys and the presentation of medals for public service to India. From time to time, the missionaries looked for more tangible benefits, such as discount prices on government construction services in the building of a new hospital.[78] Yet in a land where honours counted for a great deal, the symbolic gestures were perhaps more important in the long run.

Indore, Dhar, and Neemuch were the only stations where hospitals were built before 1914. Dispensaries were established in most other stations, however, while in several outstations medical services were provided on a part-time basis. Yet even where hospital facilities existed, by far the greatest number of patients continued to be treated in dispensaries, private homes, and impromptu village clinics. In 1896, for example, the WFMS reported that 297 patients had been treated in the Indore hospital during the preceding year, compared to 8,744 in dispensaries, homes, and nearby villages. Similar proportions were reported at other stations throughout the period. This pattern resulted in part from the types of ailments treated. But it also reflected the fact that, except in extreme circumstances, many patients were unwilling to enter the alien environment of a hospital. High-caste women feared caste pollution, despite the missionaries' assurances that distinctions would be respected. Perhaps the most striking demonstration of the reluctance to use the hospitals was the fact that no obstetrical cases were received at the Indore hospital until eight years after its founding.[79]

Except at Indore, where the hospital became an orientation centre for newly arrived doctors, only one medical missionary was generally assigned to a station. Under these circumstances the medical missionaries depended to a large extent on the help of a variety of Indian assistants – nurses, dressers, compounders, and other support staff. As in the mission schools, the quality and reliability of these workers greatly improved as the missionaries were able to train their own staff rather than rely on women who had come from other missions. No Canadian nurses came out until 1896, when Harriet Thomson arrived at Indore, and only five altogether before 1914. Given their small numbers and valuable skills, and the availability of an abundance of cheap local labour, they were freed of many of the menial tasks that fell to their counterparts at home. Training Indian nurses became their chief task, along with supervising the daily routine of the hospitals.[80] The medical missionaries were also anxious to have Indian doctors as assistants (the idea of having them as full colleagues lay well in the future), but it was not feasible to train them locally. Instead, they supported the establishment in 1895 of the Women's Christian Medical College at Ludhiana in the Punjab, an interdenominational institution for training Indian women doctors for Christian medical work. Dr Maggie MacKellar served for years as honorary secretary and then as president of the college's governing board. She and her colleagues persuaded the WFMS to provide the institution with scholarship money and other financial assistance. From time to time promising students or hospital helpers were selected and sent to Ludhiana, the understanding being that the women would return to work in the mission on the completion of their training.[81]

A large part of the medical missionaries' own practice involved the treatment of eye problems, obstetrical cases, intestinal diseases, and fevers. To improve their skills in these areas, they frequently used part of their furloughs for periods of work or study at medical centres in England or the United States. Such training, however, could do little to alleviate the problems inherent in trying to practise Western medicine under primitive conditions and among people with strong attachments to their own folk traditions. The obstetrical cases were particularly frustrating. Often the doctors were called in only after prolonged labour, unsanitary conditions, and the practices of local midwives had created tragic complications. Inevitably, they lost a good many mothers and infants, especially when, as was sometimes the case, the former were themselves barely out of their childhood.[82]

The demands of such routine work were dwarfed at the turn of the century by the famine that devastated Central India and by the plague that followed in its wake. Besides attempting to treat patients who were near death from starvation or from famine-related illnesses, the doctors joined their fellow missionaries in administering famine relief. In some respects, the plague presented an even greater challenge. In September 1903, in Indore, reportedly one of the hardest-hit Indian cities, the death toll reached 4,300. Many people refused to be inoculated for fear of being infected. Moreover, the time that elapsed between the appearance of the first symptoms of the disease and its final stages was often so short that the medical missionaries were unable to prevent deaths. This was the case with two members of the mission who died within months of their arrival from Canada. In 1907 one of the medical missionaries, Dr Agnes Turnbull, herself became an indirect victim of the plague after a long period of service in disease-ridden bazaars and a government-run plague hospital.[83] While the plague had taken its worst toll by the time Dr Turnbull died, annual flare-ups in some stations continued to make it a concern for the medical missionaries for the remainder of the period.

Despite the extent of the medical problems around her and her responsibility to work for conversions, the medical missionary was compelled to spend a significant part of her time on matters neither medical nor spiritual: arranging for the building or acquisition of new facilities, for example, and dealing with requests for charity and employment.[84] In addition, when her non-medical colleagues were absent from the station through illness, vacation, or furlough, she was expected to take over their work on a part- or full-time basis. Frequently, little more than regular supervision of Indian workers was involved, but occasionally the Women's Council made appointments that temporarily put doctors into other full-time work. In 1908, correctly anticipating that she would be put in charge of the Neemuch orphanage on her return from furlough, Dr Belle Choné Oliver protested: '[I]t is not economy to put a woman specially trained for medical work in a place where one not so trained *could* do the work.' Her fellow workers agreed that such appointments were regrettable, but especially in cases where there was more than one medical missionary per station, they were considered justifiable from time to time to prevent the closure of established work.[85]

More than any of their fellow workers, medical missionaries were thought to be vulnerable to the risk of becoming caught up in the secular aspect of their work. They therefore took pains to assure Canadian supporters that they had not lost sight of their primary mandate of saving souls. Within a year of her arrival, and before she could preach in Hindi, Dr Beatty had described for readers of the *Monthly Letter Leaflet* how she pasted Bible texts on the medicine bottles she dispensed as a preliminary form of evangelizing. And in 1891 the WFMS cited a speech Dr Marion Oliver had given to a conference of Christian women in Bombay to show that 'she always tried to keep before her, 1st, The Missionary Work, 2nd, The Prof[essional] Work.' The following year the society quoted Dr Oliver's reply to her own rhetorical question about the value to the mission of the new hospital at Indore. Significantly, her emphasis was on its spiritual utility:

The physician in India, whose best efforts are often rendered useless by even the most intelligent patients treated in their own homes, is at no loss for an answer to this question. The faithful servant of Christ can even more readily make reply, 'Great gain.' How could we have a better opportunity to tell the old, old story than by the bedsides of those who have put themselves in our care? Our prayer is not for opportunities to preach Christ, but for guidance and faithfulness in using the many which the hospital is the means of bringing to us.[86]

Medical missionaries' emphasis on the evangelistic side of their practice was not merely an attempt to reassure supporters in Canada. The evidence suggests that they took their responsibility to proselytize very seriously. Besides using bedside opportunities to speak to patients about Christianity, they made formal religious services a part of the daily routine in both hospitals and dispensaries. Their audience consisted not only of active patients and medical workers, but of all those relatives and friends who accompanied patients to hospitals and dispensaries to cook their meals and watch over them. In addition, under the medical missionary's direction, Bible women or other assistants read scripture, sang hymns, and distributed tracts to patients awaiting treatment in dispensaries and to those cared for in their own homes. Finally, the willingness with which the doctors conducted Sunday school and mid-week Bible classes and took up other forms of religious work not directly related to their medical practice was further evidence that they did not chafe at the spiritual side of their mandate.[87]

A debate about the purpose of women's medical work did take place among the Central India staff in 1892 when disagreement arose about whether Dr Maggie MacKellar should be transferred from Indore to Neemuch to open dispensary work there. At issue was the question of whether medical work should be seen *only* as a means of creating opportunities for proselytizing. Prominent champions of this position were John Wilkie and MacKellar herself; both opposed the Mission Council's action in transferring her to Neemuch. Arguing that all women's work should be seen as 'door-openers for the entrance of the Gospel,' Wilkie told home-base officials that it was 'a *serious* mistake' to continue sending lady doctors out to open new work without also sending a complement of teachers and zenana workers to follow up on the openings created by their medical practice. MacKellar herself wrote: 'We came to India to win souls for Christ, and medical work is necessary only so far as it can be used as a pioneer agent to attain this end. Personally, I do not feel that it is needed here [Neemuch] as a pioneer agent.' Dr Marion Oliver strongly opposed MacKellar's rationale: 'If our church at home looks at medical work, as a means that is to be employed only so long as doors cannot otherwise be opened, then she can afford to close it now in Central India, for there are many more open doors than labourers to enter them.' Other missionaries' responses to a circular letter on the subject of MacKellar's posting indicated that a majority of both sexes were closer to Oliver's position.[88] Moreover, Wilkie's and MacKellar's stated views need to be seen in terms of their personal concerns at the time: his, to build up a strong concentration of loyal women workers in his station; and hers, to avoid leaving congenial colleagues and superior facilities for new and solitary work at Neemuch. Significantly, however, none of the participants in the debate had challenged the assumption that the ultimate purpose of such work should be to secure converts for Christianity.

Given the great expectations associated with educational and medical work and the sizable investment of staff and money involved, it was ironic that it was neither of these forms of missionary activity but rather the rescue work begun near the end of the century in response to the great famine that brought the mission its greatest success in terms of Christian adherents.[89] Some rescue work had in fact been initiated in 1878 when a small group of children from outside the mission had been put under Marion Fairweather's care in an institution euphemistically called the Christian Girls' Industrial School and Orphanage. But the orphanage had been plagued with difficulties following Fairweather's return to Canada and was permanently closed in 1880. Two other small ventures along similar lines had been undertaken by the mid-1890s: in Ujjain, Maggie Jamieson had begun providing residential education for a few homeless blind boys, while in Indore, under John Wilkie's sponsorship, an Indian Christian woman named Mrs Johory supervised a small industrial training home for low-caste Mang women whose conversion to Christianity had alienated them from their families.[90] But it was only in response to the famines of 1897 and 1900 that the missionaries became involved in rescue work in a major way, as they recognized that children and widows left homeless by the disaster could be raised or trained as Christians in mission-run institutions. In responding in this way they were not breaking new ground: some twenty years earlier, when famine had afflicted other parts of India, large numbers of children had been rescued by other missions, eventually becoming, in the words of one missionary, 'the very backbone' of the missions' future growth.[91]

In 1897, when the worst effects of the famine remained outside Malwa, several of the ordained missionaries travelled to the most seriously afflicted regions to collect homeless children and bring them back to the mission. Some members of the mission staff were eager to claim as many such children as were available. They were constrained, however, by a number of factors. British officials, responding to Hindu and Muslim criticisms that they were promoting proselytization by allowing missionaries to collect orphans wholesale, had issued an order declaring that no children were to be taken in by mission workers unless there was clearly no one else to care for them. There was also the problem of a shortage of money to finance extensive rescue work. Faced with a sizable deficit in the early months of 1897, the FMC initially responded cautiously to the missionaries' pleas for funds. It instructed them that a large proportion of the famine relief money being provided should be reserved for the future maintenance of those orphans already rescued rather than expended on seeking out more.[92]

Given these instructions, the ordained missionaries regretfully resolved at their July presbytery meeting to try to hold the line at the 230 children they had already taken in.[93] But in a letter to R.P. MacKay in the same month, J. Fraser Campbell endeavoured to persuade the FMC that its policy was both a hard-hearted and a short-sighted one: 'My own belief is ... that if the F.M.C. had only known that this means leaving children to starve to death when we could have saved [them] from that, and we hope also from what is very much worse, they would have instructed us otherwise.' Was it right, he rhetorically asked, to expect the missionaries to bank the funds on hand and 'refuse to succour those who are actually starving now and whom we have the opportunity of not only keeping alive but evangelizing under the most favourable circumstances.' Persuaded by his letter, the FMC softened its position and authorized the presbytery to spend the Famine Fund as it saw fit. The onset of the rains, however, and the lack of sufficient housing for those children already rescued evidently prompted the missionaries to confine their efforts to arranging for their care during the remainder of the year.[94]

Among the women missionaries, only Kate (Catherine) Campbell had participated directly in the rescue operation, travelling to the Central Provinces to bring back some of the 'surplus' orphan girls collected by another mission.[95] The need to provide for the girls forced other WFMS missionaries to become involved, however, and in the process brought them into a closer working relationship with their male colleagues than had previously been the case. The rescued girls were distributed among several mission stations. Of fifty-seven initially sent to the Indore Girls' Boarding School, sixteen soon died, while older ones considered unsuitable for the school for caste or academic reasons were transferred to Mrs Johory's industrial home. Other girls were housed in makeshift arrangements in Ujjain and Neemuch. Meanwhile, in Dhar, Dr O'Hara reported that fourteen children had come of their own accord to the orphanage established there.[96]

In retrospect, the rescue activities of 1897 came to seem like a dress rehearsal for what followed. With the failure of the rains in 1899, Malwa itself was devastated by a famine whose severity was unparalleled in the preceding century.[97] Faced with an immense human tragedy at their very gates, the missionaries determined that their first task must be the saving of lives. They therefore pleaded with the church at home for the necessary funds to help feed the thousands of sufferers within their reach, and, for a time, they ceased making the conversion potential the justification for their involvement. Thus, on 21 December 1899, W.A. Wilson, who in the past had often seemed to be the very epitome of a narrow, soul-focused missionary, wrote to R.P. MacKay: 'Whether our efforts in behalf of these afflicted people open their hearts to the message of the Father's love – it is the least we can do to be as we can a channel of that love to them. Whether the fruit be as we desire or not it is the right thing to help them.' A month later, frustrated by an FMC resolution that had evidently warned the missionaries against neglecting the ordinary work of the mission for famine relief, he was even more forceful:

[S]urely it is the duty of the representatives of the Christian faith to relieve the suffering and distressed ... Our Lord in turning aside from no case of bodily suffering that came to his notice or for his help has taught us surely that not only the spiritually starving but the physically starving and diseased should have our help as we are able to give it. Perhaps I should not write thus, but that resolution seems cold – terribly chilling, to us who are in the midsts [sic] of the hungry dying multitudes of our fellows.[98]

A resolution framed by the Women's Council at its March 1900 meeting and directed to both the FMC and the WFMS graphically described the suffering that prevailed in all its stations and echoed Wilson's sentiments about the need for the church and its missionaries to demonstrate their Christianity by immediate, practical action:

As a mission we have been in Central India for more than 20 years preaching a gospel of love. How can we offer the 'Bread of Life' while refusing these dying people even the bread that perisheth? ... we would therefore earnestly entreat the F.M.C. and W.F.M.S. to take steps to put it in our power to alleviate distress by making known to the Church and to the people of Canada the unspeakable need for giving immediate relief to the suffering people of Central India.[99]

Writing from Dhar, which rivalled Neemuch as the site of some of the worst suffering in Central India, Dr Maggie O'Hara was bitter about the FMC's slow response and about its criticism of the missionaries for going outside the committee in their appeals for funds: 'What are we to do? Hear the cries for food & even water and not be able to help? ... I am going to take what help I can get from Canada or any other place and I am going to do what I believe to be my duty at this time.' Also frustrating was the fact that home-base officials seemed to be waiting for horror stories. '[W]e tell them there is a famine,' she wrote, 'and unless we give details of horror that we would much rather forget they do not seem to think it is so bad.'[100]

Notwithstanding their passionate concern to relieve immediate suffering, the missionaries' evangelistic goals had not been supplanted by a pure social gospel ideology. In describing their outdoor relief work for those at home, they made it clear that their charity was accompanied by a gospel message. In an article published in January 1900, for example, Dr Maggie MacKellar explained how, while she distributed food to the refugees who had come flooding into Neemuch, Kate Campbell conducted religious services among them, assisted by some of the orphans rescued in the previous famine.[101] As J. Fraser Campbell had done in 1897, the missionaries emphasized that the famine represented a providential opportunity to build up a Christian community in Central India through the in-gathering and training of orphan children and homeless widows. 'It seems that God is *forcing* the orphanage problem on the Church,' one of them wrote, 'and no doubt it is one of his ways of solving the problem of India's salvation.'[102]

At a joint meeting in May 1900 the women and men missionaries passed a resolution setting out their two-pronged approach to the tragedy: they would continue providing outdoor relief to as many of the needy as possible, while at the same time making arrangements for '[t]he gathering in and caring for of all the famine orphans and widows within our reach.' In the same month the FMC facilitated their plan: belatedly responding to the missionaries' calls for help, it appealed to Presbyterians to supplement their regular mission givings with generous donations to the Famine Fund. In June, the General Assembly endorsed this appeal and approved the use of famine funds for 'the saving of life by the relief of present distress and also in receiving orphan children in order to save their lives and train them up in the knowledge of the Gospel of the grace of God.'[103]

By April 1901 direct famine relief had almost stopped except in the Bhil country, where a government agent estimated that as much as one-third of the population had perished during the preceding year.[104] Elsewhere, the missionaries were free to turn their attention to those who had come into their care. Mission treasurer J.T. Taylor reported that of some 2,500 girls, boys, and women rescued, 1,083 now remained in the mission's care, 527 females and 556 males, the remainder having died, run away, or been reclaimed by family or friends.[105] As in 1897, those rescued in 1899–1900 were initially housed in makeshift facilities in various mission stations. Plans were eventually made to accommodate all the boys, with the exception of the Bhils, in one large residential and industrial training centre in the village of Rasalpura, near Mhow. The Women's Council, however, ultimately rejected the idea of one large facility and instead allocated its charges among different centres according to such criteria as age, previous social and regional background, and probable learning potential.

As the station hardest hit by the famine, Neemuch became the largest centre for girls' orphanage work. Here, Kate Campbell had initially attempted to accommodate hundreds of frail and diseased girls within the British cantonment, but, fearing the consequences of such congestion, the cantonment committee had ordered her to relocate them. The move to a hastily chosen new site tragically reduced their numbers: sixty-nine girls died of cholera in three weeks and 'as many as could ran away from what they thought certain death.'[106] Campbell was forced to move the remaining children to yet another temporary facility until, following protracted negotiations to obtain a site, a new orphanage for two hundred residents was completed in 1905.[107]

Smaller numbers of girls were cared for in other stations. In Dhar, an institution called the Victorian Orphanage had been established following the 1897 famine with funds supplied by an interdenominational Winnipeg-based group. Here, Dr O'Hara exercised such supervision over the care of the largely Bhil inmates as her other duties allowed. In Ratlam, where no single women missionaries had been stationed since 1891, Mrs Mary Forrester Campbell took charge of the orphanage, working under her husband's authority rather than that of the Women's Council. Following a somewhat controversial culling process, those girls who seemed most likely to benefit from the educational opportunities available at the Indore Girls' Boarding School were transferred there from other stations. (Headmistress Jean Sinclair, supported by the WFMS board, was anxious to prevent an influx of orphans from acting as a drain on the school's budget and a threat to its future as an advanced educational and training institution, but not all her sister missionaries were happy with an exclusive role for it.) Widows were sent to the Johory Home in Indore or to the Famine Widows' Home in Ujjain. Work with blind children having already been started in the latter station, it also became an important centre for the care and training of blind orphans.[108]

The regimes implemented in all the mission's rescue institutions had certain features in common: an emphasis on the dignity and the necessity of physical labour; a modest, even frugal, standard of living; and a strong core of religious training. Beyond this, however, there were differences that reflected the institutions' different purposes. The boys' orphanage at Rasalpura was heavily oriented towards providing occupational training for a population that, it was hoped, would soon become self-sufficient. To this end, the mission press was moved to Rasalpura, and workshops were established where weaving, carpentry, and other skills could be taught and saleable articles produced. The widows' industrial homes provided shelter, basic education, and manual employment to a group of women whose social backgrounds and widowed status left them with particularly limited options. Jobs would eventually be found for some and advanced training or marriages arranged for others, but it was tacitly recognized that a number would remain permanently dependent on the mission.[109] The girls' orphanages were both larger and more hopeful institutions than the widows' homes. In each one, the object was to instil the attitudes and skills that would later enable the residents to take their place in the outside world or become useful mission workers. Because most were eventually expected to marry, the emphasis was on teaching domestic rather than occupational skills. The routines followed in Kate Campbell's orphanage at Neemuch may be taken as roughly representative, though clearly no other missionary devoted herself so wholly and intensely to the dual tasks of surrogate mother and spiritual guide.

'We allow no drones in our hive,' Campbell told R.P. MacKay in a letter in 1904.[110] Her metaphor was more than sexually apt. The girls who lived in her orphanage were required to rise early, carry water from the well, work in the garden, grind meal, and help with cooking, laundry, and other daily tasks. In preparation for moving into their new building in 1905, they also picked stones, whitewashed, and helped level the earth and lay floors. Aside from its practical aspect in meeting the institution's needs, the work routine was intended to provide the girls with basic household training. In addition to their regular school lessons, they were given training in skills such as lace making, embroidery, knitting, and drawn-thread work, with the products of their handiwork being sold to help defray costs. As a conference of famine workers in Bombay had emphasized, industrial training of this sort could later be used by the girls in their own homes and was thus of more than short-term value.[111]

The emphasis on work in the Neemuch orphanage was paralleled by Campbell's insistence on a frugal standard of living. 'They get clothing enough to keep them clean & covered,' she reported, 'bedding to keep them warm & food enough to keep them strong & well & that is enough.'[112] If these features made her institution sound in some respects like the workhouse in *Oliver Twist,* it was also the case that her spartan approach was tempered by compassion and affection and based on a desire to ensure that the girls in her care would not be unfitted for the lives that many of them would eventually have to lead as the wives of poor men. Moreover, in striking contrast to a widespread perception that missionaries tried indiscriminately to Westernize their converts, Kate Campbell showed a remarkable sensitivity to the desirability of avoiding a wholesale assault on their culture. She believed strongly in the importance of giving her charges Indian names, Indian clothing, and Indian food.[113] On the latter subject, she described the policy she had adopted in a 1905 letter to R.P. MacKay:

I read early in my Orphanage experience an article on the food for such institutions by Mrs Darabji of Poona. She said, it was best to get a clever Hindoo woman to teach the girls how to cook cheap and economical food. That they knew how to make great varieties of food at little cost and I have kept that in mind. When the girls ask for a certain dish I try it and if it is good and cheap it is put on our bill of fare. I have a horror of our native Christians learning to eat white bread and our food stuffs. It is quite out of their reach – and certainly their own food is more tasty and their bread at least more wholesome.[114]

Kate Campbell's sensitive – and sensible – approach may help to account for the apparently lower rate of runaways in the Neemuch orphanage than among the boys cared for by the male missionaries, though the fact that orphaned girls had fewer options outside the institution obviously was also important.[115]

Unhindered by any need to be concerned about offending parents' religious views or violating the government regulations that applied in schools receiving a grant-in-aid, Campbell was free to make religious training the central element in orphanage life. The day began with prayers and a Bible lesson for everyone. Various teachers taught additional Bible lessons to different classes during the course of the day, and these Campbell reviewed on Sunday mornings. On Friday evenings there were Christian Endeavour meetings with five different groups, each one led by a missionary or by one of the senior Indian staff members. Campbell herself chose to work with the group she called 'the large dull girls': 'They are quite shoved aside by the large cleverer and the smaller cleverer ones and they will probably go out first to homes of their own so I need to give special teaching to them. It is a work that will have no show but that is of no moment.' With such girls she practised what was evidently a very intense and personal kind of evangelism: '[I] look right into their faces almost into their hearts and carry the Word there. The Lord did not give me power to move multitudes but He did give me power to get at the hearts of these girls in groups of twenties and forties, and I am content with the smaller gift if it but be to the glory of His name.'[116]

To ensure that her efforts in religious education would not be undermined by forces beyond her control, Campbell attempted to isolate her charges as much as possible from outside influences. From the time when she had first begun working with famine girls and widows, this had been her policy. In a revealing letter written in 1901, visiting China missionary Murdoch MacKenzie had looked to this approach, and to the gratitude of those rescued, to lead them into Christianity:

Miss Campbell has these women and girls thoroughly under control, away from all heathen associations, and at an age in life which leaves some of them at least particularly susceptible to Christian influences. Then they owe so much to her for what she has done in saving their lives and providing for them since, that it is natural. I count on that as among the influences that will help to win them for Christ.[117]

He was not to be disappointed. In a 1904 article entitled 'A Wonderful Sabbath at Neemuch,' Kate Campbell described for readers of the *Presbyterian Record* the remarkable phenomenon of the baptism of ninety-nine of her orphan girls. Lest sceptics should think that she had forced their hand, she explained that not all those who had expressed a desire for baptism had been allowed to go forward.[118]

At the end of the following year Campbell had a different kind of spiritual triumph to report when a revival began in the Neemuch orphanage and spread from there to young people in the mission's other institutions. Even missionaries as unemotional in their approach to evangelism as W.A. Wilson and Robert A. King wrote of the revival as a genuine and heartening development and stressed that it had not been 'worked up' by the missionaries.[119] Yet Kate Campbell's accounts of orphanage life during this period reveal how much she encouraged the phenomenon and valued subsequent manifestations of improved spiritual and moral behaviour among the girls in her care. While she recognized that the intensity of the revival could not be maintained indefinitely, she rejoiced in its quickening effect on the orphanage and on the mission generally. Later, she and her sister missionaries would look back on the revival as one of the great landmarks in the mission's history.[120]

As the residents of the orphanages grew older, Kate Campbell and the other women missionaries made momentous decisions on their behalf. The most promising girls were singled out for further training and future service within the mission as teachers, Bible women, or nurses. A few were selected to go to Ludhiana to study medicine. Marriages were arranged for many of the others, typically with orphan boys from Rasalpura, while still others became craft workers or servants. By 1914, most of the original famine orphans had left the mission's rescue institutions under circumstances such as these. In future, the facilities established for their care would increasingly function as boarding schools for the daughters of Christian parents living outside the mission stations.[121]

The care and training of the children rescued at the turn of the century had constituted a significant burden for the women and men of the Central India mission. But it was one they had no cause to regret. As missionary J.T. Taylor pointed out in 1916, 'Practically all the children who remained with the Mission when the famine ceased have since been received into the fellowship of the Church of Christ.' The rescued orphans, moreover, became the single most important source of future mission workers and the founders of families from which future generations of Christians came. Looking back over the years since the great famine, Taylor wrote, one could 'trace the good hand of God in bringing blessing out of the dread calamity.'[122]

ह॰ ह॰ ह॰

In the years before the First World War, by far the majority of the women missionaries in Central India became involved in educational, medical, or rescue work and devoted only their spare time to extra-institutional evangelism. There were plenty of precedents for and parallels to their approach. As William R. Hutchison and Torben Christensen observed in *Missionary Ideologies in the Imperialist Era,* American missionaries in particular were noted for their social-activist or 'civilizing' approach, while women missionaries generally were 'perforce civilizing agents more than evangelists.'[123] Nevertheless, there are a number of remarkable features in the Central India case. The women missionaries who served there did less direct evangelism than they had expected to do – and markedly less than they felt they should be doing, if their frequent expressions of concern about this matter can be taken as a guide. Conversely, they did more social service and institutional work than their sister missionaries in North Honan, China, during the same period and more than either their long-established American Congregationalist neighbours in the Bombay Presidency or the Canadian Baptists on India's east coast.[124] Indeed, the Central India missionaries appear to have moved proportionately further along the institutional path than even the Presbyterian women in North India who had been their most important mentors.[125]

The direction taken by women's work in Central India was determined to some degree by internal mission politics. At a more fundamental level, however, the strong emphasis on 'civilizing' in women's work was a response to the particular conditions that prevailed in the region. India was considered to be, in many ways, the most difficult of all mission fields, and, within it, the princely states presented special challenges. The Central India missionaries recognized that they were most likely to get access to the people and win support from Indian and British officials if they offered their message in a context of valued and scarce social services. Missionary institutions gave them both a place to deliver such services and a captive audience for the gospel. Once established, moreover, such work created a momentum of its own; it could not easily be scaled down, or indeed held to the same level, even if, as was the case in educational and medical work, it did not lead to conversions in the numbers anticipated. In any event, by the 1890s, as the debate over medical work suggested, the majority of missionaries were prepared to justify such work on other grounds than its door-opening capacities. Winning converts remained their priority, but as they saw how great the physical and social needs of the region were, meeting those needs became a legitimate activity in its own right.

In the rescue homes established at the turn of the century, the missionaries found the ideal institution for carrying out their work: places where the marriage of social service and religious instruction did indeed produce Christian adherents. The conditions that had given rise to the rescue homes could not, of course, be replicated. Nor, in spite of their talk about the famine as a providential occurrence, would the missionaries have wished for that. In the years after 1914, women missionaries would become more extensively involved in direct evangelism and would find more reason for optimism in such work, as new stations were opened in outlying districts where large groups of tribal and low-caste people had expressed a strong interest in Christianity.[126] But the essential character of women's work as institutional and social service activities combined with Christian instruction would remain firm.

5

Gender politics in a mission

In 1869, a writer in *Blackwood's Magazine* described mission stations as 'hotbeds of religious contention and jealousy – small men contending bitterly with one another for the exercise of a feeble and uncertain power.' Twenty years later, in the third edition of his *Indian Missionary Manual*, veteran missions publicist John Murdoch quoted the description. Such situations were not the rule, he contended, but they were especially likely to occur in small stations, where missionaries, 'often living apart and accustomed to command the natives around them, are very apt to be dogmatic and wish to have their own way.'[1]

Like much of the rest of his book, Murdoch's discussion of mission politics focused on the experience of male missionaries. Yet as he probably well knew, women were generally not indifferent to the opportunities for power in mission administration. The circumstances of their work encouraged them to seek a voice in mission decision making and gave them a convincing rationale for doing so. In Central India, the women missionaries' early involvement and superior numbers provided them with additional reasons for wanting a say in how the mission was run. At a minimum, they wanted the right to control their own work; eventually, most wanted a full and equal voice in mission government. What follows is an account of their efforts, both as individuals and as a group, to assert and increase their influence in the mission's internal affairs. In a situation in which their male colleagues were themselves sharply divided, the woman missionaries frequently found their political fortunes linked to the agenda of the mission's most powerful ordained worker.

ཞ ཞ ཞ

No formal regulations existed for the administration of the Central India mission during the first two years of its existence. In this situation, Marion Fairweather was arguably able to exercise more influence over its affairs than any woman missionary who came later. Having played an important part in advising the church about its plans for an India mission during the preceding three years, Fairweather took it for granted that she would continue to have a large role when she and Margaret Rodger joined mission founder James Douglas in Indore early in 1877 in the only accommodation he had been able to obtain. Supremely confident in her own judgments and in the value of her prior mission experience, Fairweather assumed the role of Douglas's mentor, since he was, as she later put it, a 'tyro' in mission affairs.[2] But the special circumstances that had formerly allowed her to give full rein to her ambition no longer existed once the mission was well established. In this context, her continuing attempt to play a larger role than the conventional one of 'lady missionary' proved fatal to her mission-ary career.

Fairweather's first two years in Indore were marked by a varied round of activities. In addition to her school and zenana responsibilities, she worked with Douglas on the mission press, whose establishment she had earlier supported, and joined him and their two catechists in local village visiting. She participated in his efforts to protect the two young Brahmans who were the mission's first converts and helped to arrange their transfer to the safety of another mission. As a means of gaining a stable foothold in a hostile environment, she encouraged Douglas to accept the part-time chaplaincy of the Church of Scotland troops at Mhow, a position that conveyed officer status as well as other benefits.[3] Believing that the support and eventual conversion of prominent Indians was especially important in a princely state, she began to emulate Douglas's policy of socializing with Indian gentlemen, welcoming high-caste Hindus of both sexes to her home and seizing opportunities in public places to make contact with them. Even one of her strongest supporters would later suggest that her attempts 'to convert native gentlemen' were naive and inappropriate, and when she had first come to Indore Fairweather herself had purported to find such work distasteful. But as her confidence soared, she evidently came to believe that gender was less important in the task of reaching the educated Hindu than the ability to present an intelligent case for the merits of Christianity. It is likely, too, that she found such work more stimulating than calling on illiterate women. Increasingly, the only constraints she appeared to recognize on her missionary role were those inherent in being an unor-dained worker.[4]

Additional Canadian staff joined the mission during the last half of 1877. In July, J. Fraser Campbell came up from Madras, where he had briefly worked with Scottish Presbyterians, and promptly opened a new station at Mhow. Mary Forrester (who would later marry Campbell) and Mary McGregor arrived from Canada in December, along with Douglas's wife and three children.[5] While their coming did not noticeably diminish Fairweather's expansive conception of her role, it greatly changed the circumstances in which she worked. Her continuing attempts to assert her authority and her close working relationship with James Douglas created resentment and jealousy among her fellow Canadians and gave rise to gossip among the mission's Indian assistants. Matters came to a head in the spring of 1879 when one of the assistants sent a letter to the Foreign Missions Committee in which he alleged that the behaviour of Fairweather and Douglas had been causing talk in the Indian community. A follow-up letter from Mary McGregor appeared to support the assistant's allegations. It included a copy of two notes that McGregor had reportedly received from Jane Douglas, dealing with the rumours of a sexual relationship between her husband and Fairweather. In the notes, Mrs Douglas denied giving any credence to the gossip, but she made reference to 'things done *sufficient* to cause remarks by those who did not understand English people.' McGregor, who claimed to be forwarding the notes in 'the interests of truth and justice' (Jane Douglas had asked her to destroy them), prudently avoided making any charges of her own.[6]

Confused as well as shocked by this correspondence, the FMC responded by pressing Campbell, Rodger, and McGregor for further information about the alleged scandal. All three denied any knowledge of immoral conduct by Fairweather and Douglas, but all spoke of disturbing rumours reported by mission workers or of imprudent behaviour likely to fuel such rumours. In other correspondence they complained that Douglas had been arbitrary and high-handed in his administration of the mission, interfering with their work and salaries on the one hand and demonstrating favouritism towards Fairweather on the other.[7]

Letters from other Presbyterian missions in India, however, presented quite a different picture. Two ordained Scottish workers who were familiar with the Indore staff depicted Douglas as the unjustly maligned founder of a promising mission and accused Campbell and 'the two zenana ladies' of showing 'positive indiscretion' in giving currency to scandalous rumours. The Reverend J.S. Beaumont, senior missionary of the Free Church of Scotland in India, participated in an informal investigation of the Central India troubles, and, having done so, attempted to put them into historical perspective. What had happened in Central India was not at all unusual, he wrote. Rather, jealousies and troubles were the norm in a new mission.

'As a matter of fact patent to all,' he continued, 'Miss Rodger and Miss McGregor are very jealous of Miss Fairweather, and Miss Fairweather, I am sorry to say, is far indeed from the meekest of women.' Another source of difficulty was the converts themselves: 'To play off one missionary ... against another is not a game begun for the first time in your Canadian mission.'[8]

Faced with bizarre and conflicting information from sources thousands of miles away, the FMC concluded that some action was necessary even if no firm conclusions could be reached. Without seeking an explanation from Fairweather herself, it decided in October 1879 to recall her to Canada 'on furlough.' Convenor William McLaren obviously hoped that she would quietly resign from the mission.[9] Far from doing so, she attempted to salvage her position by mounting a spirited defence. The strong testimonials she submitted from lay and ordained Westerners who had known her work in India lent strength to Beaumont's claim that she had been a victim of jealousy. Her own statements described in considerable detail the complex situation that had prevailed during the mission's first year, including the opposition from British and Indian officials that had initially made it necessary for her and Rodger to share accommodation with Douglas. It was these circumstances, she maintained, and their close working relationship that had given rise to the gossip about her and Douglas, to the jealousy of Jane Douglas and her sister missionaries, and to Campbell's resentment of what he darkly called her 'influence.' Now, by recalling her, and her alone, the committee was employing a blatant double standard and knowingly destroying her reputation.[10]

McLaren and his fellow committee members may not have believed that Fairweather was guilty of sexual misconduct – though she herself thought they did – but she had become something of a loose cannon and a focal point for resentments, and they were anxious on pragmatic grounds to keep her out of the mission. From the early months of 1880 they had additional reasons for wanting to do so, for they began to receive a series of letters from John Wilkie, their newest missionary in Central India, attacking virtually all aspects of her missionary career.[11] Acknowledging that his chief sources of information were Rodger, McGregor, and Jane Douglas (he had arrived too late to meet Fairweather personally), Wilkie wrote at various times to say that Fairweather had never acquired a proper use of native languages, had exaggerated her missionary accomplishments, and was extravagant in her use of mission funds. She had undoubtedly been ambitious and clever, he conceded, but she had lacked 'staying power' and was *too clever* for a mission agent.'[12] Though he was careful not to accuse her directly of sexual impropriety, he insisted that Fairweather's indiscreet behaviour towards Douglas and his wife and her practice of receiving Indian gentlemen had made her the deserving target of gossip, and he more than once alluded to other, discreditable rumours as yet unknown to the committee. The persistent opposition of imperial officials, continuing friction among mission staff members, and Douglas's weaknesses as a missionary administrator were also, he maintained, largely a result of her lingering, baneful influence.[13]

Wilkie's attacks on Fairweather were designed to ensure that she would not be returned to Indore. As late as 1883 he was still exercised by this possibility. The attacks were also part of Wilkie's complex and ultimately successful strategy to engineer Douglas's recall and establish his own authority in the station.[14] During the next quarter century he would use broadly similar methods to undermine other missionaries whose interests conflicted with his own. Viewed from the perspective of hindsight, his tactics appear remarkably intemperate and transparently self-serving. They did not strike home-base officials in that light, however: until his own recall in 1902, Wilkie's influence with such officials would remain greater than that of any other missionary, notwithstanding his central role in every mission controversy. Meanwhile, in 1880 his attacks constituted the final blow to Marion Fairweather's hope of returning to the mission: in June of that year the FMC notified her that as of October she would cease to be a member of its staff.[15]

໒໑ ໒໑ ໒໑

The ad hoc power that Fairweather had exercised in Central India could not have continued even if she had not been recalled. In April 1879, shortly before it received word of the troubles there, the FMC, acting on Douglas's advice, had formulated regulations for the mission. The regulations denied women any formal authority even over their own work. An all-male Mission Council, meeting quarterly or oftener, was to be responsible for all aspects of local mission decision making. It was to 'consult ... [the women missionaries] in all matters pertaining to their work,' but it was under no obligation to follow their advice.[16]

The regulations reflected existing practice in a number of other India missions and were thus not unduly harsh. Nevertheless, in a situation where a different pattern had already been established they could scarcely fail to produce discord. For three years after Fairweather's departure, only two women missionaries were in the field to be affected by them. The senior of the two, Margaret Rodger, accepted the regulations with little outward show of resentment. Mary McGregor, however, bridled at the new rules. Inevitably, her attempts to pursue an autonomous course brought her into conflict with the newly established Mission Council. John Wilkie, who had succeeded Douglas as mission treasurer and who was for several years the only ordained missionary in Indore, became her chief opponent, notwithstanding their earlier alliance to discredit Marion Fairweather.

Women missionaries' salaries and expense accounts emerged as a fruitful source of conflict.[17] As early as November 1881, in private correspondence with William McLaren, Wilkie was complaining that McGregor was unable to keep accurate financial records and flew into 'a rage' when confronted with her mistakes. The root of her troubles, he maintained, lay in the psychological difficulties single women experienced in a small tropical mission station. Two weeks later he elaborated on this theme and cautioned that, in view of the difficulties, the FMC should send out no more single women for the present:

Some few have done excellent work but the greater number have led to trouble. ... we have all had not a little trouble with their financial affairs – the only matter in which we at all interfere ... When you realize how even in Canada some excellent lady workers can hardly be kept in their place by Comts [Committees] you can perhaps understand our position here – especially as it is all much increased through the effects of an eastern climate.

As much as possible, he advised, work among women should be done by Indians, trained and supervised by missionary wives. Not only would such an approach avoid the difficulties created by having single women in the field; it would also be more economical.[18]

McGregor, in turn, complained to the FMC that she was not receiving the salary due her and that Wilkie's handling of her work-related expenses was arbitrary and unjust. As a way around the difficulties, she proposed that the women missionaries be permitted to submit their accounts directly to the WFMS board and receive their funding for salaries and expenses directly from the church treasurer.[19] Such a procedure was scarcely likely to commend itself to members of the FMC, since it would have eliminated their own role as financial monitors, as well as Wilkie's. In protest against Wilkie's handling of her affairs McGregor also refused to forward reports of her work to the FMC through the council, and, much to Wilkie's annoyance, she boycotted his mid-week prayer meetings and later his Sunday services.[20]

As the conflict between the two missionaries escalated, new charges and new tactics were introduced. McGregor accused Wilkie of getting her to sign double receipts and even of intercepting her mail. When she hired as an assistant the wife of an Indian Christian teacher whom he had earlier dismissed, he denounced the move as a deliberate act of insubordination and angrily walked out of council when newly arrived missionary Joseph Builder defended her action. (The issue was not as trivial as it seemed. Indeed, the matter of employing workers – or workers' relatives – whom other missionaries had dismissed would remain a key source of conflict in mission politics, since it effectively demonstrated to the local Christian and non-Christian communities that the judgment and authority of one missionary were being questioned by another, and that insubordination, dishonesty, or incompetent work would not necessarily be fatal to future job prospects.)[21] Wilkie also accused McGregor of conducting her schools in an extravagant fashion, deliberately misleading the FMC, and, through her high-handed behaviour, creating unhappiness among her female co-workers. Using the mission press, he printed a detailed account of his quarrels with McGregor and circulated it in Canada. In November 1884 he warned the FMC that one of them would have to be removed from Indore, though clearly he did not intend that that one should be himself.[22]

Thomas Wardrope, who had succeeded William McLaren as FMC convenor, reproved Wilkie for publicizing the mission's troubles and for complaining privately about McGregor, rather than officially, through council. He also suggested that Wilkie surrender the sensitive role of mission treasurer to another council member. On the whole, however, the FMC was inclined to accept Wilkie's interpretation of his disputes with McGregor. (Its perspective was effectively reflected in Secretary Hamilton Cassels' 1885 reference to 'the Miss McGregor trouble.') By 1886, moreover, it was clear that Wilkie had the support of two of his three fellow council members in his ongoing quarrels with McGregor. Relations between Wilkie and J. Fraser Campbell were already somewhat strained over other matters, but the senior missionary was prepared to support Wilkie against McGregor as a means of upholding the vital principle of council's authority over women's work. In January of that year, with only Builder dissenting, council asked the FMC to transfer McGregor to Mhow or recall her to Canada on furlough. Ominously, the committee opted for the latter course.[23]

Anticipating that she would meet Fairweather's fate, McGregor at first declined to return. Instead, she asked for the equivalent of her passage money to Canada and submitted her resignation, explaining that she had been asked by Indore residents to stay on and teach at their expense. Later, however, perhaps fearing that the Indore offer was more flattering than secure, she abandoned her bravado and agreed to come home when the FMC warned that she would get neither passage money nor furlough pay unless she returned at once.[24]

No final decision was made about McGregor's future relation to the mission until the spring of 1888. In the interval, she wrote and spoke to the FMC in her own defence and provided statements from Indian officials – and from the ordained missionaries themselves – about the value of her educational work in Indore. In a final attempt to destroy Wilkie's credibility, she also submitted a lengthy document from an Indian Christian contractor who alleged that Wilkie had hired him to build a mission bungalow and then treated him in a dishonest and abusive fashion. Her claims and charges prompted the committee to call Wilkie home in the autumn of 1887 in order to give him a chance to respond personally to them.[25] His account of past events in Indore was strongly supported by the testimony of Isabella Ross, a missionary who had quarrelled with McGregor soon after her arrival in India in 1883 and who had subsequently translated their personal quarrel into political support for Wilkie, even following him back to Canada to speak on his behalf. Following a meeting with the three missionaries in May 1888, the FMC decided to terminate McGregor's employment as a missionary of the Presbyterian church. Not only had a subcommittee investigating the case found 'no evidence whatever' to support her 'grave charges' against Wilkie and the council, it declared; it also found that she had deliberately misled both the council and the FMC by sending them different copies of what purported to be the same document.[26]

Like Wilkie, McGregor had resorted to charges and tactics that discredited their common vocation, but unlike him she had not become adept at disguising dishonourable methods. (Years later a China missionary investigating the long history of troubles in the Central India mission would declare that Wilkie was 'a past master at making out a good case.')[27] Nor had she been able to avoid alienating her sister missionaries with her forceful and combative personality, notwithstanding the fact that they would soon take up her struggle for a greater degree of independence. Thus, while Wilkie was sustained by a formal vote of confidence,[28] McGregor lost her job as well as her seven-year battle for autonomy in her work.

Still, the FMC was obviously somewhat uneasy about the decision it had taken. McGregor's success as a mission teacher had been acknowledged even by Wilkie, and she had clearly enjoyed excellent relations with local

Indian officials. A frequent correspondent, whose letters had appeared in various denominational periodicals, she had succeeded Fairweather as the church's most high-profile WFMS missionary, one whose departure would not go unnoticed by missions enthusiasts in Canada. Moreover, during the interval between her return to Canada and the May meeting she had been allowed, even encouraged, by FMC convenor Thomas Wardrope to do deputation work on behalf of the foreign missions cause. Under these circumstances there was a certain awkwardness in dismissing her. The committee therefore attempted to soften the blow by declaring that McGregor's unacceptable behaviour had resulted from 'the influence of the climate on her temperament' rather than from a flaw in her Christian character, and by giving her an additional two hundred dollars as a supplement to her furlough allowance. It also urged the WFMS and other interested parties to give her dismissal as little publicity as possible.[29] Whatever the reality, the FMC was anxious to avoid giving the impression of dealing inequitably with its women missionaries.

ॐ॰ ॐ॰ ॐ॰

In 1886, with five ordained missionaries in four stations on the Central India staff, the Indore presbytery was established as the body responsible for matters theological in the mission.[30] The Mission Council remained the more important body, responsible for the expenditure of funds from Canada and for the general management and extension of missionary work. In practice, the distinction in function between the two structures was somewhat arbitrary, even fictional, for they generally met at the same period, and the same men were members of both.[31] From the perspective of women's role in the mission, however, the difference between the two bodies was extremely important: since women could not be ordained as elders, they were effectively barred from presbytery, but a simple change in mission regulations could allow them membership on council.

By the autumn of 1888 the FMC was ready to consider a change in this direction. It had made no significant amendments to the regulations since their adoption in 1879. In 1884 the Mission Council had itself voted to allow women to attend meetings as 'deliberative members in regard to all matters connected with their work,' but the women missionaries had seldom done so, perhaps because, as Marion Oliver later charged, they rarely received notice of the meetings.[32] Now, both the growing importance of women's work in the mission and continuing conflict under the existing system pointed to the need for modifications that would allow women a more definite role in decisions affecting their work. Even so, it is unlikely that the FMC would have pursued discussion of such changes if the idea of making modifications had not been supported, perhaps even initiated, by John Wilkie.

Following the settlement of the McGregor case, Wilkie remained in Canada for more than two years, visiting congregations and raising funds for a new building for the college he had started in 1887. As he spoke of the value of higher education in producing Indian church leaders and of his past accomplishments and future plans in other areas of mission work, he seemed to many of his fellow Presbyterians to be an apostle of the most promising and progressive means of winning souls for Christ. By the time he left for India in the summer of 1890 his influence with home-base officials and the church press was higher than that of any of his colleagues. The ideas for changes in mission administration that he had begun to put forward at the end of 1888 at the FMC's request were therefore assured a respectful hearing.[33]

Wilkie's advocacy of a greater voice for women missionaries was ironic but understandable. As the number of women missionaries in Central India grew, and as the acceptability of their educational and medical work became increasingly evident, he recognized that as the only ordained missionary permanently stationed in Indore he would be well advised to promote their efforts and cultivate their support. Thus, notwithstanding his earlier strictures against single women workers, he began to advocate substantial and costly advances in women's institutional work. As this policy, and his methods of work, alienated him from his male colleagues – by 1890 he would be at odds with all but one – he also began to call for a greater role for women in mission politics. At the same time, he effectively presented himself to the WFMS board as the ordained missionary most in sympathy with women's work and thus persuaded it to support his plan for concentrating its most important institutions in Indore.

The other men in the mission recognized the strong element of expediency in Wilkie's new policy, but the majority of women missionaries either failed to see it or else chose to ignore it in view of the increased leverage his support gave their causes at home. Still, there were costs as well as benefits in the alliance. Most of the male missionaries were undeniably hostile to 'women's rights' in a mission, and some, such as J. Fraser Campbell, were clearly anxious to divert part of the flow of WFMS dollars into their own endeavours.[34] At the same time, they were demonstrably far from being opposed to women's missionary work. Pragmatism alone would have precluded such an attitude. The specific projects championed by Wilkie, however, frequently seemed to them to be extravagant attempts to build up his own missionary empire in Indore. Responding from this perspective, they dug in their heels in resistance, first on the matter of costly structures and then on the issue of political rights.

Wilkie's new approach to women's work had first become evident in 1884 in connection with the proposal for a girls' boarding school in Indore. In August of that year Margaret Rodger had written to the WFMS suggesting such a school. In the same month Wilkie had sent preliminary plans to the FMC for the construction of a boarding school facility and had proposed Rodger as its head. In subsequent correspondence it became clear that the idea of the school had originated with him and that his advocacy of Rodger as headmistress had more to do with her 'steady' nature than her executive ability.[35] Later, when the matter came before council and a majority of the ordained missionaries objected that a boarding school on the scale proposed was premature and extravagant, he interpreted their views to the women missionaries and to home-base officials as a product of their jealousy of him, their indifference to women's work, and their personal opposition to Rodger.[36]

During his extended stay in Canada in 1888–90 Wilkie succeeded in persuading the FMC to authorize construction of the boarding school, notwithstanding his ordained colleagues' continuing reservations. Later, back in Indore, he supervised the school's construction and that of the new hospital for women, readily obtaining additional funds from the WFMS when the cost of both buildings substantially exceeded estimates. By the end of 1892 the two structures stood as impressive monuments to his newfound concern for women's work. For Rodger, however, the outcome was a less happy one. In 1886, frustrated over delays on the boarding school project, she had submitted her resignation to the FMC. It had been greeted with surprise and not accepted. But three years later when she offered to retire so that a newcomer could be appointed to the headship of the school as a means of ending controversy, the committee hesitated only briefly before acting on her offer.[37] Its appointee, Amy Harris, died before she could move her students into the new building, but no one, including Wilkie, suggested that Rodger be brought back for the job. Wilkie, in fact, specifically cautioned the FMC against considering such a step and instead urged that incumbent Jean Sinclair be appointed on a permanent basis.[38] In Sinclair he appeared to have found both a client as tractable as Rodger and one who also possessed other attractive qualities.

No similar controversy arose in connection with the advancement of women's medical work. Nevertheless, the Indore medical missionaries came to believe that except for Wilkie and W.A. Wilson, the ordained missionaries were generally unfriendly to women's work. An issue arose in 1887 that Wilkie skilfully exploited to further that impression. Even by the standards of the mission's politics it appears to have been remarkably petty: the council voted to increase the salaries of three women employed by Joseph Builder as assistant missionaries in Mhow.[39] The three were sisters of European parentage who had been raised and educated locally. Since no WFMS missionaries were then stationed in Mhow, no objections were raised to his having hired the women to conduct school and zenana work. Wilkie, however, apparently convinced Dr Elizabeth Beatty and Dr Marion Oliver that their own status – and hence their usefulness – as full-fledged missionaries would be diminished in the eyes of British and Indian residents if domiciled Europeans of inferior education and background were given salaries that even approximated their own. Moreover, such increases would put the salaries of the Mhow assistants above that of two European women employed as assistants in Indore. Though she had been in India only three months, Dr Oliver wrote several letters to home-base officials detailing the likely injurious effects on women's missionary work if the proposed increase were implemented. Wilkie and Wilson, who had opposed the increase, were the true friends of women's work in the mission, she assured the officials, not the three men who had voted for it.[40] Won over by such arguments, the FMC disallowed the increase. Not surprisingly, council rejected a subsequent proposal that Dr Beatty's European assistant be given a raise. Frustrated by the divisions that had arisen over the salary issue, Builder deplored Wilkie's divisive tactics in a letter to the FMC and suggested that if the women missionaries were to attend meetings of council themselves, they could avoid being misled and angered by second-hand summaries of its deliberations.[41]

It was with controversies such as this fresh in its mind that a special FMC subcommittee took up the task of formulating new regulations for the Central India mission. In 1889, its secretary, Hamilton Cassels, solicited the missionaries' views on the best way to restructure local mission government. The questions he asked them to consider did not deal exclusively with women's role, but it soon became clear that it was the key issue for most. In Canada, Wilkie enlarged on the suggestions he had made in 1888. '[A]s far as possible,' he wrote, 'the ladies should be allowed to arrange all matters connected with their own special work directly.' The format he recommended was a separate women's council, reporting to the FMC through presbytery and consisting of all the unmarried women sent out from Canada.[42] Not surprisingly, the responses Cassels received from the men in the field contained quite different proposals.

Not only were most of them committed to retaining formal authority over women's work; they were anxious to make that authority more effective in practice. Campbell, the chief spokesman for the most conservative position, drew on information that council had solicited from other India missions about the role of women in their government in order to support his case. He rejected the system recently adopted by the Scottish missionaries in neighbouring Rajputana of admitting women to council to vote on their own affairs. It would prove impossible in practice to make clear distinctions between men's and women's work, he wrote. In any event, the presence of women would inevitably lead to conflict and defeat their own best interests. His own recipe was classic paternalism: 'I believe that at least Christian gentlemen will be likely to feel more generously careful of the comfort of ladies who put themselves under their care than of those who assume a position of independence on "women's rights." ' Like John Buchanan and George McKelvie, the two most recently arrived male missionaries, Campbell cited the Irish Presbyterian mission as the model he found most congenial: there, women had no vote in council and were unable to hire new staff or open new work without the permission of their station's ordained missionary. Much as he valued their help and cooperation, he added, he would rather do without women workers in his station than share authority with them.[43]

Adopting a more liberal position, W.A. Wilson recommended admitting women to council to vote on 'all matters relating to their own work.' Like Campbell and the newly arrived men, however, he insisted that 'no lady should be sent to ... [an ordained missionary's] field against his wishes.' To underline the position they had taken in their individual responses, council members passed a resolution unanimously declaring that all aspects of work undertaken by women missionaries should be 'acceptable to the Miss y [sic] in charge of their respective stations.'[44]

The women missionaries were in substantial agreement with one another on the question of their roles. Like the council, they had investigated methods of mission government in other India fields, and they recommended to the FMC the practices they found most acceptable. Women should either have their own council, they argued, or else (preferably) the right to vote in a mixed council on matters affecting their work. But if the former model were to be adopted, Dr Beatty warned, it should exclude missionary wives, since a brief experiment with a council of single women and missionary wives in Rajputana had shown that the latter merely acted as mouthpieces for their husbands. Once their general estimates had been approved, the women missionaries wrote, they should have maximum independence in the conduct of their own work and in the hiring of Indian assistants. In regard to the latter, the only right they conceded to council or to the ordained missionary in their station was that of proscribing the hiring of workers previously fired or disciplined for improper conduct. In an uncharacteristically strong expression of her views, Margaret Rodger wrote that if women missionaries were not considered capable of taking charge of their own work they should not have been sent from Canada in the first place.[45] Moreover, they all agreed – and this was really their trump card – attempts by men to exercise close oversight over their work were futile as well as offensive. To make this point Dr Oliver used an analogy whose significance none could miss:

... to speak of oversight of women's work among women in India even by such an august body as a Presbytery sounds very like sending a man to the kitchen to oversee his wife's cooking. The wife might be good natured enough to suffer him, but it is not in the power of the zenana missionary to permit any gentleman inside a zenana, a woman's hospital or any department of her work unless it be a low caste girls' school. Nor can I imagine any gentleman save from a love of showing authority being willing to assume the oversight of work of which he can have no thorough knowledge ...[46]

Having been asked by the FMC for their views on mission government, the women missionaries made no attempt to hide their resentment of their male colleagues' paternalism. They firmly rejected the notion that they were the subordinates, or employees, of the ordained missionary in their station, allowed there only on his sufferance. In a sly reversal of the latter position, Dr Beatty suggested that women working in a particular station ought perhaps to have a say in the choice of the ordained missionary sent to labour among them, just as women and men in Canada had a say in calling a pastor. Beatty also deplored the fact that 'young men' straight from Canada immediately had a voice in mission affairs simply by virtue of their sex. Like W.A. Wilson she recommended that missionaries of both sexes should meet minimum language and residency requirements before being allowed to vote on mission business. Finally, to underline their rejection of a subordinate role, Beatty and the other women missionaries declined council's suggestion that they forward their views through it and instead wrote directly to the FMC.[47]

If Beatty and Oliver showed particular spirit in pressing the claims of women missionaries, it was in part because they were already seasoned veterans of gender politics. Prior to the establishment of the Women's Medical College at Kingston, the two had attended mixed medical classes at Queen's. There, they had experienced the opposition of those male classmates and instructors who most strongly resented women's presence. Beatty, one of the first three women to attend the mixed classes, had been singled out for harassment, but she had also shown herself especially well equipped to cope. Classmate Elizabeth Smith had admiringly observed: 'She's a master of sarcasm, a wrestler in argument ... would go through a mountain rather than go round it.' Though she had less zest for combat than her older classmate, Oliver, too, had shown resilience in the face of the opposition. She had also learned the valuable lesson that 'women's rights,' when presented and perceived as a strategy for doing good, could win widespread public acceptance (on a weekend home at the height of the fray, the intending missionary had 'met with almost an ovation'). Having profited by their experiences as pioneer women medical students, Beatty and Oliver were well prepared for Indore.[48]

As the FMC subcommittee pondered the missionaries' views on mission government and conducted its own investigation into the administrative practices sanctioned by other societies, the factionalism in Central India increased. Writing from the mission in May 1891, some six months after her arrival, Dr Maggie MacKellar wryly observed, 'I am not half so much surprised at the state of the heathen as I am at the state of the missionaries.'[49] George McKelvie had quarrelled bitterly with Wilkie, resigning from the mission in a flurry of charges and countercharges whose negative effects on mission fund raising and recruiting the FMC frantically sought to contain. Even W.A. Wilson broke with his former ally, distressed by his determination to have his own way, especially on the matter of the mission college, and by his obvious efforts to manipulate the women missionaries and exacerbate tensions between them and the other ordained men.[50]

Wilson and his colleagues probably overestimated the extent to which Wilkie was able to shape the women missionaries' agenda at this time. Their specific recommendations on mission government, for example, by no means duplicated his. Nevertheless, such matters as their willingness to reverse themselves on a site for the boarding school in response to a suggestion from him served to illustrate his remarkable ability to persuade them that their interests and his were in harmony.[51] And as more women workers arrived from Canada, he was able to win a majority to this view, a task made easier by his ordained colleagues' inflexibility on the matter of mission government.

In 1891 the FMC at last adopted new regulations and forwarded them to India. It had received conflicting advice from other foreign missionary societies as well as from its own workers, and it was itself divided on the issue of women's role in a mission. On the whole, however, it opted for a 'liberal' position. Women missionaries were given the right to participate in all council deliberations and 'to vote on all matters affecting their own work,' though in line with the recommendations of Beatty and Wilson no missionary was to be allowed voting privileges until she or he had spent a year in the field and passed the first language examination.[52]

Far from ending conflict among the Central India staff, the new regulations simply made it more direct. As Campbell had predicted, attempts to make distinctions about what constituted men's and women's concerns proved unworkable in practice. Was the selection of a site for a new church exclusively a men's matter, for example? Or, though women could not themselves be officers on the council, could they participate in the election of officers? On occasion, some ordained missionaries seemed prepared to give a broad interpretation to the phrase 'matters affecting their own work.' More typically, however, the majority insisted on a narrow construction. Thus, at only the second council meeting held under the new regulations, Wilson protested when a woman tried to nominate a male council officer.[53] Since, next to Wilkie, he had earlier been the most liberal ordained missionary on the question of women's role, it was not an auspicious beginning.

By 1893, in response to an FMC inquiry about how to deal with the ongoing conflict in the mission, Wilson, on furlough in Canada, was calling for an end to the joint council. The arrangement only promoted discord, he wrote, and it effectively gave women control: 'Some maintain that everything the Council has up for consideration has some relation to women's work and therefore the women may deliberate and vote on every matter discussed, which means that the mission is to be controlled by the women, since the women are in the great majority.' As an example of the harm done by a broad interpretation of the matters on which women could vote, he cited the case of a colleague (Campbell) who had been forced to discharge a qualified female Indian medical assistant when the women in council had contended that only a WFMS medical missionary should supervise such a worker. As a result of that decision Campbell had lost the services of the woman's husband as well, since the couple had left for a situation where both could find employment. Acknowledging that a return to the 1879 regulations would not be feasible, he suggested the creation of separate deliberative bodies for men and women missionaries, with the former having the right to make recommendations about the plans and estimates sent home by the latter.[54]

The problems arising from a broad interpretation of women's voting rights were increased, from the perspective of Wilson and his colleagues, by the fact that Wilkie frequently made use of their votes to pursue his own goals. The council minutes for July 1893 contained an example of the kind of practice to which they objected. As a way to avoid his brother missionaries' perennial criticisms of his spending and accounting practices, and to escape from further confrontations with the mission treasurer, Wilkie proposed the introduction of a system whereby each missionary would receive drafts for salary and estimated expenditures direct from the church treasurer in Canada and send quarterly accounts to him, with a local professional auditor rather than a fellow missionary inspecting each one's accounts on a yearly basis. Apparently by prior arrangement, Jean Sinclair seconded Wilkie's proposal. Challenged on her right to do so, she and her sister missionaries, and Wilkie, insisted that this was in fact a matter affecting women's work.[55] No immediate action was subsequently taken on the substance of the proposal, but the episode served to heighten the ordained missionaries' suspicions that the women were in Wilkie's pocket.

In March 1894 several ordained missionaries seized an opportunity to dissolve the council. Norman Russell, the key figure behind the move, subsequently described it to the FMC as 'something in the nature of a revolution, though a peaceful one.'[56] In the absence of a male quorum, the March council meeting lapsed after two days. A 'Committee of Presbytery' was immediately created to finish off urgent business and to outline past problems and propose new arrangements to the FMC. Because of ambiguities in the existing regulations, the self-appointed committee claimed, the WFMS missionaries were 'constantly led to deal with the affairs of the ordained missionaries.' Declaring it to be 'not in the interest of the Mission that the ladies should be on an equal footing with the men in a *common* council to discuss *all* business,' it recommended two new structures: a 'Canadian Finance Committee,' consisting of all the Canadian members of presbytery, and a separate women's council to oversee women's work. Or, if the women missionaries and the FMC preferred, the women's council could include the Canadian Finance Committee and have missionaries' wives as corresponding members![57]

Not surprisingly, Wilkie and many of the women missionaries denounced both the manner and the purpose of the March revolution. Responding to their criticisms in a joint letter to the FMC, Russell, Buchanan, and Wilson denied that any ordained missionaries had deliberately absented themselves from council in order to have it lapse. They readily acknowledged, however, that their intention was to 'shut out the ladies from participation in our business ... this is the very point we are contending for.' And by 'our business,' they made clear, they included Wilkie's: '[T]hough we recognize a good motive in the attempt of some of the ladies to adjudge Mr. Wilkie's affairs we cannot recognize either their right to do so or the wisdom of such action.'[58]

On furlough in Canada later that spring, J. Fraser Campbell wrote separately to the FMC about the recent developments in the mission. While he, too, objected strongly to the way in which women's participation in council had added to Wilkie's leverage, what chiefly offended him was the principle of women's being able to vote on, and even control, the work of ordained men. 'Why should any of our fellow-presbyters at home propose thus to lower our position and authority as ministers?' he asked in an aggrieved tone. He went on to warn that the recruitment of men for the India field would become even harder when the relative indignity of their position became fully known in the church.[59]

Most FMC members deplored the break-up of the Mission Council. In part, their angry response reflected the continuing impact of Wilkie's persuasive abilities. Returning to Canada on sick leave promptly after the March meeting, Wilkie effectively strengthened the impression that his brethren in Central India were opposed to progressive mission policies and personally jealous of him.[60] His task was made easier by the fact that their only representative on the ground was the dour and inflexible Campbell, and that R.P. MacKay, the FMC's first full-time secretary, was a personal friend and thus even more disinclined than his predecessors had been to question Wilkie's claims and motives. But even if Wilkie had not been present to fan the flames of their displeasure, the majority of FMC members would have been affronted by the fact that a self-appointed committee of missionaries had deliberately set aside the regulations the FMC had formulated some three years earlier. Always jealous to defend their prerogatives as the makers of mission policy, FMC members were now more inclined than ever to disregard the advice of the ordained majority in India and reassert their own authority.

In September 1894 MacKay sent the presbytery committee interim regulations for re-establishing the council. The regulations provided for only a minimal expansion in women missionaries' role. He warned, however, that some FMC members were now pushing for the creation of a mission council in which women would have full equality.[61] Meanwhile, he contacted other mission societies to ascertain their practices on mission government, as Cassels had done several years earlier, and he sought the views of the women missionaries themselves.

A majority of the women took a more militant position than they had done in 1889. On furlough in Canada, Dr Marion Oliver told the FMC that she was unwilling to return to Central India if the mission's troubles were not resolved and the women not given an equal voice. Five women in the field threatened to resign if this goal was not met. One of the five, Dr Minnie G. Fraser, justified her stand with a characteristic blend of religiosity and belligerence.[62] Most, however, avoided such an approach. In rationalizing their call for equal rights they focused instead on the irritants and lack of harmony that prevailed under the existing system, on the rightness and logic of their being treated as co-workers, and, predictably, on the 'best interests of the work.'

Responding to R.P. MacKay's reproach for their threatened resignations ('The self-denials of missionary literature ... do not look in the least like that'),[63] Dr Maggie MacKellar at first denied the threat and then reiterated it: 'The Canadian Mission in Central India,' she pointedly reminded him, 'is not "the world" to which He has commanded us to "Go" to.' MacKellar went on to explain why the exceptional nature of women missionaries' calling entitled them – even as good Presbyterians – to seek rights not enjoyed by women in the church courts at home:

We hear it often given as a reason, why we should not have equal privileges with the men, that women in church courts at home have not. Has the church laid any responsibility upon the women at home as she has upon the women, whom she has sent to the foreign field? I think not.

How can a woman in the mission field be looked upon as being in anyway upon a different footing from her brother missionary in the same field? Is she simply a member of his congregation just as the woman convert out from heathenism is and therefore, in her work, subject to him as her pastor, teacher etc? *She is not* and if not, then she is not on the same footing as a woman in a Church at home ...

You perhaps and other ministers of the Church will lay great stress upon the fact, that most of our brother missionaries are ordained and that therefore it is not right and proper for us to have the same footing according to Presbyterian teaching. Away with such a reason, for Christ taught differently and we have been *'foreordained'* by God Himself to engage in this grand and glorious work of winning souls for Him.[64]

In her letter on the subject, Jean Sinclair attempted to undermine the argument that in the case of the Central India mission equal rights for women would, in effect, mean women's control:

With our forces so unequal, it might be a dangerous thing to suggest, if the women, for instance, voted in a body; but they have not done so in the past, and there is no reason to suppose that if co-ordinate powers are granted us, it will lead to 'petticoat government' in the Mission. On the contrary, I would like to hope that the women of the C. India mission would be influenced by no other motive than an honest, earnest desire to advance Christ's cause and Kingdom, and that to this end every power of body, mind and Spirit would be consecrated.[65]

Sinclair's letter alluded to a second distinctive feature of women missionaries' response to the latest consultation on their roles: their lack of unanimity. Four women dissociated themselves from the call for equal rights. Two of the four, Dr Maggie O'Hara and Maggie Jamieson, had earlier supported women's right to deliberate in council and to vote on their own work. Now, however, together with two of the newer women missionaries, they declared in a joint response that to go beyond that arrangement was 'unnecessary and would in no wise tend to make peace and harmony.' Kate Calder, one of the two newcomers, also wrote a separate letter in which she deprecated the other faction's 'childish threat' to resign and declared that its members were not seeking God's glory but their own. Holy scripture had decreed separate roles for the sexes, she argued, and in pressing for equal rights in mission government, women risked destroying 'what is womanly in us.'[66]

The call for equal rights by a majority of the women missionaries undoubtedly owed a good deal to the influence of John Wilkie, as Norman Russell promptly suggested. But there were also grounds for Wilkie's countercharge that Russell and the other ordained missionaries had been influencing the minority who opposed equality.[67] At Mhow, having quarrelled with her two pro-rights co-workers following their engagements to British soldiers, Calder was obviously anxious to avoid alienating the station's ordained missionaries by opposing their stand on the question, while, in Neemuch, Maggie Jamieson's views largely mirrored those of her missionary brother, whose station and home she shared.[68] The position of Dr O'Hara, the leader of the minority faction, was somewhat more complex. O'Hara's devotion to Presbyterian teaching, which, for her, precluded ecclesiastical equality between the sexes, was undoubtedly sincere: in 1925 she would be one of the few India missionaries to retain her connection with the Presbyterian Church. Paradoxically, however, she was one of the most independent-minded and assertive of the woman missionaries then serving in Central India, and these qualities made her unamenable to Wilkie's 'feminist' blandishments. At the same time, her eagerness to open medical work in Dhar (an initiative that Wilkie opposed) dovetailed with Norman Russell's desire to start a station there and gave her a pragmatic as well as a principled reason for adopting a moderate position on the council question.[69]

The draft regulations that the FMC sent to Central India in October 1895 largely represented a triumph for the equal-rights faction: women missionaries were given the same council rights as men 'to speak, vote or hold office, except that the President shall always be a male missionary.' An executive, consisting of three women and three men, in addition to the president, was to take care of mission business between full meetings of council, while in each station a 'station council' was to be responsible for such matters as preparing local estimates. Since a full council meeting was now to be held only once a year, the executive would have effective day-to-day power, possessing the right, for example, to assign new missionaries to their stations where the FMC had not done so, and to set the qualifications and salaries for Indian assistants. A number of other provisions not directly related to women's role removed some of Wilkie's long-standing grievances about the financial management of the mission. Like the equal-rights faction of women missionaries, he complained about what had not been obtained, but on the whole both he and they had reason to be pleased.[70]

The other ordained missionaries were so strongly opposed to the principles embodied in the draft regulations that they declined even to discuss the details in council as the FMC had intended.[71] In a joint statement, they outlined their now-familiar objections to equal rights for their women colleagues and introduced a new concern. Because the council in Central India still performed many of the functions that would normally fall to a presbytery, they argued, the new regulations would effectively mean that even the affairs of the emerging Indian church would be controlled by women. Ignoring the overall age similarity between women and men missionaries, they also made several references to the inappropriateness of 'young ladies' having equal rights with 'ordained missionaries.' Their statement was co-signed by the four women who had opposed equal rights, and it concluded with a personal postscript by Dr O'Hara. The draft regulations, she wrote, appeared to her to be 'unscriptural, unpresbyterian and inexpedient,' but she would 'readily accept them' so long as they were to become the basis of policy for the *entire* church and not just for its branch in

India.[72] As O'Hara well understood, her postscript would have troubling implications for the FMC, which had no wish to apply equal-rights principles to its relations with the WFMS board.

The FMC instructed the mission that the new regulations were to go into effect by October 1896, but in view of the fact that a majority of the staff had reacted so negatively to them, it was not sanguine about the outcome. In September, in a conciliatory reply to the majority's joint statement, it attempted to downplay the extent to which the regulations would empower women and slyly suggested that more of the mission's business should be transferred from council to presbytery.[73] But the ordained missionaries were not to be mollified by any such arguments or strategies. They would not resign, they told the FMC, but neither would they attend council meetings or serve on the council executive. Instead, acting on the advice of some of the most senior India missionaries, they would go over its head and appeal as a presbytery direct to the General Assembly for relief from the regulations.[74]

To obtain ammunition for their case, the ordained missionaries had sent copies of the new regulations to their counterparts in other Presbyterian missions. As they had anticipated, by far the majority of those consulted joined them in denouncing the regulations.[75] Among this group was a figure well known to the Canadian church, the Reverend S.H. Kellogg, an eminent American missionary and translator who had served on the FMC a few years earlier while temporarily holding a Toronto charge. Kellogg and other respondents predicted or described a variety of difficulties as the fruit of an equal-rights system. They enlarged on the Canadians' claim that a good deal of what would normally be presbytery business in the home church came before council in an India mission, with the result that, under the new regulations, women missionaries could conceivably control ecclesiastical affairs. Moreover, since even the personal conduct of Indian workers was sometimes dealt with in council, women missionaries – 'often young unmarried ladies!' – would be involved in such 'unseemly' matters as investigating charges of adultery and fornication. Nor was the granting of equal rights in the Canadian mission a matter of merely academic concern to its neighbours. Rather, as Kellogg and others pointed out, it was 'sure to affect in a most mischievous way other surrounding Missions.'[76] Finally, with such regulations in place, other missions would be reluctant to undertake co-operative ventures with the Central India staff. In an unofficial letter to W.A. Wilson, the Reverend John McInnes of the Scottish mission in Rajputana enlarged on this drawback, explaining that he and his colleagues would be unprepared to join their Canadian brethren in a joint program for training Indian pastors until the matter of the regulations was satisfactorily settled. Eschewing the lofty tone and impersonal language of most other respondents, he wrote:

[W]e are so disgusted with your Board's wild action in regard to the ladies that we won't even speak of union till it comes back to reason and Scriptural position, and *please tell your home men so.* We very deeply sympathize with you in your trouble ... So far as I know, not a soul of us sides with Wilkie and his band of Graces, – rather *ecclesiastical Amazons.* [77]

The responses of such men provided the ordained missionaries with a powerful tool in their appeal to the General Assembly. In the past, the FMC and the home church had been influenced by the argument that peculiar cultural conditions in India justified giving women workers there an inordinately large role. Now, here was a body of missionaries 'of the ripest knowledge and experience'[78] saying quite the reverse. The appeal was also supported by the O'Hara faction and was signed or informally endorsed by the three newest male missionaries in the field. Wilkie, of course, dissented from it.[79] The majority of women missionaries, to their intense frustration, had no opportunity to examine and challenge its claims until after it had done its work.[80]

Though the appeal was directed to the General Assembly, the FMC received an advance copy. Having considered its contents, and the untenable state of affairs in the mission, most members concluded that they had little choice but to prepare for the scrapping of yet another set of regulations.[81] In May 1897 R.P. MacKay wrote to advise Wilkie that the FMC would recommend to the upcoming General Assembly the abandonment of the equal-rights council and the creation of separate councils for women and men missionaries. The FMC was confident that it could 'fight and win before the Assembly' in a defence of its 1895 regulations, he told his friend, but it would rather accept the appearance of a 'backdown' than risk the break-up of the mission. Then, openly acknowledging that Wilkie's acceptance of the new regulations would be even more important than that of the women missionaries, he went on to add, 'If you accept I fear nothing else.'[82]

As he had sometimes done in the past, MacKay conveyed an impression of greater unanimity in the FMC than actually existed. The committee's divisions on the India troubles were in fact sharp and ironic. George Monro Grant, whose general views on women's rights were well in advance of their time, had advocated the abolition of the equal-rights council and the creation of two separate bodies as a way out of the Central India difficulties, while William Moore, whose strong anti-feminist sentiments as convenor have already been noted, pressed for the council's retention. Loyalty to Wilkie, and a desire to resist the ordained missionaries' challenge to FMC authority, rather than a concern for women missionaries' rights, were obviously the motivating factors for Moore and those who stood with him. Grant, on the other hand, had all along held somewhat aloof from the general enthusiasm for Wilkie.[83] It was largely his proposal that the FMC forwarded to the General Assembly and that became the basis of new regulations prepared by an assembly committee.

Under the new regulations, a Finance Committee composed of all the ordained Canadian missionaries was to oversee men's missionary work; constituted as presbytery, the same men would take charge of ecclesiastical matters. A Women's Council would 'supervise and direct the work of each individual [woman] missionary.' Its autonomy was limited, however, by the fact that its estimates were to be forwarded to the FMC through presbytery for comment. A mission treasurer, appointed by and responsible to the FMC, would have clear and considerable powers as the gatekeeper of mission funds, and appeals past him to the church treasurer in Canada would henceforth be prohibited. Overall, the new regulations gave greater responsibility to missionaries in the field than the FMC had been inclined to do earlier, while at the same time providing that the Finance Committee or the Women's Council, rather than individual missionaries, would plan and execute building projects and other costly initiatives.[84] The effect, clearly, would be to reduce the opportunities for individual appeals to home-base officials such as had, in the past, allowed Wilkie to circumvent the wishes of his ordained colleagues and obtain substantial sums for his own projects and those of his women allies.

In Central India, initial reactions to the new regulations suggested the likelihood of yet another round of protracted conflict and complaint. While a majority of presbytery thankfully accepted them as 'probably the best possible under the circumstances,'[85] other missionaries expressed strong disapproval. Anticipating their displeasure, MacKay asked the women who had earlier sought an equal-rights council to swallow their disappointment and accept the new system for the good of the mission. He was particularly concerned about winning the support of Dr Marion Oliver and Jean Sinclair, two of the most senior and influential women in the field and the two with whom both he and Wilkie had been most friendly. 'I only feel that at this point much depends on yourself and Miss Sinclair,' he told Oliver in a July 1897 letter. 'If you two take the attitude of acceptance and patient hopefulness you can do much to save the Church from serious harm.'[86] Refusing this responsibility, they instead joined a majority on the Women's Council in protesting the regulations. The new system denied them their right to perfect equality in all non-ecclesiastical matters, they declared, and it would not promote the best interests of the work. To illustrate the latter claim, they argued that having women missionaries' estimates go to the FMC through presbytery would eventually have the unfortunate effect of allowing ordained Indians to decide on them, since they, rather than Canadian men, would some day comprise the majority of presbyters. The issue was a red herring – not a single Indian was then a member of presbytery – but it sounded more disinterested than merely objecting to the presbytery's right to comment on their estimates, and it was calculated to appeal to home-base fears of Indian control of Canadian funds. As in the past, some of their criticisms, including this one, indicated that they had worked out a common strategy with John Wilkie, whose protest ran to ten printed pages.[87]

Responding separately as a Women's Council minority, the O'Hara faction – reduced to three with Mary Dougan's return to Canada – lamented the fact that a partial-rights council had not been restored and that they would thus be deprived of opportunities to benefit from an exchange of the ideas and experiences of missionaries of both sexes. Interestingly, their view was shared by one of the men who had earlier signalled approval of the new regulations. Writing privately to R.P. MacKay, A.P. Ledingham explained that he had gone along with the presbytery endorsement to put an end to immediate difficulties, but that in reality he anticipated that two separate councils would violate 'the essential oneness of the work' and that they would soon become narrow and stagnant.[88]

Notwithstanding these initial protests, the new regulations marked a positive turning point in the mission's acrimonious history. A subtly worded amendment, enacted in 1898, put an end to the need for the Women's Council to submit its estimates to presbytery for comment and transfer to Canada.[89] The result, of course, was a significant increase in its autonomy. With this important change in place, the path was cleared both for improved relations among the women missionaries themselves and between them and the male staff. John Wilkie, however, became an increasingly isolated figure.

Especially as it became clear that the new system of mission government would remain in place, the two factions in the Women's Council made practical efforts to bury past differences. The process was made easier by the resignations of three women whose political differences had been sharply accentuated by personal quarrels.[90] By early 1898 several of the Indore missionaries had made social visits to Dhar to mend fences with Maggie O'Hara; others took care in official letters to speak of her in friendly terms. O'Hara, in turn, sent one of her 'adopted' Indian Christian girls to the Indore boarding school, a move of some significance, since, in the past, Jean Sinclair had complained that for political reasons missionaries in other stations had refused to send girls to her.[91]

Inevitably, old hostilities and former alignments sometimes surfaced in Women's Council proceedings, especially during the first few years. On the whole, however, the resurgence of old quarrels became the exception rather than the rule. The advent of the famine provided a timely basis for united action and a compelling diversion from past troubles. The growth of harmony within the Women's Council was symbolized in the election of Dr O'Hara as president near the end of 1899 and in unanimous support for Jean Sinclair's desire to advance the boarding school to high school status.[92] In a letter to R.P. MacKay in January 1901, newly arrived missionary Mary Leach reported a delightful spirit of unity among the women. '[T]hey are really congenial & friendly both in & out of council,' she wrote.[93] This was too rosy a picture; personal rivalries and divisions within the council certainly did not cease to exist. Increasingly, however, Women's Council policies appeared to be adopted or rejected on their merits rather than on the basis of who had proposed them. And as the ranks of the council members were joined by new missionaries with no direct knowledge of former quarrels, the factionalism of past mission politics became increasingly irrelevant.

The removal of women's right to 'interfere' with their work went a long way towards dissolving male missionaries' resentment of 'lady workers.' Freed of what many had regarded as a continuing affront to their dignity as men and (in most cases) ministers, they even came to terms with the fact that they no longer had an automatic right to comment on women's estimates.[94] Meanwhile, several developments after 1898 contributed to improved relations between the two groups of missionaries. An exchange of minutes between their respective organizations generally kept them informed of each other's plans and prevented the misunderstandings that had been predicted as an outgrowth of separate mission organizations. Beginning in 1899, conferences were held to discuss mutual concerns. The famine served as an effective unifying force between the men and women, as among the women themselves, involving them in joint planning for relief efforts and for the future care of the orphans. In a more limited way, the plague and the revival appear to have had similar effects by channelling the missionaries' energies and hopes into common and compelling concerns.

There were, of course, some persistent irritants. Some male missionaries wanted to have the drawing power of women's institutional work in their stations without having that work under the authority of the Women's Council. In the past, when a male missionary had established work among girls or women, it had typically been in a station where no woman missionary was present, and often it was conducted under his wife's supervision. Sometimes, as with J. Fraser Campbell's employment of a female Indian medical worker in 1893, the women missionaries had formally objected to such arrangements; in other cases, no protest had been made, and the WFMS board had occasionally met the estimates. With the establishment of the Women's Council, however, the board refused to be responsible for any estimates for women's work that did not come through the council, even work by missionary wives.[95] Despite some grumbling, most male missionaries recognized that a new era had come and did not persist in work among girls or women.

There were two notable exceptions. Campbell, predictably, was one of them. The girls' orphanage established at Ratlam at the time of the famine and supervised by his wife remained under his rather than the Women's Council's authority. Additionally, he and a male medical missionary in Ratlam both operated dispensaries in which large numbers of women were treated. Campbell coveted WFMS funds and valued WFMS missionaries, but he remained adamant that he would do without both so long as they impaired his authority in 'his' station.[96] The other determined hold-out was Dr John Buchanan. Buchanan's unwillingness to concede authority to the Women's Council reflected both his desire to have full control of his special work among the aboriginal Bhils and his conservative views on women's rights. Unlike Campbell, however, he was not prepared to forgo the services of a woman missionary on a permanent basis. Over the strong objections of the Women's Council, he managed in 1912 to persuade the FMC to allow him to employ Bertha Robson, a Queen's MA graduate from his home community, under his rather than council's authority. Especially since Robson knew and accepted the terms of the arrangement, there was little the Women's Council could do to prevent it.[97] As frustrating as some of the women missionaries found the situations with Campbell and Buchanan, they were able to keep them in perspective. The arrangements were, after all, anomalies. And the women believed that the work being undertaken would be productive of much good, however administered.

No factor was more important in healing the breach between the women and men missionaries than the decline of Wilkie's influence over his former allies and his removal from the mission in 1902. With the introduction of the new regulations in 1897, there was no longer a basis for the reciprocity in mission politics that had previously existed between Wilkie and a majority of the women. In this situation, and in the face of other changes, he lost the support of Sinclair and Oliver, the two women who had formerly been his most influential supporters in the mission field.

Though she acknowledged that her troubles with Wilkie went back several years, Sinclair did not openly criticize him to the FMC until 1900. At that point, his efforts to prevent her from raising her boarding school to high school status in order to further his own plans for coeducation brought matters to a head. In an unofficial letter to R.P. MacKay, Sinclair denounced Wilkie with a bitterness that was all the greater for her sense of having been betrayed:

In the light of recent years, I do not hesitate to say that it has ever been his policy to *crush* what he cannot *control.* I must speak now, tho I have hesitated ever since my return from Canada in '96 to say a word against one whom I, with others, now believe to be unscrupulous in the using of all & any means to further his own ends. For 5 years I believed in him implicitly. Then I went on furlough. I heard from him only once while I was in Canada, & that was when he wanted me to back up his scheme for a Training School. – & because I still believed the man to be honest & upright I saw as he wanted me to see. Immediately I returned to India, I found everything different. I believe Mr. Wilkie had hoped to see someone in charge of the Boarding School whom he could twist round his little finger. – a nominal head with himself as referee ... I believe there was a determination to somehow control *all* the work at Indore.[98]

In the same year, on furlough in Canada, Dr Marion Oliver criticized Wilkie to WFMS officials for making inflated claims about his industrial home for women in Indore.[99] Such criticism from his male colleagues had long since become routine, but it was a striking departure for Oliver. It was followed in March 1902 by a much more sensational charge: in private letters, Oliver informed R.P. MacKay of her belief that Wilkie had become addicted to 'pernicious drugs.' She drew on the correspondence of two missionaries who privately shared her suspicions, the Reverend J.T. Taylor, with whom Wilkie was then living in Indore, and Dr Margaret Wallace, a China missionary who had come to Central India in the wake of the Boxer uprising and who, she claimed, had first drawn her attention to the possibility that Wilkie's erratic behaviour might be explained by such an addiction.[100] Oliver agreed to allow MacKay to use her letters if necessary. In June, however, in the absence of any solid evidence to support her suspicions, the FMC pressured her to withdraw her allegations in order to avoid possible legal action by Wilkie; and, like Taylor and Wallace, she was formally rebuked for giving the drug rumours currency. (Wallace was subsequently dismissed from missionary service for refusing to accept the rebuke and return to China as ordered.)[101]

During the same week, by a vote of ten to three, the FMC accepted the recommendation of the presbytery in Central India and terminated Wilkie's connection with the mission.[102] None of his fellow presbyters had made public reference to the drug rumours, and the committee unequivocally denied that the rumours had played any part in its decision. This may well have been the case. In the face of mounting evidence that Wilkie was becoming increasingly quarrelsome with his colleagues and unreliable in his claims, there were plenty of other reasons for the FMC to conclude that he could no longer be left in the mission. Similar reasons for recalling him had been advanced, and rejected, in the past. Now, however, two ordained China missionaries who had temporarily been serving in Central India had joined in recommending his recall, and their very moderation and lack of vested interest gave their opinions compelling weight. One of the two, Murdoch MacKenzie, had returned to Canada as the presbytery's special envoy. After a long and depressing examination of relevant historical records, he had become even more convinced that Wilkie was the chief cause of the mission's troubled past.[103] In the face of such testimony, it was no longer possible for the committee to believe that Wilkie was merely a victim of jealous colleagues, much less, as some admirers had claimed, a modern-day Moses harassed by lesser men. Still, the drug rumours may have been a factor in at last bringing some FMC members to abandon their support for the controversial Wilkie. And the fact that the rumours had been brought to the committee's attention by Marion Oliver, a qualified physician and a missionary in whose judgment MacKay had always placed great stock, made it difficult to dismiss them as simply malicious.[104]

Wilkie's influence on mission relations did not end abruptly with his recall. Early in 1903 while he was attempting to have the FMC's decision reversed, six women missionaries, led by Dr Maggie MacKellar, forwarded a memorial to the committee declaring their continuing confidence in him. In September, furlough and retired missionaries in Canada lined up decisively for or against him in testimony before a General Assembly commission that had been appointed to look into his long and controversial role in the mission.[105]

In 1904 a group of Canadian supporters headed by J.K. Macdonald, the managing director of Confederation Life, established an independent mission for Wilkie in Jhansi, north of Central India.[106] When he briefly visited Indore, en route to Jhansi, several of his women friends pointedly organized an entertainment for him on the night of a mission-sponsored function. Reporting on the event, Principal Robert King confided to MacKay that Wilkie's return had had the effect of reopening 'old sores' among the mission staff. The phenomenon proved to be a temporary one, however, as even lifelong Wilkie apologists like MacKellar learned to work in harmony with those who had opposed him. And significantly, while a number of the mission's Indian employees followed him to Jhansi, attracted by his promise of better salaries, none of his missionary supporters did so.[107] Indeed, with the exception of Wilkie's daughter, no woman missionary would be employed in Jhansi during the mission's fourteen years outside the Presbyterian church.[108]

No move was made in the post-Wilkie era to seek the restoration of a single mission council in Central India. The male missionaries no longer routinely suspected a hidden agenda in the proposals and actions of the women workers, but their views about the impropriety of sharing authority equally with women evidently remained unchanged, and there was no reason for them to believe that a partial-rights council would be any more workable, or acceptable, than it had been in the past. Most women missionaries, in any case, now seemed resigned to the separate spheres arrangement. After several years of managing their own affairs, some may actually have preferred it.[109]

One of the younger missionaries, Dr Belle Choné Oliver, was a notable exception. In 1913, having just returned from a mixed missionary conference in Calcutta, she spoke in a letter to R.P. MacKay of 'the feeling of good fellowship' she had experienced there:

As I sat in the Conference with men and women ... I thought again and again how good it w'd be to have a united Council for our mission in Central India. We c'd do better work together, provided we came together in the right spirit, and I hope to be in C.I. when this comes to pass, as I believe it will. Both the men and women have suffered for lack of it.[110]

She went on to cite an example of the kind of problem that could occur under separate systems: in response to a request from the FMC for a projection of future mission needs, the male missionaries had taken up the question in their own committee; since they had not been specifically instructed to do so, they had made no effort to contact the Women's Council, whose members only learned of their report when they read it in the *Presbyterian Record*. To Choné Oliver, it seemed perfectly obvious that the two groups of missionaries should have co-operated on such a report. But as the older women perhaps recognized, so long as the male missionaries held the kind of attitude that had led to such an 'oversight,' there was little likelihood that the two groups could come together 'in the right spirit.' With vivid memories of a time when a joint mission council had proven to be anything but an arena for good fellowship, Choné Oliver's sister missionaries were in no hurry to resurrect such a body. It would be a decade after the end of this period and in a climate that had greatly changed as a result of religious and social ferment in Canada and India before they would again propose a system of mission government in which women and men were united and equal. Then they would be successful.[111]

ह‌ो ह‌ो ह‌ो

In her account of American women missionaries in turn-of-the-century China, Jane Hunter suggests that American Protestant women found so much satisfaction in the power they wielded in their relationships with the Chinese that the matter of political equality with male missionaries remained largely a non-issue.[112] This study of Canadian Presbyterian women in India has revealed a very different pattern. As candidates, the Canadians had stressed their desire to serve God and their 'heathen sisters.' This was not empty rhetoric. Yet after they had spent some time on the mission field, many developed a desire for power and authority not only in their dealings with converts and mission employees but also in their relationships with their male co-workers.

While the circumstances of their work and the nature of their calling provided the women with a rationale for seeking autonomy in their daily routines and a voice in mission government, it could not overcome their own prior conditioning, or the objections of their male colleagues. Thus, two early women missionaries, asserting themselves on an individual basis, appeared so aggressive and unwomanly that they alienated colleagues of both sexes, notwithstanding their marked ability. It was only when they spoke as a group, and when the cause of women's rights on a mission field was taken up by an influential ordained worker, that the women missionaries achieved a measure of success. Acting out of expediency, their male mentor championed – even stimulated – their demands and played a key role in convincing home-base officials that a greater role for women in mission politics would advance the missionary cause. His advocacy, however, spurred other male missionaries to fierce resistance: not only did they object on theological grounds to sharing authority with women; they deplored the fact that that authority was used as a means of gaining acceptance for policies to which they were opposed. Their objections ultimately led to the creation of separate spheres in missionary politics. Initially opposed to the separate spheres arrangement, the women missionaries later accepted it as a relief from the conflict and factionalism that had marked the mission's history and as an opportunity to manage their own affairs without male tutelage.

6

Beyond the romance of missions

In 1887, reluctantly contemplating the possibility that persistent illness might force her to return to Canada after only three years in Central India, Dr Elizabeth Beatty wrote, 'Much – I might perhaps say, *all* – the romance has been rubbed off my ideas of mission life, but I am not the less in love with it.'[1] Her response was not unusual. For missionaries in all foreign fields, the process of adaptation involved not only learning a new language and adjusting to a new climate and culture, but coming to terms with the fact that foreign mission work, and indeed foreign missionaries, were very different from the way they had appeared back home. The discrepancy between their preconceptions and the reality of life in a foreign mission field may occasionally have contributed to the health problems or other personal difficulties that led some workers to withdraw after only a few years of service. Yet in Central India a surprising number survived the encounter and went on to long and satisfying missionary careers. Hopeful expectations about the future and the encouragement provided by occasional breakthroughs helped to sustain them in the face of generally meagre spiritual results. There were also tangible and immediate rewards arising from the more secular aspects of their work, as well as satisfying personal relationships with those among whom they lived. Taken together, these things enabled the missionaries to weather the loss of their illusions and achieve a sense of belonging and well-being in their adopted corner of the Empire.

ॐ ॐ ॐ

In 1890, while he was still serving in China, the Reverend James Frazer Smith ruefully summarized his experiences in that field:

It is now two years since I landed, and the work ... appears vastly different from what it appeared in Canada two years ago. Now that anything that savored of romance has disappeared, we find ourselves face to face with a stern, cold, indifferent heathenism, which clings most tenaciously to the past, and which is not going to be moved by merely going through the streets with a Bible in one hand and a hymn book in the other, singing hymns and repeating texts of Scripture.[2]

His Central India colleagues could understand and sympathize: even when they accompanied their religious message with educational and medical services and presented it to people in wretched social and economic circumstances, the number of their converts remained dismally small. Perhaps fearful of the effect on recruitment and fund raising of reports that showed minimal gains, most missionaries avoided citing specific conversion data. The Reverend W.A. Wilson did give some figures in his 1903 book, *The Redemption of Malwa.* 'Since the beginning of the Mission,' he wrote, 'over five hundred and fifty persons have professed faith by receiving baptism. Of recent years a goodly number have come from the orphanages.'[3] Wilson could have made the picture more complete – if also more depressing – by noting that some of those who did 'come out' after years of patient nurturing subsequently reverted to their former faith, while others, professing admiration for the person of Christ over a period of many years, nevertheless remained relentlessly 'heathen,' simply adding the name of Jesus to their list of favourite deities and ignoring the missionaries' claims for the exclusiveness of their god.[4]

Inevitably, the missionaries sometimes became discouraged in the face of the paucity of converts. When this happened, however, they did not question the feasibility of the missionary project or their own personal calling for the work, but instead pointed to the many barriers to conversion or blamed themselves for insufficient effort or a temporary lapse of faith. While the latter approach could sometimes result in intense personal anguish, it was a short-term phenomenon rather than a permanently debilitating despair. In general, a set of rationalizations and beliefs that appear to have been common coinage in many India missions enabled the missionaries to respond to their situation with optimism rather than despair. Two of these responses are particularly noteworthy for their persistence and wide currency. One was the missionaries' contention that the eventual collapse of Hinduism was inevitable; the other was their belief that many of the Indians whose lives they had touched were already 'secret believers.'

Optimism about Hinduism's vulnerability was especially striking during the early years of the mission. In 1878, mission founder James Douglas reported that while they might not yet be ready to embrace Christianity, many educated Hindus were already aware of the moral and intellectual bankruptcy of their religious system and privately searching the Bible for guidance. Marion Fairweather wrote in a similar vein. Though she had no illusions that the pace would be rapid or that India's Christianity would replicate that of the West, she was confident that with the spread of literacy and the rise of indigenous church leadership, India would be Christianized. Such a perspective made it possible to view such Hindu reform movements as *Brahmo Samaj* and *Arya Samaj* either as way stations on the road to India's acceptance of Christianity or as signs that the ancient edifice was making desperate but futile efforts to sustain itself. They should really take heart when they encountered such opposition as that provided by *Arya Samaj,* Fairweather and others wrote, for however difficult it made their task, it was a sign that the work they were doing was indeed having an effect.[5]

Of course, assurances that the task before them was not an impossible one were provided by the missionaries at least in part to sustain home-base support. Carried away by such strategic concerns, some workers spoke confidently about the imminence of change. During his fund-raising tour in 1889, John Wilkie reportedly referred to 'the fast disappearance of caste, [and] the wonderful thirst for Biblical knowledge.' Similarly, Norman Russell, pressing on R.P. MacKay the need for more workers, warned in 1893, 'The people are awakening and we may have a harvest any day.'[6] From time to time, more cautious missionaries warned against the long-term dangers of too-sanguine estimates of Hinduism's weaknesses or frankly acknowledged that the people were not in fact 'longing for the gospel.' One young realist, writing to former Knox College classmates from his perspective as a teacher in the mission's college, confessed that, though he found many Indians attracted by the life and teachings of Jesus, he doubted there would ever be a large Christian church in India.[7] Yet such sober predictions were not the norm. Rather, as low-caste and tribal groups responded positively to district itinerating in the last years of the period, the tendency to predict breakthroughs and make optimistic pronouncements became almost universal, and a concern for maintaining home-base morale was by no means the sole motivating factor.

It was this sanguine attitude in the face of tremendous obstacles that the FMC's J. McPherson Scott wished to stress for readers of the *Presbyterian Record* in 1913 following the conclusion of his tour of the church's China and India fields. Especially given the tyranny of caste, he wrote in his piece on India, the workers there had 'a harder job on their hands' than their counterparts in other fields. And yet, 'Confidence in the ultimate triumph of the gospel in India possesses and inspires every one of them. There is no discouragement, no shrinking from any difficulty.'[8]

The gap between what they had so far accomplished and what they ultimately expected in regard to the Christianization of India was accommodated and explained by the missionaries within a framework of familiar metaphors. In the early part of the twentieth century, evangelist Bella Goodfellow, labouring without any visible gains in the ancient and holy city of Ujjain and out in the districts beyond, could comfort herself with the thought that her work was a leaven whose results would eventually show. Maggie Jamieson used the analogy of a lighthouse to describe her educational work among the low-caste chamars of Neemuch:

[T]here is always much preliminary labour to be done first in building the foundation below the surface of the water. But when all this is accomplished the structure begins to rise in shapely beauty. We are still at the foundation here. But the grand purpose shall be achieved, the light shall appear and go on to shine forever.[9]

For missionaries with rural or small-town backgrounds and for those engaged in itinerating, the metaphor of seed-sowing was an especially congenial one: the ground might appear impossibly stony and they might not themselves be present to reap the harvest, but somewhere in the future it would surely come. 'Let us remember the Law of the Kingdom,' Jean Sinclair wrote in 1908; ' "first the blade, then the ear, after that the full corn in the ear." '[10]

A component of the faith expressed in such images was the missionaries' conviction that they were working in partnership with God and within the framework of a divine plan whose unfolding they could only dimly understand. In *Tales from the Inns of Healing*, an overview of medical mission work published near the end of her career, Dr Choné Oliver quoted an unidentified writer who expressed this view. While there had been few open converts after a lifetime of work, the writer acknowledged, many had been drawn closer to God, and 'may we not leave it to Him to draw them still closer?' 'Who can say what the result [of hospital-based evangelism] will be?' another of Oliver's contributors asked. 'God has said, "My word shall not return unto me void," and we believe it.' A variety of frustrations and disappointments could be rationalized and accepted with such an outlook. Even such apparent obstacles as the continuing conflict among mission staff members could be seen as part of God's mysterious plan for the ultimate redemption of India.[11]

However naive it appears in retrospect, such optimism was not entirely rooted in blind faith or wishful thinking. As various facets of Westernization altered urban India, it appeared reasonable to hope that the social reforms introduced under the British and taken up with such zeal by many educated Indians would gradually radiate outward to the entire country, destroying caste, the zenana system, and Hinduism generally as they went.[12] Moreover, incipient mass movements in Central India and more advanced movements elsewhere suggested that India's millions of poor and oppressed might at last be prepared to seek a way out of their plight by turning to Christianity. Certainly, such developments would come to be seen as cause for alarm by nationalists such as Gandhi. Finally, while census data near the turn of the century showed that Christians were still a tiny minority in the subcontinent, the same data also revealed that the Christian community was increasing far more rapidly in percentage terms than the Indian population generally.[13]

Contemplating their small number of converts, the missionaries also consoled themselves with the thought that many of those among whom they had laboured had been permanently impressed, and improved, by Christian teaching. Among this group, they further believed, a significant number had become Christians in all but name. Assumptions about the likelihood of a sizable population of 'secret believers' arose in part from experienced missionaries' keen awareness of the high cost of converting. In a 1913 letter to R.P. MacKay accompanying a report on her work, Choné Oliver lamented the absence of 'souls won for Christ,' but went on to quote the views of a recent eminent visitor to India on the importance of recognizing the barriers to open conversion:

[I]t is not a question of religious conviction! it is a question of forfeiting everything which seems to make life worth living. The pressure which is immediately brought to bear by the organization of Hindu society upon any intending ... [convert] must deter all but the most heroic. To lose property, children, parents, to be absolutely repudiated and outcast, to become an alien in one's own country, a stranger to one's own people – that is a high price to pay for accepting the creed of the heart.[14]

When what constrained well-to-do and intelligent Indian men from openly professing Christianity was 'only' a fear of losing their status and material well-being, some missionaries were impatient, even scornful, of their caution. But they had a good deal of sympathy for women who held back, especially in cases where conversion would mean giving up husbands and children. And as Dr Elizabeth McMaster acknowledged, 'it is little that we can do to share their sorrows with them.'[15] The question of how many women refrained from converting only out of a fear of the consequences is of course impossible to answer. Undoubtedly, some who had come to care personally for the missionaries told them this as a solace.[16] Yet even as cautious a reporter as W.A. Wilson believed that the number was considerable. 'So many believers are in the zenanas,' he wrote in 1903, 'that some churches are discussing the question of authorizing women missionaries to administer the rite of baptism.'[17] His own church was not one of those that took up the subject, and there is no indication that the women missionaries of Central India pressed it to do so. They were perhaps not anxious to test the sincerity of those who claimed to be secret believers by offering them the option of private baptism at the hands of a woman. In any event, they wanted converts who could stand up and be counted for Christ, and they realized that baptizing women privately behind the zenana walls, however personally satisfying, would not accomplish that end. Meanwhile, as they came to realize what conversion would involve, especially for women of good caste, they were at least able to substitute more realistic expectations for personal self-reproach and to allay Canadian church members' suspicions that the slow growth of the Christian community in Central India was the result of half-hearted efforts or the tragic but inevitable by-product of long years of internal strife.

The missionaries sometimes seemed to be more depressed by the quality of their converts and paid Christian workers than by their small numbers. As cautious Presbyterians, most of them took care to discourage 'rice Christians' – those women and men whose prime motive for converting was clearly the expected material benefits – and they delayed recommending baptism for individuals who might have been carried away by a spiritual whim.[18] Even so, their letters and reports recorded a litany of disappointments: Indian Christians were unreliable, dishonest, insincere, licentious, and childlike; they were inclined to expect jobs or other material benefits simply because they were Christian, and they depended too much on revivals and artificial stimuli for the maintenance of their faith.[19]

While criticisms of this sort were almost universal, they were least likely to be voiced by newly arrived workers and by those whom long years of experience had inured to disappointment. Two letters written by WFMS missionaries in 1893 are useful for illustrating contrasting pictures of converts. The first, by Mary Dougan, was rich in the rhetoric of an enthusiastic newcomer: 'I wish in my heart that the home people could be transported here for one day that their hearts might yearn as ours do for the souls of these benighted people who sit in darkness and know it not. And that they might see the peace and joy and abiding rest in the faces of those who have found the light.' As she looked at 'their earnest happy faces,' Dougan said of the latter group, she was proud to call them brothers and sisters. The second letter, by Dr Maggie MacKellar, who had been almost three years in the field, candidly acknowledged disappointment:

The state of our Christians is uppermost in my mind to-day, so if my letter partakes of the hue of the waters of the Mediterranean it will be because I want to convey to your minds the fact that the indifference and inconsistencies of our Christians is one of the great barriers against the progress of christianity in India ... You think, no doubt, (as we all did before coming here) that the converts are so happy in the possession of such a wonderful Saviour, that they are yearning to tell those around them of a full and free Salvation through Christ. But such is not the case. It is not because they cannot talk and preach, for they are born preachers ... but is due partly to the placid indifference which is so characteristic of them as a people. Let the missionary appoint a meeting and ask a convert to preach, he will do so readily, but as to their going out of their own accord to tell the heathen about Jesus, they do not do it ... At times, too, they give way to the superstitious beliefs of the heathen. ... Then again some of them are very shiftless and get into debt, and then clear out if possible, leaving the heathen shop-keeper crying loudly to the missionary for his money. Is it any wonder that we sometimes hear from the lips of the heathen, 'If this is all that the religion of Jesus Christ does for one, we do not want it.'[20]

If the missionaries sometimes seemed more critical of the native Christians than of Indians who had resisted conversion, it was in large part because their most frequent and intimate contacts were chiefly with the former group and because, as MacKellar observed, they were held accountable by the non-Christian community for converts' failures and shortcomings. In their less pessimistic moments, they acknowledged that, especially given the deprived backgrounds from which most of them had come and the daily testing they had to undergo, many Indian Christians would compare favourably with their counterparts in Canada.[21] Meanwhile, the few who measured up to their exacting standard of what a convert should be helped to compensate for previous disappointments. Writing to a friend about her first convert in Dhar, a teenaged mother named Sonubai whom she had informally adopted, Dr Maggie O'Hara declared, '[E]ven if my coming to India had done nothing more than been the means of bringing this dear girl to Christ I would not cease to thank our Father for that.'[22]

O'Hara's satisfaction with Sonubai, and with the two infant girls whom she had adopted at the same time, was attributable to the fact that she had direct control over their training. The evangelistic significance of the famine, as Chapter 4 demonstrated, was that it gave the missionaries an opportunity to replicate her venture in Christian nurture on a large scale. In the hothouse conditions of their orphanages, they were able to take advantage of the 'natural' responsiveness to religious instruction that they had long noted in Indian youth and to raise hundreds of children in closer conformity to their own notions of ideal Christian citizenship. Laments about the shortcomings of native Christians by no means died away as a result of this development. But as the missionaries were able to substitute the alumni of their orphanages for the itinerant opportunists who, in the early days, had comprised an embarrassing number of their staff of native Christian assistants, and to create core Christian families through the marriages they arranged, they also began writing enthusiastic accounts about a new generation of Christians who were proving to be a credit rather than a disgrace to their creed.[23]

ॐ ॐ ॐ

Lacking the consolations of family life that helped to sustain most of their male colleagues, single women missionaries might have succumbed to long periods of despair if there had not been something other than long-term expectations and the windfall of souls provided by the famine to divert their attention from the millions of Indians who remained outside their orbit of influence and altogether ignorant of the Christian message. The day-to-day demands and satisfactions of the more secular aspects of their work were significant factors in this regard. The relationships they developed with those around them were also vitally important. In their dealings with Indians and British officials, women missionaries found opportunities for power and recognition without parallel in Canadian society, while in their relationships with fellow workers they formed strong bonds of affection and mutual sympathy to compensate for the severing of former ties.

Especially because they knew that in many areas of their field they were providing social services that would not otherwise be available, the women missionaries of Central India took a good deal of interest in increasing the availability of those services and upgrading their quality. Given their limited resources and the many local constraints that existed, they realized that they could not expect to emulate the most advanced Western standards in education and medical care or indeed do more than scratch the surface of the needs around them. Yet within these limits, and because of them, they found good reason for pride in their accomplishments. Establishing schools and medical facilities in new and remote districts, erecting proper hospitals after years in makeshift quarters, raising the boarding school to high school status – all these were milestones in the development of the mission. Similarly, learning successful techniques for relieving widespread obstetrical problems, winning prizes for orphanage handiwork in national competitions, and helping gifted students to excel in government examinations were positive, tangible, achievements.[24]

Such milestones and accomplishments did not come often, of course, and they could be only an indirect source of gratification to most missionaries. But even providing relatively simple services could give the women a feeling that what they were doing was worthwhile when the people among whom they chiefly laboured were woefully needy by Western standards. Thus, Maggie Jamieson, teaching low-caste boys to read for a few hours at dawn before they went off to work, observed, 'It gives pleasure in the highest sense to help such earnest students.' And nurse Margaret Coltart, writing in retirement, recalled that even the sulphur they had given to villagers to be mixed with ghee as a treatment for scabies had been received with eagerness and gratitude.[25] In India, such women learned, one did not have to be wealthy to practise *noblesse oblige,* for their skills as Western teachers, nurses, and doctors and their access to scarce resources enabled them to make a significantly greater social contribution than they could have made back home. Their work, quite simply, counted for more.

Furthermore, in moving about freely in Indian society and practising their professional skills, the women missionaries knew that they were doing more than providing needed social services. They were also functioning as agents of social change for Indian girls and women. As such, they were part of a widespread phenomenon, much praised by contemporary social reformers in India and the West. Some historians have argued that the training and example the missionaries provided were the most important factors behind the revolutionary changes in Indian women's lives in the late nineteenth and early twentieth centuries. In his *Modern India and the West,* published in 1941, L.S.S. O'Malley, for instance, wrote:

It would ... be difficult to exaggerate the part played by Christian missions in the emancipation of Indian women. To-day Indians are rejoicing in women's wide and spontaneous response to the call for national service, and it is of the happiest augury for a self-governing India that so many of them are able and willing to undertake onerous tasks. But no amount of willingness would have made them competent to undertake professional responsibilities in colleges and hospitals, had not Christian missionaries, in the face of apathy and open hostility, steadily and patiently pursued their self-appointed task of emancipation and equipped Indian women for the responsibilities which they to-day are undertaking.[26]

It is important to treat such claims with some caution. O'Malley, writing in anticipation of Indian independence and with a view to reminding Indian nationalists of their debt to the West, undoubtedly overstated the case. More recent studies of forces for social change in nineteenth- and early twentieth-century India, even by writers sympathetic to missions, have also noted the important role played by indigenous (if Western-influenced) reform societies in improving the position of women. Reacting against the notion that Indian women's emancipation was a gift from the West, and minimizing the question of human agency, some nationalist feminist writers have posited the resurgence of an ancient and never entirely suppressed tradition of female strength and assertiveness as the key to the changes in women's roles in this period. Finally, it is worth recalling that even the 'dark' period of Indian women's history furnished illustrations of outstanding female leadership, women like the widow Ahilya Bai, the most talented and widely celebrated of the early Holkar rulers, and the Rani Lakshmibai of Jhansi, whose determination and martial skills in the uprising of 1857 became the stuff of countless legends.[27] Clearly, Indian women were not without indigenous sources of assistance and inspiration in contemplating and preparing for non-traditional roles.

These caveats notwithstanding, it is probably true that women missionaries were the most accessible and directly helpful mentors for many of the thousands of Indian girls and women who forsook centuries of tradition during the late nineteenth and early twentieth centuries to obtain a formal education and enter professional life. In backward regions like Central India, women missionaries facilitated the educational and career goals that Parsis and some Westernized Hindus were beginning to have for their daughters, and they implanted similar ambitions in the minds of many other girls whose parents regarded education for females as at best useless and at worst pernicious. The missionaries had not, of course, come to India to liberate women for secular reasons, and the fact that by far the majority of the girls who passed through their schools remained unconverted was an ongoing disappointment. Nevertheless, the Canadian missionaries (and their WFMS sponsors) were proud of the role they were playing in helping to open doors and create firsts for Indian girls and women. Boarding school head Jessie Duncan signalled the importance she attached to this aspect of her career in entitling one collection of her reminiscences 'India's Womanhood on the March.'[28]

Moreover, there were some remarkable successes throughout the subcontinent among Indian Christian girls. During the first decade of the twentieth century, the number of Christian girls passing matriculation examinations and attaining literacy in English was higher than that for any other religious group in some parts of the country, not just in proportionate but in absolute terms. In part because Hindus regarded it as unclean and degrading, nursing remained a profession almost entirely dominated by Christians. The nurses' training programs run by the missionaries tended to admit younger and less-promising candidates than those accepted in upper-level academic studies. Nevertheless, as one study noted, they gave 'thousands of women not only an economic advantage which otherwise they could not have had, but a sound preparation for home life.' Similarly, as in China, mission medical schools laid the foundation for medical education for women, and for many years Christians were significantly overrepresented in the population of Indian women doctors.[29]

Relative to their own numbers and the size of the Christian community on which they could draw, the missionaries in Central India contributed significantly to the creation of such patterns. Strongly motivated by their desire for assistants and successors, they watched over the development of the girls in their care like anxious talent scouts, singling out and promoting those they thought most likely to benefit from advanced training. Maggie O'Hara's plans for Hira and Mariam, the two girls she had adopted along with Sonubai, may be taken as the epitome of the missionaries' zeal in this regard. By 1902, O'Hara had enrolled both girls in the boarding school at Indore. 'I sometimes dream of them taking my place when I lay down the burden,' she wrote. 'Anyhow, if they have the aptitude and show the inclination for it I shall give them a good education.' About Mariam she later observed, 'She is a very clever girl and I am looking for great things from her some day.'[30]

O'Hara planned for and educated her girls in the context of an affectionate, motherly relationship. To a lesser extent, the same pattern prevailed in the various institutions where the women missionaries raised or trained Christian girls. With less need than their male counterparts to instil sturdy independence in their charges, with smaller institutions in which to raise them, and with no families of their own to vie for their attention, they were freer to care personally for their charges as well as to train them. Emotional attachments were undoubtedly strongest for those missionaries who had direct responsibility for the institutions. (Describing Kate Campbell's involvement with the Neemuch orphans, a male colleague observed, '*Miss Campbell's life is in these girls.*')[31] But other missionaries also had contact with the orphans, and with other Christian girls: through Sunday school teaching or YWCA work, for example, through their later vocational training, or in connection with marriage arrangements. As a result, they came to take an interest in the girls as individuals and not merely as mission trophies, and to be guided by personal concern as well as pragmatic calculations in making plans for their futures.

One must be cautious, however, about painting too rosy a picture. Given the racist attitudes of the period and the circumstances that had brought them together, the relationships between the missionaries and the girls in their care seldom developed into equal or truly sisterly ones, even when the latter became adults. Whether paid fellow workers in the missionary cause or wives and mothers with homes of their own, the Indian women remained clients, and the missionaries remained patrons. In the idiom of Anglo-India the latter were *ma-bap* – mother and father – to their Indian 'children,' with all the privileges and obligations that such a role involved.[32]

The influence that the missionaries exerted as resource persons and role models and the very real authority they exercised over the Christian girls and women who became their wards were probably the most typical and significant manifestations of the power they acquired in their dealings with Indians. But there were other points of contact with the Indian population that also provided missionaries with varying degrees of power, influence, and prestige. These aspects of the missionary experience were obviously gratifying ones. However sincere they were about their desire to 'serve', many missionaries clearly became somewhat imperious in the face of the opportunities for self-assertion created by their jobs and fond of the deference shown them as putative representatives of the raj.

Women missionaries' first experience of such opportunities typically came within their own households. In spite of their modest backgrounds, they readily adapted to a domestic world of household servants, gardeners, grooms, etc., most of whom were male. Their retinues, though generally small by comparison with those of British officialdom, freed them from such familiar responsibilities as cooking, cleaning, and laundry. Nor did they have to apologize to the home-base constituency for this aspect of their lives, for the cost of such help was so low and their vocational duties were deemed so important that even missionary wives were urged by advice manuals to leave household chores to servants. The keeping of servants could also be justified in terms of maintaining their image as Britons in

India. As Mrs Minnie Shaw Scott explained in a 1914 letter to friends, 'We have a certain position to keep up and we would not be respected if we did not do it.'[33]

The single women were also quick to learn that however small their personal salaries and mission budgets might seem to them, to Indians seeking jobs or other benefits, missionaries were figures of comparative wealth and therefore persons to be cultivated, and sometimes feared. Converts who had been low-caste or untouchable Hindus typically transferred to the missionaries the deference they had formerly shown to their Indian superiors, their poverty as well as the severing of former ties making them heavily dependent on their new patrons. Those who became mission employees were particularly vulnerable. Women missionaries exercised a large measure of control over their workers' lives, notwithstanding the struggles they had to engage in to win formal authority over their own work. Private 'immorality,' even more than incompetence, could cost workers their jobs. Furthermore (when it was not undermined by internal mission squabbles), the missionary's word could prevent a dismissed worker from finding a place in another station or even another field.[34]

Admittedly, a variety of forms of insubordination could exist behind an outward show of obedience. There were also practical constraints on how much authority missionaries could exercise over Christian workers while the supply of such labour was scarce. (Because of this, some, like Jean Sinclair, actually preferred non-Christian employees.) Towards the end of the period, moreover, there was occasionally some open resistance to the unequal power relationships that had traditionally existed between Indian Christian workers and missionaries, as the former, influenced by the rise of nationalist sentiment, began agitating for a voice in mission policy making and in the distribution of mission funds. The missionaries, however, held the upper hand, and they were determined to keep it that way. Like their counterparts in other India missions, they had always paid lip service to the concept of devolution, but in practice they showed little inclination to respond positively to Indians' requests for responsible roles. Using the financial aspect as her rationale, nurse Harriet Thomson wrote in 1913, 'I don't feel like giving up hospital management to Indians yet, for they have little knowledge of close economy. The money comes so easily, and if they had full control there would be waste.'[35]

The reluctance of missionaries of both sexes to give Indian Christians control, especially in financial matters, meant that within the hierarchy of a mission station, women missionaries generally outranked Indian men. In the absence of the ordained missionary, therefore, they sometimes exercised a supervisory role over his workers as well as their own.[36] It was a graphic illustration of the fact that within the Central India mission racism ran even deeper than sexism.

The deference that high-born and wealthy Indians paid to women missionaries differed considerably in motivation and form from that shown by converts and mission workers. The Canadian women in Central India enjoyed a certain regard among prominent Indians simply because they were Western ladies who appeared to represent the Empire. At the same time, their vocation, and perhaps their colonial background, made them more approachable socially than the memsahibs who were the wives of British civil and military officials, whose disdain for Indians was legendary.[37] What particularly commended the missionaries to the Indian elite, however, was the fact that they were the purveyors of scarce Western skills and services.

The positive effects of this interest on the development of women's work have already been noted, but it also had gratifying personal implications for the missionaries involved. This was especially striking in the small state of Dhar, where the incumbent maharaja when Dr Maggie O'Hara arrived there in 1895 was, like her, an ardent imperialist and perhaps more than usually interested in Western medicine because of his own physical infirmity.[38] Having successfully obtained a medical missionary for their state, the maharaja and his officials were careful to cultivate her on an ongoing basis. There were thus florid tributes to 'Madame O'Hara' in 1897 when more than 1,000 people gathered for the official opening of the new hospital. Two years later when she returned from furlough, the prime minister's carriage was made available to meet her at the end of the railway line at Mhow, and four relays of horses hastened her return to her station. The prime minister, his assistant, and the former personal secretary to the maharaja (who had died during her absence) called to welcome her back. Subsequently, on occasions such as the accession and marriage of the new ruler, her services to the state were gratefully acknowledged in public tributes. Some expressions of princely regard fell dramatically outside the usual patterns of garlands and effusive speeches, as, for example, in 1908, when O'Hara was summoned to pose for photographs with the maharaja and his party and the corpse of a panther following a successful royal hunt.[39]

O'Hara remained in Dhar until she retired in 1927. Gifted with a confident, attractive personality and a regal physical presence, she obviously commended herself to the royal family on the basis of her personal qualities as well as her utility, and in turn developed a genuine affection for its members. Other missionaries in Dhar, and in larger stations, were praised by Indian officials for their services to women and children and were invited from time to time to socialize with their rulers, but in no other case do the bonds seem to have become as personal and enduring as those between O'Hara and the Dhar royal family. To former missionary Mary Leach Addison, writing in 1920, they 'g[ave] the lie to the too-oft stated "There can be no social life between Europeans and Indians." '[40]

Occasionally, Indian princes sought to obtain missionaries' professional services exclusively for the use of their own court. Dr Clara A. Swain, the first woman medical missionary appointed to any field, was eventually lost to the American Methodist mission at Bareilly in this way, though according to R. Pierce Beaver she accepted her royal appointment 'primarily for the opportunity of Christian witness.' An offer of this kind was apparently made to Dr Marion Oliver in the late 1880s. While visiting in Kashmir, Oliver treated the maharaja's wife and was subsequently asked to stay on as court physician. In a somewhat similar development in 1902, Jean Sinclair was asked by the AGG to become personal guardian to the rani of Dewas as part of an imperial policy of placing young princes and their wives under tutelage.[41] Neither offer was accepted. Nevertheless, especially in the context of contentious mission politics and other discouragements in the work, these were comforting reminders of yet other opportunities beyond the missionary frontier.

The nature of the relationship between British officials in Central India and the rulers of the princely states was such that, as the missionaries' stock rose with one group, it also rose with the other. Thus, the regard that women missionaries were shown by ruling princes and their officials was significantly increased by the acceptance and honours they received from the raj. In their reports of various tokens of imperial recognition, the missionaries liked to imply that they cared about such things only for this spillover effect, that is, for the increased leverage it gave them in promoting the interests of 'the work.'[42] Yet their protests of personal indifference failed to mask the immense satisfaction they took in such recognition. Especially for the most imperially minded among them, the nods of approval from British officialdom were probably among the most personally rewarding aspects of their missionary service.

So far as purely social relations were concerned, it is unlikely that the missionaries, as a group, were regarded by the British elite in Central India as quite up to the mark. An Indian Christian author in 1889 attempted to paint a bright picture of such relationships. The missionary, he wrote, 'moves on the most intimate terms with the Collector or Doctor or Engineer of the station; and receives the same homage from the natives, which they ungrudgingly give to the Collector Sahib and those who move in his circle.' In all likelihood, this rosy assessment reflected the writer's perspective as an Indian, as well as his desire to encourage missionary vocations. Charles Allen, a social historian of British India, was probably nearer the truth in suggesting that 'missionaries ... were given a limited role on the fringes of "Anglo-India" and were, by and large, left to their own devices.' Allen's assessment is vividly supported in Sara Jeanette Duncan's somewhat auto-biographical *The Simple Adventures of a Memsahib* and in the novels in Paul Scott's *Raj Quartet*.[43]

Still, the nature of the relationship probably varied a good deal from one part of India to another, and even from station to station. In Indore, there were a number of functions to which all respectable Europeans seemingly were invited – Residency garden parties, for instance, and con-certs for fund-raising purposes. Because that was so, the missionaries had recognized the extent of the snub when in 1880, plagued by opposition from without and scandal from within, they had been altogether excluded from the AGG's twenty-fourth of May durbar. From that low point they had advanced considerably until, in the early twentieth century, they were blessed with the arrival of an AGG whose friendship with one of their members, the daughter of a former officer of the Black Watch in India, brought the mission 'many things that otherwise would not have come to it.'[44] In the military cantonment at Mhow, a large number of English people were reportedly available for social contacts. Within a month of her arrival there in 1884, missionary wife Kate Builder was already familiar with local calling hours and proud of having dined with a titled lady. Several missionaries at Neemuch also referred to pleasant social relations with British residents in the cantonment there. Not surprisingly, there seems to have been a greater likelihood of frequent and truly close social contacts in those stations where the British had fewer of their own kind to socialize with. Thus, in out-of-the-way Dhar, where a very small imperial presence was maintained, the political agent was evidently on very friendly terms with the missionaries, so that when his wife died in 1906, Frank Russell conducted her funeral service, and Maggie O'Hara wrote of her death as a considerable personal loss.[45] When missionaries were as demonstrably sympathetic to the imperial cause as O'Hara, there was additional reason, besides their small numbers, for friendly relations between the two groups.

When missionaries spoke of their contacts with the British in letters to home-base officials, it was not generally to describe social relations, whether satisfying or otherwise, but rather to report on expressions of appreciation for their work. British officials, whatever their personal religious views, were primarily concerned with the political repercussions of missionary activity and therefore most inclined to support those aspects of the work that were conducted through the agency of social services. In practice, in Central India, this meant that the most formal tokens of recognition went to women workers.

In the period before 1914, five of the Central India missionaries were awarded Kaiser-i-Hind medals in recognition of 'important and useful service in the advancement of the public interest in India.' The only male recipient among them, and the last of the five to receive the award, was John Buchanan, an ordained medical missionary whose work among the remote and largely un-Hinduized Bhil tribespeople around Amkhut the British were anxious to encourage.[46] Since, as the AGG indicated in presenting the medal to Dr Agnes Turnbull in 1906, only thirty-six out of a total of some three hundred medals had so far been given to women,[47] the pattern of rewards in Central India was especially significant.

Invitations to receptions for visiting dignitaries, and the order of precedence at these events, were also understood to be tokens of recognition. The receptions held on the occasion of viceregal visits were normally the most important of these affairs. In November 1902 Maggie O'Hara proudly reported on such a dinner for Lord Curzon:

[W]e were invited to dine with the Viceregal party. I had the honour of sitting at his immediate left and found him very interested in all I had to tell him about our work ... His words of appreciation have done us good ... it was a real help to have the highest British authority in all India give us a word of cheer and commendation.[48]

Eleven years later, when Lord and Lady Hardinge visited Dhar, the same pattern was repeated; this time, however, the honorific treatment was made even more evident. The viceregal aide, who had become quite friendly with the Canadian missionaries during a previous posting in Central India, called for O'Hara and evangelist Mary Herdman in his car and personally escorted them to the luncheon. Meanwhile, in Indore, in 1905, while all the station's missionaries had been invited to a Residency reception for the Prince and Princess of Wales, only Dr Agnes Turnbull had been personally introduced to the royal couple. Reporting on this event, Janet White, who taught in and administered the Women's Industrial Home, showed no resentment that one of their number had been thus singled out.

Indirectly, she seemed to feel, they had all been honoured by the attention paid to Dr Turnbull.[49]

In Neemuch, as in other stations, the women doctors were particularly esteemed. In 1909, a senior British medical officer in the cantonment wrote to R.P. MacKay to describe his harmonious professional relationship with them and to explain that they had caused him to change his mind about 'lady doctors':

When I landed in India I started with the strongest prejudice against lady doctors and I confess that this prejudice still obtains so far as home is concerned. As concerns India, however, Dr. MacKellar and Dr. [Belle Choné] Oliver ... have entirely converted me ... Both these ladies have earned my highest respect and liking for their arduous and conscientious work and their breadth of mind.[50]

For MacKellar, formal recognition soon followed this private tribute. In 1911 a public outdoor dinner was held to mark her fiftieth birthday and her twenty-first year of service in Central India. While the celebrations were organized by the local Christian community, British and Indian officials and ordinary local citizens evidently joined in. Describing this affair for home-base officials, a male medical colleague explained that MacKellar was also to be the AGG's guest at the upcoming Delhi durbar: '[I]t will place at least one phase of our cause in a position of some prominence on that great day,' he observed. 'We don't seek medals and honours but in a land like India they have their place and it is not a mean one.' The following year at the official opening of the new Neemuch hospital, the AGG presented MacKellar with the Kaiser-i-Hind medal.[51] For someone as ardently imperialistic as MacKellar, and as fond of the public-relations aspects of mission work, this series of tributes was clearly enormously satisfying.

Notwithstanding his friendly remarks about missionaries' educational and medical activities on the occasion of the presentation to MacKellar, the AGG and his agents did not automatically support the social service aspects of mission work. Just how directly their aid and encouragement were tied to hard calculations of immediate or long-term political interest was illustrated by a series of setbacks in men's work that took place at about the same time. In the face of growing nationalist agitation in the region around Sirdarpur, the men's Mission Council was refused permission to set up a dispensary there unless it would pledge that no religious instruction would accompany medical treatment. A similar problem prevented the opening of work in Barwani.[52] In 1911, British officials in Mhow reportedly reneged on an agreement to let the mission run the cantonment school because of local objections. In the same year, the AGG halved the government grant to Indore Christian College after Principal King failed, in his view, to deal harshly enough with youthful nationalist sympathizers.[53] Women's work, meanwhile, continued to be encouraged, since not only was it seen as providing services for the needier sex, its religious elements did not come so noticeably before the public and were therefore less vulnerable to nationalist attacks.

As the bearers of scarce and politically attractive social services, then, and as Western ladies who valued rather than ridiculed the society of native elites, the women missionaries were often the recipients of helpful, gratifying attention from both Indian and British officials. It is likely, however, that a third element contributed to the *entente cordiale* that developed: whether by virtue of disinclination or the exercise of discretion, the women and men missionaries in Central India – but especially the women – generally eschewed public comment on issues that were awkward or politically sensitive for their imperial and Indian hosts.

Disinclination is sufficient to explain the women missionaries' silence on the nationalism question. Convinced as they were that British rule had brought immense benefit to India, and particularly to Indian womanhood, they had no wish to see the clock turned back, as they thought it would be, by a move towards independent rule. Nor, at the local level, did they wish to encourage a spirit inimical to their own authority. No self-restraint was required, therefore, to keep them from espousing a cause that was as uncongenial to most princely rulers as it was to imperial authorities. On the rare occasions when they acknowledged the existence of nationalist agitation in India in letters and reports to Canada, it was to assert their unqualified support for the raj.[54]

Discretion rather than disinclination probably accounted for their failure to take a public stand on an important social and political question that came to the fore in India and England during the late nineteenth century and that should have been particularly germane for missionaries in Central India – that is, the issue of imperial involvement in the production and sale of opium. As we have seen, Malwa was one of the chief opium-producing regions of the subcontinent. Besides being the opium agent for Central India, the AGG when the Canadians arrived in the late 1870s was also a prominent spokesman for the view that the harmful properties of the drug had been greatly exaggerated. For their part, the Maharaja Holkar and a number of other princes relied on opium as a key source of direct and indirect revenue.[55]

As the missionaries' correspondence makes clear, they deplored official sponsorship of opium production. To Dr Marion Oliver, for instance, writing in 1897, it seemed horrifying that the British should be profiting from the opium harvest in the face of widespread famine. But precisely because imperial and Indian leaders alike were involved in the trade, the missionaries faced double jeopardy if they opted to set themselves up as vocal critics of that involvement. A striking lesson was provided in 1894 when one of Norman Russell's Christian workers appeared as a critical witness before the Commission of Enquiry into opium production, appointed a year earlier by a reluctant British government. Angered by what he saw as missionary interference, Holkar declared that the mission need expect no further assistance from him for some time to come. An editorial in the *Times of India* gave prominent exposure to a letter from Holkar's chief minister ridiculing the mission's role in the matter. Given the risks involved in speaking out, even as indirectly as in this case, it evidently seemed to the Canadians that it was the better part of valour to forgo public statements on the opium question – and on other controversial issues such as child marriage – and instead work for change in a quiet, behind-the-scenes fashion. In 1893, in England, the prominent clergyman and social reformer Hugh Price Hughes had denounced missionary pragmatism on the opium question as 'the most appalling proof of the demoralizing effect of associating with Indian officialdom.'[56] Perhaps it was. But from the perspective of the vulnerable missionaries in Central India, there was little to be gained and much to be lost by taking on two establishments.

Genuine friendships occasionally developed out of the women missionaries' symbiotic relationships with Indian and British officials. Not surprisingly, however, their closest personal ties were among themselves. The particular friendships that developed among some women workers formed one of the enriching dimensions of their lives, sustaining them in times of difficulty and carrying over into old age. In her study of American women missionaries in turn-of-the-century China, Jane Hunter likened such 'special friendships' to earlier patterns of affection among middle-class women in the United States, as described in a much-cited article by Caroll Smith-Rosenberg. For the single Canadian women in India in this period, the comparison also seems apt: uninhibited by a knowledge of psychological theories that would later make such friendships seem pathetic or even aberrant, they spoke unselfconsciously about their regard for each other, and the close bonds between them were accepted as perfectly natural in the society in which they lived.[57]

What was most striking about the women missionaries' relationships in the early days, of course, was not the blossoming of friendships but rather the absence of harmony. A similar situation evidently prevailed in many fledgling missions: writers of advice for intending women missionaries warned of the need for patience and forbearance in relationships with sister workers, especially in cases where strong, uncongenial personalities were forced to coexist for long periods in the same station, sometimes even in the same household, with little recourse to other society. In Central India, tendencies towards dissension were aggravated as quarrels that began in the political realm spilled over into personal relationships, and *vice versa*. Thus, the bond that developed between Mary McGregor and Margaret Rodger out of their common jealousy of Fairweather soon dissolved in the face of McGregor's own ambitions, so that by 1885 McGregor was left to live on her own in one of the ladies' bungalows, while the other three single women in the station shared the other.[58]

At the same time, the factionalism of mission politics sometimes proved to be a building block for enduring friendships. The relationship that developed between Dr Marion Oliver and Jean Sinclair was a case in point. Oliver had been in Indore for two years when Sinclair arrived in 1889. Like Oliver, Sinclair soon became a strong apologist for John Wilkie and an aggressive champion of women's rights in a mission. The relationship survived – indeed was probably strengthened by – the break with Wilkie. Each supported the other's position, and Oliver occasionally attempted to soften the impact on R.P. MacKay of some of her friend's more forceful remarks.[59] Even Sinclair's marriage in 1906 did not create a rift, though one suspects that it left Oliver a somewhat lonely woman. Seven years after Oliver's death in Canada in 1913, Sinclair wrote a brief account of her friend's life. Designed as an inspirational booklet for use by the WMS, it omitted all reference to the ordinary human ambitions and weaknesses that had made Oliver such an interesting and sympathetic character and passed quickly over her medical work to highlight the spiritual aspects of her career. The hagiographic style was all the more regrettable in that Sinclair could be a lively and effective writer. Nevertheless, the booklet served as a memorial to a cherished colleague whose life and work had not been honoured in other ways.[60]

In contrast to a pattern noted by Hunter among American women missionaries in China, the relationship between Oliver and Sinclair was not a case of a career-oriented, dominating figure being complemented by a more domestic and 'feminine' one: both were strong-minded, sometimes outspoken women with firm commitments to their work. But as with several of the women whose friendships Hunter described, there was a similar pattern of a considerable age difference. Oliver was eleven years older and therefore probably served in the early years as something of a mentor to her younger, less-experienced friend.

This was clearly the case in another strong missionary friendship, that between Dr Maggie MacKellar and Dr Choné Oliver. MacKellar was forty-one years old and had been an India missionary for some twelve years when twenty-seven-year-old Choné Oliver arrived in 1902. The nature of the relationship had been established years earlier when MacKellar's designation in Ingersoll, Ontario, had served as a crucial factor in Oliver's decision to become a medical missionary. Before leaving Ontario, MacKellar had promised to be waiting in Bombay to welcome Oliver personally when she too had completed her training and was ready to begin her life's work. Following her arrival, Choné Oliver practised medicine with MacKellar in Neemuch at various intervals and, like Marion Oliver and Jean Sinclair, the two women corresponded frequently when apart.[61]

The bond between 'Paul' and 'Timothy,' as the older and younger doctor sometimes styled themselves, was not disrupted when Choné Oliver formed a friendship with a third woman, nurse Margaret Coltart, that eventually developed into the most important in her life. The friendship began in 1916 when Coltart took care of Oliver following an operation and at a time when she was still depressed over the sudden death of a young missionary whom she had personally recruited for India. The three were not posted to the same station during the years of their common friendship, but they sometimes took holidays together, and in 1920 Oliver and Coltart co-operated on a small booklet about MacKellar for the WMS.[62] The continuity in their friendship, and something of its nature, was reflected in the birthday greetings Oliver received from MacKellar and Coltart in 1930: from the former, a quoted passage celebrating the stern virtues of independence and trail blazing, and from the latter a stanza by Walt Whitman dealing with precisely the same theme. The quotations were evidently intended as tributes to Oliver's courage in deciding to leave regular mission service for a new post as full-time secretary for medical work to the National Christian Council of India (NCC). In view of the fact that some members of the mission staff opposed the move, Oliver was particularly grateful for her friends' support.[63]

In 1934, just prior to another birthday, Choné Oliver commented in her diary on the important role that friendships had played in her life. Looking back, she wrote, she could see that 'the outstanding values were in the friends I had made, and personal contacts. Life has been rich in these and He has surely come to me in these Himself.'[64] By the time she made the observation, Oliver's work as a missionary bureaucrat had taken her to another part of India. Through her new position, and extensive travel, she had greatly widened her circle of acquaintances. Yet the earlier friendships remained vitally important, especially that with Coltart. Oliver wrote almost weekly to the younger woman, whose support and approval she greatly desired in her new line of work. She also made regular visits back to the mission, and from time to time Coltart came to stay with her in Nagpur. In 1946, when it became clear that Oliver was fatally ill, Coltart accompanied her back to Canada and was with her a year later when she died. After the funeral, a nephew who had helped to care for Oliver observed, 'Miss Coltart will miss Aunt a great deal.'[65] He knew that even if he was one of Choné Oliver's dearest relatives, he was not her chief mourner.

When the political troubles in Central India began to ease at the turn of the century, special friendships such as those just described were supplemented by a more general sense of community among the missionaries. On the basis of their shared hopes and experiences, and out of a desire for the society of those with whom they had most in common, the missionaries developed close ties with one another, not just along individual and factional lines, but within stations, and as a collective group. 'Single ladies' and married couples got together for dinner parties and evenings of music, charades, or other games. On special occasions such as Christmas, the entire staff, even in a large station like Indore, sometimes held a joint celebration.[66] The births of healthy babies and other cheerful developments in the lives of mission families were enthusiastically reported by the spinster missionaries as well as by those most directly concerned. By the same token, deaths within the missionary circle were felt as personal as well as professional losses. In 1913, after belatedly receiving the news from Canada of Marion Oliver's death, the Reverend J.T. Taylor tried to convey this sense of community to R.P. MacKay. Mildly reproaching the secretary for his failure to cable word of the event, he wrote: 'It is perhaps not realized at Home that those who work together in a heathen land, against common difficulties, are more to each other than possibly fellow-workers are in the Home land.'[67] Certainly for the women missionaries, Taylor's observation was an understatement.

ह़∾ ह़∾ ह़∾

Over time, many missionaries came to feel more at home in India than in their own country. The process was accelerated by the bittersweet experience of being on furlough. Returned workers welcomed the opportunity to revisit their families and to publicize the missionary cause, and they could hardly fail to take some pleasure in the favourable attention they attracted, especially in their own communities. But after the initial joys of the homecoming and the satisfaction in being a local celebrity had faded, there could also be a good deal of pain and dislocation associated with the furlough experience. As the years passed, missionaries returned to communities where aged parents had died and where siblings and old friends had families or new interests of their own. Both groups made them feel welcome as visitors, but they were conscious of the fact that they no longer had a Canadian home of their own. Married missionaries sometimes managed to rent a place where they could live independently for the duration of their stay in Canada, but the single women workers with their woefully inadequate furlough allowances usually had no such option.[68] Figures of independence and comparative wealth in the mission field, they were forced to live like poor relations and to practise close economies unless they had private means. Finally, after a period of years in a culture where poverty and spirituality were powerful forces, life in the homeland seemed increasingly given over to secular concerns and material self-indulgence.[69]

In 1905, following her return from furlough, Jean Sinclair contrasted for R.P. MacKay the sense of rootlessness she had experienced while in Canada with the feeling that, in India, she had a worthwhile role to play:

The maddening sense of freedom from responsibility when on furlough, the feeling of being a supernumerary in the work of the church at home, the outlook from the wretched pedestal on which many of the dear good home folk insist on placing the returned missionary, – the difficulty of fitting in & being natural, – all this & much else contribute to a state of restlessness & longing – undefinable but very real, – and one rejoices to be back in the place where great things await the doing, & where each little duty, however insignificant in itself ... tends to the consummation of 'that far-off divine event towards which the whole creation moves.'[70]

Sinclair was more articulate in describing the phenomenon of furlough alienation than most of her sister missionaries. Yet public and private documents reveal that the feelings she had experienced were not unusual. Nor were they confined to those who had been a long time in the field. Depressed by the sense of dislocation she felt on her first return visit to Canada, Choné Oliver looked forward to the arrival of her India mail and to her own return to the field. A poignant diary entry in the winter of 1908 briefly recorded her feelings: 'Long, *long* to go back to India.' In these circumstances, a poem called 'On Furlough,' given to her by Maggie Mac-Kellar and dealing in a highly sentimental way with the broad themes in Sinclair's letter, struck a responsive chord. The last two stanzas in particular expressed her own feelings:

> My brain is dazed and wearied
>   With the New World's stress and strife
> With the race for money and place and power,
>   And the whirl of the nation's life.
> Let me go back. Such pleasures
>   And pains are not for me;
> But oh! for a share in the Harvest Home
>   Of the fields beyond the sea!
>
> For there are my chosen people,
>   And that is my place to fill,
> To spend the last of my life and strength
>   In doing my Master's will.
> Let me go back! 'Tis nothing
>   To suffer and to dare;
> For the Lord has faithfully kept His word
>   He is with me always there![71]

Choné Oliver's reaction to her furlough was all the more remarkable in that the last years of her first term had been darkened by intense personal anguish over her failure to make converts.[72] Equally striking is the fact that even those missionaries whose work went largely unrecognized by Indian and British officials experienced a similar restlessness when back in Canada and a similar desire to return to the field. Evangelists Edith Hanna Menzies and Bella Goodfellow, for instance, strained against the illnesses that detained them in Canada near the end of the period, the latter refusing to bow even to the tuberculosis that would result a few years later in her death.[73]

What drew them and their sister workers back to India was the sense of belonging and personal significance that they had in the mission field. The feeling was by no means unique to single women missionaries, but given the relatively unattractive position of spinsters in contemporary Canadian society, it was perhaps especially powerful for them. By contrast with the spectre of redundancy that shadowed them on furlough, each was conscious of having in India what Marion Oliver in 1895 had called 'a little corner of my own into which I fit,'[74] and of being in a place where, in Jean Sinclair's words, 'great things await the doing.' As Anglo-Saxon Christian women among a subject people, they could contribute to the accomplishment of those 'great things' in however small a way and at the same time enjoy the superior status and authority that their race and role conferred. Among themselves, they could rejoice in some close and enduring friendships, and, eventually, in a genuine sense of mission community. Finally, despite the loss of many of their illusions, there was a lingering spirit of adventure, as well as religious faith, in their continuing enthusiasm for foreign missionary work. Some lines from Walt Whitman's 'Passage to India,' used in a memorial tribute to Jean Sinclair in 1946 and said to have been favourites of hers, effectively captured this spirit:

Take ship, my soul!
Joyous launch out on trackless seas,
Fearless for unknown shores to sail –
Are they not all the seas of God?[75]

7

'A sphere less injurious'

The concept of the zenana served Western women well. An ideal rather than a reality for millions of Eastern women, it nevertheless provided a rationale that enabled millions of British and North American women to play a part in the foreign missionary movement in the nineteenth and early twentieth centuries.[1] Complementing this rationale was the perception that the movement constituted a 'less injurious' sphere to true Western womanhood than others being contemplated or pursued by the era's restless 'new women.' However ironic that view may have been, and however ultimately self-serving for the male leaders who voiced it, it played a crucial role by creating a sympathetic, even enthusiastic, climate for women's home-base and overseas participation. That climate, in turn, made the movement an attractive option for women who wanted to assert themselves without repudiating contemporary social and religious ideas on appropriate gender roles.

As the largest of the three regional organizations established by Presbyterians in the late nineteenth century to support women's missionary work, the Toronto-based Woman's Foreign Missionary Society had an important impact on churchwomen's lives and, through that, on the larger society. Several features stand out in an assessment of its character and significance. The first is its strong denominational focus. Having looked to their counterparts in the United States for a constitution on which to model their own society, WFMS leaders continued to have close ties with women's missionary societies in the Presbyterian Church (North), sending delegates to their annual meetings and drawing on their experience for guidance on a variety of matters. In this they resembled the women who led the missionary societies of the three other large Canadian Protestant denominations:

bonds with co-religionists across the border were often more important than relations with missions-minded women in the same city. Organizational empire building, as well as theology, entered into this pattern.

Called into existence at a time when it did not have to compete for attention with a host of other women's organizations, the WFMS found a ready welcome and inspired a lasting allegiance. At the grass-roots level, the monthly auxiliary meeting provided women with an opportunity for personal and spiritual growth and a chance to socialize on behalf of a good cause. These elements were present to an even greater degree at the Board of Management level. For the women who comprised the board, however, work for foreign missions was more than just a worthwhile diversion. It was serious business, and it absorbed their energies and drew on their abilities in a way that belied its status as a volunteer activity. Because that was so, the members of the board quickly acquired a reputation for being good at what they did. Their achievements as fund raisers and publicists and their organizational skills were acknowledged both by those who believed in the unique importance of their work and by those in the home missions constituency who regretted their single-mindedness.

The latter aspect was perhaps the most characteristic feature of the WFMS and the key to its success. WFMS leaders remained steadfast in their belief that the spiritual and physical needs of Eastern women made a claim on their energies that could not be made by any other religious or secular reform cause coming to the fore in Canada. Shut away in seclusion, denied the gospel as preached by male missionaries, suffering from ignorance and a lack of medical care, these 'heathen sisters' could be reached only by other, Christian, women. Facilitating such a ministry at the home base was uniquely, compellingly, 'woman's sphere.' This rationale both inspired board members to work vigorously for the cause and gave them a pragmatic basis for defending their organization's integrity. In conjunction with the mystique associated with *foreign* missionary work, it also gave their endeavour special prestige.

The single-mindedness of the WFMS leadership had implications for the contemporary woman's movement as well as for the church's home missions program. As early as 1887 a Presbyterian journalist was suggesting that what women were doing on behalf of foreign missions demonstrated that they deserved the vote and were fully capable of exercising it. In the same decade a Montreal clergyman whose specific object was the creation of a deaconess order advised his fellow Presbyterians to grant women a larger role in the church. If they failed to do so, he warned, then as the wealth and influence of women's organizations grew, their leaders would reject all restraints from within the church and perhaps look beyond it for outlets for their desire to be of service.[2] These statements, and others like them, suggest that WFMS leaders could have traded on their accomplishments to work within the church for autonomous status for their organization and full laity rights for women, and to lobby outside it for woman's suffrage. Yet none of these things happened. Autonomy did not become an issue even in the negotiations leading up to the 1914 merger with the Women's Home Missionary Society, and WFMS leaders did not call for laity rights for churchwomen as their Methodist counterparts did.[3] Presbyterian women lagged behind Methodists and Anglicans in representation in the leadership of the suffrage movement despite the fact that by 1911 theirs was the largest denomination in Canadian Protestantism. Their minimal involvement is all the more striking in that Presbyterian men were strongly represented in the ranks of acknowledged suffrage advocates.[4]

Having taken the stand that the spiritual and physical needs of Eastern women made a unique and full claim on their energies, WFMS leaders risked putting themselves in a false position if they began agitating for feminist goals. They could only justify a call for a larger, more formal role in their church's foreign missions enterprise, and in church decision making generally, if they could effectively demonstrate that such a change would expedite their task. While they were prepared to argue strongly in the late 1890s that their women missionaries needed equal rights in mission government in order to be able to do their best work, WFMS leaders were evidently unprepared to make an analogous claim for themselves.

Arguments linking the interests of their work with votes for women in the secular sphere would have been even more problematic. Such arguments made sense for temperance spokeswomen and even for home missions leaders, but the maternal feminist ideology that provided the rationale for such women could not, for all its versatility, be stretched to the point of sustaining a convincing claim that woman's suffrage in Canada would hasten the spread of the gospel in India, China, and Korea. Nellie McClung attempted to make the case for the Methodist Woman's Missionary Society (whose focus was home as well as foreign work) when in 1914 she spoke to the Manitoba Conference branch on 'The Relation of the Woman's Suffrage to the Missionary Cause.'[5] Presbyterian women, however, had no feminist of McClung's stature and inventiveness either inside or outside the WFMS. If the society's members were going to advocate suffrage, therefore, they would have to do it while wearing a different hat. Even then they would risk jeopardizing their image as selfless women who had left home duties only in response to 'heathen women's' pathetic cries for help.

But it was not merely a question of the lack of a convincing rationale. WFMS leaders' strong convictions about Eastern women's disabilities and about their own incomparably more emancipated status undoubtedly served as an effective damper on any tendencies towards militancy. The influence of this 'foreign' factor was not, of course, confined to the society's leadership. It extended to the grass roots of the WFMS and other women's missionary societies, and probably well beyond. Its significance for the turn-of-the-century woman's movement in Canada should not be underestimated. Women could not repeatedly hear sermons about how much better off they were than their sisters in non-Christian lands, read heart-rending accounts of the latter's brief, constricted lives, and view such artifacts of 'Oriental oppression' as the tiny shoes worn by footbound Chinese women without being drawn to the conclusion that they had little reason to protest woman's lot in Canada. Radical feminists like Elizabeth Cady Stanton and Matilda Joslyn Gage in the United States and Flora MacDonald Denison in Canada might deplore the false consciousness that this church-generated propaganda promoted, but their attempts to counteract it met with little success.[6] Given its strength and pervasiveness, it was hardly surprising that women's missionary societies in Canada (including the Methodist WMS, McClung's efforts notwithstanding) generally declined to associate themselves with the suffrage cause[7] and that maternal feminism became the chief basis on which the case was made by other groups. For their part, WFMS leaders, as prime purveyors as well as recipients of the view that the women of Western Christendom were uniquely blessed, continued to regard agitation for women's rights primarily as an activity that was suited to their foreign fields.

None of this meant that they were indifferent to the attractions of power. Within their own denomination, however, they already possessed in the WFMS a significant power base. In her study of women's historical role in the Christian church, undertaken following the first meeting of the World Council of Churches, Kathleen Bliss wrote: 'It is nonsense to say that women have never had any power in the Churches: they have had immense power, but power in the form of influence, which is irresponsible power.'[8] Especially in the context of the far-reaching changes that the World Council of Churches was meant to further, Bliss was anxious to have women move beyond the stage of exercising irresponsible power in the churches. Yet as this study has indicated, WFMS leaders found some advantages in their lack of formal authority. Moreover, when they tried to slip past the executive members of the Foreign Missions Committee even small changes that would have enlarged their official role, they found out how vigilant such churchmen could be in guarding their prerogatives. In such circumstances, it was easier for WFMS leaders to continue exercising their influence indirectly and without fanfare than to risk a direct challenge to the organization that had called their society into being. Given their close personal ties to FMC personnel and to the church hierarchy generally, and their reverence for Presbyterian tradition, this behind-the-scenes approach to the exercise of power was a particularly understandable one. Inevitably, it was sometimes accompanied by WFMS leaders' efforts to maintain or enlarge the scope of their activities at the expense of their sisters in the church's other women's missionary societies.

For the single women who found careers in the movement, becoming a foreign missionary was both the right and the attractive thing to do. The belief that missionary work was God's will for their lives gave women the courage to leave secure routines and familiar settings for distant and reportedly hazardous lands. The call placed heavy burdens on them, but it also created attractive possibilities for well-educated women facing spinsterhood in a society with few options and little status to offer them. The church's foreign mission fields in India and the Far East provided women with career opportunities that were virtually unavailable in Canada. Through foreign missionary service, moreover, even respectable women could become adventurers, and even ordinary women heroines.

In the mission fields, women filled positions more authoritative than those to which they had been accustomed in Canada. But the possibilities for self-assertion were not limitless. Carried away by the fluid situation that existed in the early days of the Central India mission, and by a naive confidence in the value attached to her prior experience and abilities, Marion Fairweather tested the limits. Her dismissal in 1880 made it clear that not even the peculiar needs of a mission field would be allowed unduly to blur long-standing notions of appropriate womanly behaviour. Fairweather's assertive behaviour, like that of colleague Mary McGregor, who followed her into enforced retirement eight years later, offended co-workers of both sexes and effectively served to establish the boundaries of what would be tolerated in female missionary conduct.

Other women missionaries who came to Central India took a more cautious and orthodox approach to their roles. Unlike WFMS executives, they were not content to remain indefinitely in a subordinate relationship to their male colleagues, but they were uninclined to press for a formal voice in mission politics until an influential male missionary came forward to champion their cause as a means of promoting his own mission agenda.

An effective strategy in the short run, this approach ultimately backfired when a majority of the male workers succeeded in convincing the FMC that their colleague's advocacy of equality for women in mission politics was motivated by self-interest and that such equality would be detrimental to the mission's best interests.

Their failure to secure on a permanent basis a joint mission council in which both sexes had full and equal representation was a serious disappointment to a majority of the women missionaries. Yet a separate women's council proved in some respects to be a more effective and certainly a more peaceful way to manage their affairs. Moreover, the political issue, despite the furore it created in the mission for many years, was only one element in their lives as career missionaries. In the growth and variety of their work, in the power and prestige they experienced in their relationships with Indians of both sexes, in the recognition they received from imperial officials, and in the close friendships they established with one another, they found ample rewards to offset their political disappointments.

The largeness of what women were doing in foreign mission fields was recognized and honoured in Canada. When they returned on furlough, they were treated as celebrities in their home communities and given a willing and respectful hearing in a variety of church forums. After Jean Sinclair shattered Presbyterian tradition by addressing the General Assembly during her 1896 furlough,[9] other eminent women missionaries were given the same opportunity on an almost annual basis. Similarly, at the congregational level, ministers regularly gave up all or part of the Sunday 'diet of worship' in order to allow them to present the claims of their work. The practice became so routine, in fact, that when an elder in one church session objected to it in 1909, R.P. MacKay could only respond with astonishment.[10] Senior women missionaries were among the earliest women to be granted honorary doctorates by the universities they had attended. When they died, their funerals and obituaries were a final token of the stature they had achieved.[11]

To the extent that they received such recognition, missionaries came prominently before the public as role models. Yet the fact that they were extending the boundaries of women's roles through their work in the mission fields seems not to have been used as a rationale for calling for new and larger opportunities for professional women in Canada. Women missionaries ran their own schools and hospitals, and on occasion taught young college men in the 'backward' countries of the East, but what did that signify at home? They faced the challenging task of presenting Christianity to women strongly tied to ancient faiths and lacking in the skills of literacy, but that was not construed as evidence of women's fitness for the ordained ministry in Canada.[12] For many Canadians, the message of the movement appeared to be that the place for women to play innovative roles was outside the country, in lands whose flawed religious and cultural systems made such activity necessary. The special needs of those lands, and the fact that women missionaries had been 'called' to their work, made large roles justifiable for them. By the same token, it made their experiences irrelevant for women living in Canada.

The question of their impact as role models in Canada was undoubtedly a non-issue for most missionaries. As the years passed, their concern was increasingly with the place that had become their home and, more particularly, with the work that had become their lives. Aside from the bonds they maintained with family and friends, their chief interest in Canada came to be in its potential for supplying recruits and money for the cause. The subject of church union attracted their attention and won their support because of its expected positive impact on the future of missionary work, but many other matters were of scant concern. To the extent that it came to their notice, the movement for a larger role for women in church and society in contemporary Canada had the potential to engage their sympathies, especially given their own struggles in the realm of mission politics, but their correspondence suggests that it was not something in which they invested much thought.[13]

The missionaries' chief concern was, of course, to change women's lives outside Canada, and notwithstanding their failure to make large numbers of converts, they did have an effect. Their impact went beyond the obvious matters of providing educational and medical services. Even in cases where families were most resolute about making use of Western women's skills and services without surrendering control of the religious and cultural values of their wives and daughters, the missionaries could sometimes function as agents of ideological as well as practical change. This was particularly likely to happen with students who attended mission schools for a period of many years. The potential for influence was naturally greater with the daughters of Christian families, and, in Central India, greatest of all with the widows and orphans who came into mission care as a result of the great famine. Through the example and training provided by the missionaries, hundreds of girls and women were given at least a somewhat larger range of options than would otherwise have been available to them and encouraged to resist the notion that seclusion was the highest social and religious ideal to which a woman could aspire.

Their significance as agents of cultural change has been one of the most frequently noted phenomena in traditional appraisals of women missionaries' roles. What has less often been recognized is the extent to which the missionaries were themselves altered by their experiences. This happened at a number of levels. The simple, arrogant beliefs about 'the heathen' that were part of the missionaries' intellectual outfit as they left Canada gradually gave way to more complex understandings as they came to know non-Christians as individuals and to learn something of the tremendous variety of other societies' religious beliefs and practices. Maggie MacKellar's gentle hint to the WFMS in 1912 that the term non-Christian be substituted for heathen[14] seems not to have had much immediate impact on the society's literature and rhetoric, but it was a vivid illustration of the change that had taken place in her own outlook during twenty-two years of service.

In the same way, any idea the missionaries may have had about its being their job to transplant all aspects of Western culture to their new environment as part of a Christian 'package' was soon abandoned. In India, they signalled this at an early stage in small but significant ways, by asking, for instance, that dolls sent from Canada as gifts for their pupils be left unclothed so that they could be dressed by their future owners in garments like their own.[15] In the larger matters of favouring Indian rather than Western names for their orphans and adopting the custom of arranging marriages when it came time for them to marry, the missionaries were also practising cultural adaptation. These things did not mean that they had become indifferent to the matter of obtaining conversions, or that they had abandoned their belief in the cultural superiority of the West. Indeed, such adaptations were dictated in part by simple expediency. But as compassionate, comparatively well-educated women, the missionaries also responded to the situation in which they found themselves by developing a measure of cultural understanding and sympathy.

Inevitably, changes in attitude were also reflected in their approach to their work. While the social services they provided continued to be viewed as a tool for securing converts and were justified primarily on those grounds to missions supporters at home, the missionaries came to regard such work as having a value beyond its potential for proselytization. Especially as they saw that even basic educational and medical services were often not available in many parts of their fields, they took pride and satisfaction in providing such services and would have scorned the idea that the only legitimate function for their schools and hospitals was to obtain a captive audience for the gospel.

Women who became missionaries also changed at a more personal level.

As a result of their vocation they were forced to abandon the notion of 'a meek and quiet spirit' as a woman's most priceless possession. Dr Marion Oliver could sit mutely by at the 'At Home' held prior to her departure for India in 1886, allowing her minister to respond on her behalf after William McLaren had presented her with a Bible as a gift of the WFMS.[16] But such behaviour was hardly conducive to effective work as a medical missionary. Nor was it in keeping with the spirit of assertiveness that must surely have been present even in comparatively shy women like Oliver when they opted to leave the rural and small-town communities that had typically been their homes for a distant and wholly different way of life. The transforming magic of 'the calling' was that it effectively liberated that spirit. Some five years after her low-key role in the 'At Home' held in her honour, Dr Oliver was standing before Indian and Canadian fellow workers in the mission's new hospital and delivering a speech of welcome to the wife of the viceroy. In the interval, she had acquired a new language, come to know at least two princely families, learned to practise medicine under new and challenging conditions, and played a vigorous part in the mission's political battles. The distance she had travelled since leaving Canada was more than could be measured in miles.

At its height, the foreign missionary movement appeared to many Canadian Protestants to be attracting some of the churches' most outstanding men and women. Whether or not they thought this was a good thing frequently depended upon whether their chief interest was in foreign or home missions. To some Canadians, not particularly concerned about either enterprise, the 'brain drain' to foreign mission fields was cause for wonder and regret. One of the instructors at the Woman's Medical College in Toronto where Dr Jean Dow had studied in the 1890s belonged to this group. Having heard that her beautiful, gifted ex-pupil had gone as a missionary to China, the instructor reportedly asked, 'Can you tell me how that wonderful woman, Dr. Jean Dow, came to throw her life away by going out to that heathen country?'[17] Especially for someone uncommitted to the movement and conscious chiefly of dismal conversion statistics and mission horror stories, it was a logical question to ask. What it failed to recognize was that women like Dow had been drawn to the movement from childhood, and that missionary work held rich possibilities for personal and spiritual fulfilment. Far from feeling that they had thrown their talents away, the women who made careers in foreign missions believed that their lives had been given unique value and significance.

Appendices

Appendix B
Women missionaries, by field, including biographical data (listed alphabetically)

Name	Main childhood residence	Father's occupation	Size of family	Educational background	Pre-service work experience	Dates of service in specified area†
EASTERN DIVISION MISSIONARIES – INDIA						
Phillipina Johns (?–1876)	Halifax, NS	N/A*	N/A	N/A	School principal	1874–6 (retired; ill)
EASTERN DIVISION MISSIONARIES – TRINIDAD						
Adella Archibald (1869–1960)	Salmon River, Colchester Co., NS	Farmer	9	Normal school, Truro	Teacher	1889–1935 (broken service)
Minnie Archibald (?–1887)	Truro, Colchester Co., NS	N/A	2	N/A	Teacher	1886–7 (died in field)
Annie Blackadder (1850–1939)	Wolfville, Kings Co., NS	Cabinet maker	8	Normal school, Truro	Teacher	1876–1914
Christina Copeland (N/A)	Pictou, Pictou Co., NS	N/A	N/A	N/A	N/A	1884–9 (retired to marry)
Lucy Fisher (N/A)	Middle Stewiacke, Colchester Co., NS	N/A	N/A	N/A	N/A	1890–1900 (retired to marry)

Name						
Margaret Graham (N/A)	Colchester Co., NS	N/A	N/A	N/A	N/A	1889–91 (retired; ill)
Amy Hilton (N/A)	Yarmouth, Yarmouth Co., NS	N/A	N/A	N/A	N/A	1884–6 (retired; ill)
Martha Kirkpatrick (1866–?)	Shubenacadie, Colchester Co., NS	N/A	N/A	N/A	N/A	1891–7
Mary Layton (N/A)	Upper Stewiacke, Colchester Co., NS	Minister	N/A	N/A	N/A	1900–2
Elizabeth McCunn (1877–?)	River John, Pictou Co., NS	N/A	N/A	Pictou Academy Teacher	N/A	1901–7
Marion Outhit (1885–19?)	Halifax, Halifax Co., NS	N/A	N/A	MA, Dalhousie	N/A	1912–16

*N/A – Information not available
†Dates of service may include a final year of furlough service in Canada.

Appendix B (continued)

Name	Main childhood residence	Father's occupation	Size of family	Educational background	Pre-service work experience	Dates of service in specified area
EASTERN DIVISION MISSIONARIES – TRINIDAD *(continued)*						
Agnes Semple (1856–1943)	Brule, Colchester Co., NS	N/A	N/A	N/A	Teacher	1883–9 (retired to marry)
Cecilia Sinclair (1868–19?)	Lochaber, Guysborough Co., NS	N/A	N/A	N/A	Teacher	1894–9 (retired to marry)
EASTERN DIVISION MISSIONARIES – NORTH KOREA						
J. Hazel Kirk (N/A)	East River, St Mary's, NS	Minister	N/A	Nurse's training, Halifax	Nurse	1913–21 (married)
Elizabeth McCully (1862–1941)	Truro, Colchester Co., NS	Postmaster	N/A	Normal school, Truro; missionary training, NY	Teacher	(1909–34)
Louise McCully (1864–1945)	Truro, Colchester Co., NS	Postmaster	N/A	Missionary training, NY; Bible school, Boston	Postal assistant; China missionary	1900–34

Dr Catherine McMillan (1867–1922)	Jacquet River, Restigouche Co., NB	Farmer	5	Normal school, Fredericton; medical college, Baltimore and Cornell	Teacher; doctor	1901–21 (died in field)
Catherine Mair (1880–1919)	Campbellton, Restigouche Co., NB	Businessman	8	Normal school and BA, Dalhousie	Teacher	1906–9 (married in field)
Jennie Robb (1870–1954)	Saint John, Saint John Co., NB	Harness maker	10	Bible normal school; high school, 3 years	Secretary, NB Sunday school association	1903–39
Maud Rogers (1883–1963)	Stellarton, Pictou Co., NS	N/A	N/A	Domestic science, Boston; Ewart, 4 months	Nurse/ housekeeper; assistant matron, YWCA	1909–47

WESTERN DIVISION MISSIONARIES – CENTRAL INDIA

Dr Elizabeth Beatty (1856?–1939)	Lansdowne, Leeds Co., Ont.	Farmer	N/A	Medical college, Kingston	N/A	1884–91 (retired; ill)

Appendix B (continued)

WESTERN DIVISION MISSIONARIES – CENTRAL INDIA (continued)

Name	Main childhood residence	Father's occupation	Size of family	Educational background	Pre-service work experience	Dates of service in specified area
Margaret Brebner (1881–1927)	Sarnia, Lambton Co., Ont.	N/A	N/A	Ewart, 1 session	N/A	1912–16 (married in field)
Catherine Calder (1858–19?)	Beaverton, Ont. Co., Ont.	Farmer	4	Normal school	Teacher	1892–9 (retired to marry)
Margaret Cameron (1879–1969)	Kirkhill Glengarry Co., Ont.	N/A	8	Nurse's training, U.S.: Ewart, part of session	Teacher	1911–44
Catherine Campbell (1865–1937)	Molesworth, Perth Co., Ont.	Farmer	10	Normal school, Ottawa	Teacher	1894–1935
Rachel Chase (1870–19?)	Orillia, Simcoe Co., Ont.	Grain dealer	6	BA, University of Toronto	Teacher	1895–9 (retired; ill, and father's request)

Name	Origin	Father's occupation	No.	Education	Role	Years
Florence Clearihue (1878–1969)	Guelph, Wellington Co., later Toronto, Ont.	N/A	5	Business college; Ewart, 1 year	Stenographer; shorthand teacher	1906–47
Margaret Coltart (1881–1965)	Melbourne, Man. (born Scotland)	Farmer	10	Nurse's training, Winnipeg	Head nurse; city mission nurse	1911–48
Mary Dougan (1869–19?)	Thorold, Lincoln Co., Ont.	Merchant	8	Normal school	Teacher	1893–1900 (retired; ill)
Margaret Drummond (1885–1977)	Minnedosa, Man.	N/A	7	Normal school; Ewart, 2 years	Teacher	1911–54
Jessie Duncan (1866–1952)	Stratford, Perth Co., Ont.	Hide dealer	6	Normal school, Toronto, Chautauqua courses; Moody Institute	Teacher; principal	1892–1932
Marion Fairweather (1846–1923)	Bowmanville, Durham Co., Ont.	Shopkeeper	4	Normal school, Montreal; Ottawa Ladies' College	Teacher	1873–80 (dismissed from service)

Appendix B (continued)

WESTERN DIVISION MISSIONARIES – CENTRAL INDIA (continued)

Name	Main childhood residence	Father's occupation	Size of family	Educational background	Pre-service work experience	Dates of service in specified area
Mary Forrester (1847–1931)	Dartmouth, Halifax Co., NS	Minister; superintendent of education	N/A	Ottawa Ladies' College; normal school	Teacher	1877–9 (married in field)
Dr Wilhelmina G. (Minnie) Fraser (1862–19?)	St Elmo, Glengarry Co., Ont.	Minister	6	Medical college, Kingston; postgraduate study [?]	Practical nurse	1890–6 (retired; ill; later married)
Ethel Glendinning (1880–1976)	Bendale, York Co., Ont.	N/A	N/A	Moody Institute; Ewart, 1 year	N/A	1909–45
I.A. (Bella) Goodfellow (1862–1918)	Thornbury, Grey Co., Ont.	N/A	7	Ewart, 2 years	Church work	1899–1916 (retired; ill)
Jessie Grier (1869–1948)	England, and Toronto, Ont.	N/A	N/A	N/A	Teacher; Bible woman	1893–1936

Amelia Harris (1865–92)	Montreal, Que.; Toronto, Ont.	Merchant	N/A	Normal school, Toronto; university courses	Teacher	1889–92 (died in service)
Mary Herdman (1859–1947)	Pictou, Pictou Co., NS	Minister	8	Bible normal school; nursing short course	Church work; assistant missionary, India	1903–20 (colleagues urged retirement)
Margaret Jamieson (1860–1944)	Megantic, Inverness Co., Que.	N/A	3	N/A	Head teacher	1889–1904 (became travelling secretary for WFMS)
Mary Leach (1875–19?)	Bradford, England	Army officer	0	Brantford Ladies' College; Ewart, 2 years	Housemaid	1900–8 (retired to marry)
Jean Leyden (1873–19?)	Almonte, Lanark Co., Ont.	Wool sorter	5	Normal school, Ottawa	Teacher	1896–1900 (colleagues urged retirement)
Dr Susie McCalla (1871–1970)	St Catherines, Lincoln Co., Ont.	Merchant	9	Normal school; medical college, Toronto; Ewart, 1 summer	Teacher	1900–2 (married North Honan missionary)

Appendix B (continued)

Name	Main childhood residence	Father's occupation	Size of family	Educational background	Pre-service work experience	Dates of service in specified area
WESTERN DIVISION MISSIONARIES – CENTRAL INDIA (continued)						
Mary McGregor (?–1901)	Brockville, Leeds Co., Ont. [unconfirmed]	N/A	N/A	Few months hospital training to prepare for foreign field	Teacher	1877–88 (dismissed from service)
Margaret McHarrie (1881–1964)	Scotland	N/A	7	Domestic science; nurse's training; Ewart, part of session; Bible Training Institute	Housekeeper; practical nurse	1910–52
Dr Mary Mackay (1864–1935)	Pictou Co., NS	Farmer	N/A	Mount Allison Ladies' College; medical college, Toronto	N/A	1888–9 (married in field)
Dr Margaret MacKellar (1861–1941)	Bruce Co. and Oxford Co., Ont. (born Scotland)	Seaman; farmer	4	Medical college, Kingston; postgraduate study, England	Milliner; dressmaker	1890–1931

Mabel MacLean (1878–19?)	Orillia, Simcoe Co., Ont. (born England)	N/A	N/A	Ewart, 2 years	Teacher	1912–19 (retired; married in Canada)
Dr Elizabeth McMaster (1871–1956)	St Mary's, Middlesex Co., Ont.	N/A	5	Normal school; medical college, Toronto; Ewart, 6 months	Teacher; intern, Philadelphia	1904–41
Elizabeth McWilliams (1862–?)	Waterloo Co., Ont.	N/A	6	N/A	Teacher	1891–4 (retired; ill; worked later in Northwest)
Charlotte (Lottie) Madill (1881–1942)	Shelburne, Dufferin Co., Ont.	N/A	N/A	Normal school, Toronto; Ewart, few months	Teacher	1909–11 (married in field)
Bertha Manarey (1886–1972)	Gorham, Grey Co., Ont.	Farmer	10	Ewart, 2 years	Teacher; deaconess	1913–45
Mrs Edith Hanna Menzies (1870–1961)	Streetsville, and Fort Frances, Ont.	Wool spinner	5	Common school	Work in family home	1904–42
Anna Nairn (1878–19?)	Galt, Waterloo Co., Ont.	N/A	3	Ewart, 1 year	Teacher, public school and business college	1906–9 (married in field)

Appendix B (continued)

Name	Main childhood residence	Father's occupation	Size of family	Educational background	Pre-service work experience	Dates of service in specified area
WESTERN DIVISION MISSIONARIES – CENTRAL INDIA (continued)						
Dr Margaret O'Hara (1855–1940)	Port Elmsley, Lanark Co., Ont.	Farmer	5	Medical college, Kingston; postgraduate study, NY	Teacher	1891–1927
Dr Belle Choné Oliver (1875–1947)	Chesterfield and Ingersoll, Oxford Co., Ont.	Businessman, MPP	10	Medical college, Toronto; Ewart, few months	Teacher; intern, Philadelphia	1902–46
Dr Marion Oliver (1855–1913)	Avonbank, Perth Co., Ont.	Farmer	9	Medical college, Kingston	Teacher	1886–1912
Bella Ptolemy (1867–19?)	Saltfleet, Wentworth Co., Ont.	Carpenter	6	Normal school; some university study	Teacher; head teacher	1895–1904 (called home to care for mother)

Name	Origin	Father's occupation	No.	Education	Occupation	Service
Elizabeth Robertson (1877–1952)	Winnipeg, Man.	N/A	N/A	Normal school; BA, University of Manitoba; Ewart, few months	Teacher; stenographer	1911–41
Bertha Robson (1884–1948)	Glen Morris, Brant Co., Ont.	Farmer	3	MA, Queen's; School of Pedagogy, Queen's	High school teacher; extramural tutor, Queen's	1912–33
Margaret Rodger (1847–1929)	East Settlement, near Lachute, Que.	Farmer	7	Normal school, Montreal; Ottawa Ladies' College	Teacher	1873–91 (retired because of mission conflicts)
Isabella Ross (1856–19?)	Beaverton, Ont.	Farmer	7	3 months hospital training as preparation for foreign field	Teacher [?]	1883–8 (broken by extended furlough; retired to marry)
Elizabeth Scott (1866–1938)	Pilot Mound, Man. (born Ontario)	Farmer	N/A	Matriculation; medical college, Kingston, 1 year	Teacher	1889–90 (retired; ill; married in Canada)

Appendix B (continued)

Name	Main childhood residence	Father's occupation	Size of family	Educational background	Pre-service work experience	Dates of service in specified area
WESTERN DIVISION MISSIONARIES – CENTRAL INDIA (continued)						
Janet E. Sinclair (1865–1944)	Toronto, Ont.	N/A	5	Normal school, Toronto; Ewart, 1 year	Teacher, kindergarten specialist	1910–15 (retired; ill)
Jean V. Sinclair (1866–1946)	Medoc, Hastings Co., Ont.	Harness maker	4	Model school; medical college, Kingston, 1 year	Teacher	1889–1906 (married in field)
Harriet Thomson (1864–1950)	Scarborough, York Co., Ont.	Farmer	2	Nurse's training, Toronto; Toronto Bible Training School	N/A	1896–1929
Dr Agnes M. Turnbull (1866?–1907)	Franklin Centre, Que.; later, Montreal, Que., and Belleville, Ont.	Minister	N/A	Normal school, Montreal; medical college, Kingston; postgraduate study, NY	Teacher	1892–1907 (died in field)

Name (dates)	Origin	Father's occupation	Siblings	Education	Position	Years
Jessie Weir (1872–1953)	East Zorra, Oxford Co., and Burford Twp, Brant Co., Ont.	Farmer	10	High school; normal school, Toronto	Teacher	1896–1937
Janet White (1855–1921)	India and Scotland	Army officer	N/A	Normal school, Scotland	Teacher	1893–1920

WESTERN DIVISION MISSIONARIES – NORTH HONAN, CHINA

Name (dates)	Origin	Father's occupation	Siblings	Education	Position	Years
Margaret Brown (1887–1978)	Tiverton, Bruce Co., Ont.	Farmer	5	Normal school, Ottawa; BA, Queen's	Teacher	1913–56
Ethel Cameron (1887–1934)	Lucknow, Bruce Co., Ont.	N/A	4	High school, 3 years; model school; Ewart, 2 years	Teacher	1911–14 (ill; did church work in Canada)
Leah Dinwoody (1879–1960)	Wychwood and Toronto, Ont.	Merchant	N/A	College of Music, Toronto; Ewart, 2 years	Deaconess	1912–45
Dr Jean Dow (1870–1927)	Fergus, Wellington Co., Ont.	Farmer	4	Model school and medical college, Toronto	Teacher	1895–1927 (died in field)

Appendix B (continued)

WESTERN DIVISION MISSIONARIES – NORTH HONAN, CHINA (continued)

Name	Main childhood residence	Father's occupation	Size of family	Educational background	Pre-service work experience	Dates of service in specified area
Margaret Gay (1886–1973)	Toronto, Ont.	N/A	N/A	Ewart, 2 years	Stenographer	1910–41 (broken by study leave)
Jennie Graham (1858–?)	Simcoe Co., and Toronto	Retailer and real estate agent	7	Nurse's training, Toronto	N/A	1889–91 (ill; married in Canada)
Dr Lucinda Graham (1862–94)	Simcoe Co., and Toronto	Retailer and real estate agent	7	Normal school; medical college, Toronto	Teacher	1892–4 (died in field)
Agnes Hall (1884?–1978)	Blackheath, Wentworth Co., Ont.	Farmer	7	High school, 3 years; model school; Ewart, 1 year	Teacher	1909–11 (married in field)
Bertha Hodge (1878–1963)	London, Middlesex Co., Ont.	Doctor	3	University of Western Ontario, 2 years; music training	Volunteer church work	1913–47

Name	Birthplace			Education	Work	Years
Mina Logan (1878–?)	Ireland	Minister	4	MA, Royal University, Ireland	Teacher, high school and college	1912–18 (married missionary in another China field)
Margaret Macdonald (1871–1945)	Toronto, Ont. (born Scotland)	N/A	N/A	Toronto Bible Training School; University of Toronto 1 year	Volunteer church work; missionary, China Inland Mission	1909–27
Edith McGill (1882?–19?)	Neepawa, Man.	Magistrate	N/A	Normal school, Winnipeg; Ewart, 2 years	Teacher	1906–13 (married in field)
Isabel ('Bella') MacIntosh (1870–1950)	Lucknow, Bruce Co., Ont.	N/A	6	Ewart, 2 years	Bible woman and city mission worker	1903–27
Margaret McIntosh (1857–1945)	Guelph, Wellington Co., Ont.	Merchant's clerk	9	Nurse's training, Toronto	Volunteer church work	1889–1927
Elizabeth McLennan (1868–1947)	Williamstown, Glengarry Co., Ont.	Farmer	7	Normal school, Ottawa; BA, Queen's; Ewart, 1 summer	Teacher	1905–39

Appendix B (continued)

WESTERN DIVISION MISSIONARIES – NORTH HONAN, CHINA (continued)

Name	Main childhood residence	Father's occupation	Size of family	Educational background	Pre-service work experience	Dates of service in specified area
M.E. ('Maisie') McNeely (1891–1977)	Carleton Place, Lanark Co., Ont.	N/A	8	Nurse's training, Toronto and NY	Private nurse	1913–16 (married in field)
Mary Annie O'Neill (1877–1963)	Rutherford, Ont.	Farmer [?]	7	Ewart, 2 years	Work in family home	1909–45
Minnie Pyke (1870–1955)	Brantford, Brant Co., Ont.	N/A	N/A	Normal school, Ottawa	Teacher	1896–1926 (broken by health leave and work in Canada)
Mrs Jeannette McCalla Ratcliffe (1876–1952)	St Catharines, Lincoln Co., Ont.	Merchant	9	Nurse's training; university, 1 year	N/A	1910–41 (originally as matron in school for missionary children)

Name (dates)	Origin	Father's occupation	No.	Education	Role	Service
Davina Robb (1872–1956)	Toronto, Ont. (born Scotland)	N/A	6	BA, University of Toronto; Bible Training School	Teacher	1896–7; 1923–38 (married in field; later rehired as widow)
Minnie Robertson (1878–1952)	Carleton Place, Lanark Co., Ont.	Miller	5	Some high school; Ewart, 2 years	Deaconess	1903–5 (married in field)
Harriet Sutherland (N/A)	Cobourg, Northumberland Co., Ont.	N/A	N/A	Nurse's training, Toronto	Nursing instructor	1888–9 (married U.S. missionary)
Grace Sykes (1890–1982)	Lethbridge, Alta.	N/A	N/A	Normal school, Toronto; Ewart, 2 years	Student teacher	1912–47
Mary Thomson (1879–1961)	Lanark, Lanark Co., Ont.	N/A	7	High school; Ewart, 2 years	Teacher	1906–10 (married in field)
Margaret Walks (1887–1948)	Paisley, Bruce Co., Ont.	Farmer	5	BA, Queen's	Teacher	1913–16 (married in field)

Appendix B (continued)

Name	Main childhood residence	Father's occupation	Size of family	Educational background	Pre-service work experience	Dates of service in specified area
WESTERN DIVISION MISSIONARIES – NORTH HONAN, CHINA *(continued)*						
Dr Margaret Wallace (1869–1963)	Essex, Essex Co., Ont.	N/A	6	Normal school, Toronto; medical college, Toronto	Teacher	1898–1903 (forced to resign; rehired for India, 1929–38)
Winnifred Warren (1885–1971)	Walkerton, Bruce Co., Ont.	N/A	3	Normal school, Hamilton	Teacher	1913–37 (originally as teacher of missionary children)
WESTERN DIVISION MISSIONARIES – SOUTH CHINA						
Agnes Dickson (1877–19?)	Fenelon Falls, Victoria Co., Ont.	N/A	N/A	BA, University of Toronto	YWCA worker	1904–23 (later did church work in Canada)
Florence H. Langrill (1890?–?)	Killarney, Man.	N/A	N/A	Normal school	Teacher	1913–29 (retired; family needs)

Name (dates)	Birthplace	Father's occupation	Siblings	Education	Mission role	Years of service
Harriet Latter (?–1937)	Ellesmere, York Co., Ont.	School principal	3	BA, University of Toronto; Bible College, NY	Teacher	1909–11 (retired; family ill)
Dr Isabel Little (?–1909)	White Hill, Simcoe Co., Ont.	N/A	N/A	Medical college, Toronto; Bible normal training, NY	Teacher; intern, Philadelphia	1904–6 (left mission to marry)
Dr Jessie McBean (1878–1945)	Toronto, Ont.	N/A	6	Medical college, Toronto; Ewart, part of session	varied summer employment	1905–25 (later with American mission)
Rachel McLean (1878–19?)	Bradford, Simcoe Co., Ont.	N/A	7	Normal school, Toronto	Teacher	1907–14 (retired)
Ethel Reid (1881–1957)	PEI	Farmer	5	Normal school, Charlottetown, PEI, and Toronto	Teacher	1912–25 (retired, ill; later married China missionary)

WESTERN DIVISION MISSIONARIES – NORTH FORMOSA

Name (dates)	Birthplace	Father's occupation	Siblings	Education	Mission role	Years of service
Lily Adair (1873–1971)	Three Rivers, Que.	N/A	N/A	Three Rivers Academy; Ewart, 2 years	Teacher; deaconess	1911–41

Appendix B (continued)

WESTERN DIVISION MISSIONARIES – NORTH FORMOSA (continued)

Name	Main childhood residence	Father's occupation	Size of family	Educational background	Pre-service work experience	Dates of service in specified area
Mabel Clazie (1879–1968)	Shannonville, Hastings Co., Ont.	Farmer	5	Normal school, Ottawa; Ewart, 2 years	Teacher	1910–45
Hannah Connell (1869–1931)	Alliston, Simcoe Co., Ont.	N/A	10	College of Music, Toronto; Ewart, 2 years	Music teacher	1905–31 (died in field)
Isabel Elliott (1881–1971)	Agincourt, York Co., Ont.	Farmer	4	Nurse's training NY; Ewart, 1 year	Private nurse	1912–39
Jane Kinney (1877–1965)	Florenceville, NB	Farmer	8	Normal school; BA, University of New Brunswick	Teacher	1905–40

WESTERN DIVISION MISSIONARY – SHANGHAI, CHINA, SPECIAL APPOINTMENT

Name	Birthplace	Father's occupation		Education	Occupation	Dates
M. Verne McNeely (1885–19?)	Carleton Place, Lanark Co., Ont.	N/A	8	BA, University of Toronto	Stenographer and office assistant	1909–14 (retired as WFMS-assisted non-denominational literary worker; remained in China)

WESTERN DIVISION MISSIONARIES – NORTH KOREA

Name	Birthplace	Father's occupation		Education	Occupation	Dates
Ethel MacEachern (1882–1959)	King Twp, York Co., Ont.	Farmer	N/A	Normal school, London; Ewart, part of session	Teacher	1913–41
Ethel McFarlane (1881–1933)	Manitoba	Minister	3	Normal school, Winnipeg; BA, University of Manitoba; Ewart, few weeks	Teacher	1913–16 (retired; ill)

Appendix B (continued)

Name	Main childhood residence	Father's occupation	Size of family	Educational background	Pre-service work experience	Dates of service in specified area
WESTERN DIVISION MISSIONARIES – NORTH KOREA (continued)						
Edna McLellan (1883–1975)	Noel Shore, Hants Co., NS	N/A	N/A	Normal school, Truro; Ewart, 2 years	Teacher; work in family home	1913–41
Esther Smith (1880–19?)	Quebec City, Que.	N/A	9	Normal school; BA and MA, McGill	High school principal	1913–15 (retired; ill)

Appendix C
India male missionaries and missionary wives (listed alphabetically)

Name	Home community	Dates of service*
Rev. Frederick J. Anderson, BA Mabel Twaddell	Montreal, Que. Burke, NY	1901–47
Rev. John Buchanan, BA, MD Dr Mary Mackay, former missionary†	Glenmorris, Ont.	1888–1939
Rev. Joseph Builder, BA Kate (surname unknown)	Caledonia, Ont. Hamilton, Ont.	1883–8
Rev. J. Fraser Campbell, Mary Forrester, former missionary	Baddeck, NS	1876–1927
Rev. Daniel G. Cock, BA 1. Ella Maxwell, BA 2. Winnifred Butler Jamieson	West River, NS Halifax, NS Woodsville, NH	1902–40
Rev. W. John Cook, BA Ruth Bremner	Orton, Ont. Minesing, Ont.	1910–25
Mr Louis D.S. Coxon Margaret Brebner, former missionary	Mooresfield, NJ	1914–27
Rev. D.J. Davidson, BA Dr Isabella Thomson	North Guillimbury, Ont. Scarborough, Ont.	1904–44
Rev. James M. Douglas Jane Smith	Scotland, and Peterborough, Ont. Darlington, Ont.	1877–82
Rev. Alex. Dunn, MA (unmarried)	Scotland, and Arthur, Ont.	1908–10
Rev. James R. Harcourt, BA 1. Edith Blaine 2. Mary Stockbridge	Smithville, Ont. Blackheath, Ont. Mhow, India	1900–35

*Dates of service may include a final year of furlough service in Canada.
†For information on missionary wives who had themselves been Canadian Presbyterian missionaries see Appendix B.

Appendix C
India male missionaries and missionary wives (listed alphabetically)

Name	Home community	Dates of service
Rev. William J. Jamieson	Megantic, Que.	1890–8
Winnifred Butler	Woodsville, NH	
Rev. Robert A. King, MA, BD	Scotland, and Brandon, Man.	1903–11; 1916–29
Annie Murray, BA	Brandon, Man.	
Rev. A.P. Ledingham, BA	Durnoch, Ont.	1895–1920
Minnie Hogg	Winnipeg, Man.	
Mr D.E. McDonald	Ont.	1911–25
wife (name unknown)	Ont.	
Rev. James S. MacKay, BA	Harrington, Ont.	1904–33
Jean V. Sinclair, former missionary		
Mr Kenneth G. MacKay, BSA	Heath Bell, NS	1906–12
Anna Nairn, former missionary		
Rev. George McKelvie, MA	Que.	1888–91
M. Stockbridge	Mhow, India	
Dr A.G. McPhedran, BA	Stroud, Ont.	1909–15
Maude (surname unknown), RN	(unknown)	
Dr George Menzies, BA	Ailsa Craig, Ont.	1902–3
Edith Hanna	Streetsville, and Fort Frances, Ont.	
Rev. Robert C. Murray, BA	Pictou, NS	1885–7
Charlotte Wilson	Pictou, NS	
Dr Alexander Nugent, BA	Reaboro, Ont.	1899–1932
Margaret Reid	Reaboro, Ont.	
Rev. Frank Russell, MA	Toronto, Ont.; Winnipeg, Man.	1893–1940
Margaret Evans	England, and Mussoorie, India	

Appendix C
India male missionaries and missionary wives (listed alphabetically)

Name	Home community	Dates of service
Rev. Norman Russell, BA	Toronto, Ont.; Winnipeg, Man.	1890–1902
Minnie Hodgins	Toronto, Ont.	
Rev. William G. Russell, BA (unmarried)	Motherwell, Ont.	1901–13
Rev. Robert Schofield, MA	Calgary, Alta.	1910–18
Jeannie Robson, BA	Regina, Sask.	
Rev. Alexander A. Scott, BA	Carleton Place, Ont.	1912–52
Minnie Shaw	Carleton Place, Ont.	
Rev. James A. Sharrard, BA	Uxbridge, Ont.	1907–14
Edith Murray	Brandon, Man.	
Rev. David F. Smith, BA	Scotland, and Hamilton area, Ont.	1906–37
Charlotte (Lottie) Madill, former missionary		
Rev. James F. Smith, MD	Latona, Ont.	1896–1900
Minnie Waugh	Hamilton, Ont.	
Rev. John T. Taylor, BA	Cambridge, Ont.	1899–45
Harriet Copeland	Collingwood, Ont.	
Dr John J. Thompson	Motherwell, Ont.	1895–7
Emily Lick	Oshawa, Ont.	
Dr James M. Waters	Lobo, Ont.	1903–23
Henrietta Alexander, RN	Kinkardine, Ont.	
Rev. John Wilkie, BA	Scotland, and Guelph, Ont.	1879–1902; 1904–28 (Gwalior Mission)
Agnes Nielson	Almonte, Ont.	
Rev. William A. Wilson, MA	Nelson, Ont.	1884–1917
Margaret Caven	Toronto, Ont.	
Dr Claude R. Woods	Mallorytown, Ont.	1893–1903
Birdie Mallory	Mallorytown, Ont.	

Appendix D
Central India mission stations of the Presbyterian Church in Canada, 1914

Station	Year established
Indore	1877
Mhow	1877
Neemuch	1885
Ratlam	1886
Ujjain	1887
Dhar	1895
Amkhut	1897
Kharua	1910
Rasalpura (originally part of Mhow station; no women on staff during this period)	1910
Barhawa (no women on staff during this period)	1911
Jaora (no women on staff during this period)	1913
Sitamau (no women on staff during this period)	1913
Banswara	1914

Notes

For full references for works cited in abbreviated form in the Notes see the Select Bibliography.

Introduction

1 UCA, FMC, General Correspondence, box 1, file 15, Queenie McCoy to RPM, 9 Jan. 1893; ibid., box 2, file 18, Mrs M. Simpson to RPM, 28 Feb. 1894; *Presbyterian Review,* 15 July 1897, 40; FMC, General Correspondence, box 4, file 66, AEA to T. Eaton Co., 29 July 1912, and UCA, FMC, Minutes, 25: 26 July 1912, 5. In the last of the situations referred to, Eaton's tried to protect itself by informing the committee that in future it would charge 5 per cent of the value of missionaries' goods to guarantee safe delivery.
2 Latourette, *The Great Century;* Neill, *A History of Christian Missions,* especially chs 8 and 9
3 For information on prominent businessmen involved in the foreign missionary movement, see Foster, 'The Imperialism of Righteousness'; for Canadians' proportionately high numbers in the fields, see Foster, 66.
4 MacMurchy, *The Woman – Bless Her,* 10–11; Bacchi, *Liberation Deferred?,* 71; WFMS, *Thirty-Eighth Annual Report,* 1914, 76–7; Morris Wolfe, ed., *A Saturday Night Scrapbook* (Toronto: New Press 1973), xii
5 Daniel Kubat and David Thornton, *A Statistical Profile of Canadian Society* (Toronto: McGraw-Hill Ryerson 1974), 30
6 Douglas, *The Feminization of American Culture;* Cott, *The Bonds of Womanhood*
7 Hageman, 'Women and Missions,' 167
8 Hunter, *The Gospel of Gentility,* quotation at 226; Hill, *The World Their Household.* Mention should also be made of R. Pierce Beaver's *American Protestant Women in World Mission* (originally published as *All Loves Excelling*), an overview of home-base and overseas developments that contains some material on Canada. Largely unanalytical and at times verging on the hagiographic, it is nevertheless invaluable as a source of information on chronology, personalities, and key developments.
9 Malmgreen, ed., *Religion in the Lives of English Women,* Introduction; Bailey, *Women and the British Empire,* ch. 3, 'Missionaries.' Bailey refers readers to American literature for illustrations of the kind of work that still needs to be undertaken on British women. There is, of course, valuable relevant material in such works as F.K. Prochaska's *Women and Philanthropy.*
10 Mitchinson, 'Canadian Women and Church Missionary Societies,' 57–75; Strong-Boag, *The Parliament of Women,* 95–6
11 Recent works include Ridout, 'A Woman of Mission'; and Gagan, ' "Here I am, Send Me" ' (Gagan's PHD dissertation, 'A Sensitive Independence: The Personnel of the Woman's Missionary Society of the Methodist Church of Canada, 1881–1925' [McMaster University 1987], was not yet available through the National Library when this work was being revised); Johnston,

'The Road to Winsome Womanhood'; and Brouwer, ' "Far Indeed from the Meekest of Women," ' and 'Opening Doors Through Social Service.' Alvyn J. Austin's *Saving China* pays a good deal of attention to Catholic as well as Protestant women missionaries and may well stimulate further research.

CHAPTER 1 Precedents

1 Hutchison, *Errand to the World*, 44, 93; Shenk, 'The "Great Century," Reconsidered,' 133

2 Latourette, *The Great Century*; Neill, *A History of Christian Missions*, and Neill, *Colonialism and Christian Missions*

3 Neill, *A History of Christian Missions*, 261–6; Drewery, *William Carey*

4 Bearce, *British Attitudes towards India*, 60–3, 94–5; Neill, *The Story of the Christian Church in India and Pakistan*, 64–6

5 Warren, *Social History and Christian Mission*, 37–9, and, for the quotation, 56; see also Walls, 'The British,' 60.

6 Phillips, *Protestant America and the Pagan World*; Rabe, *The Home Base of American China Missions*, 1–5; Forman, 'The Americans,' 54. While Forman and other recent scholars of the movement agree that the simultaneous flowering of the missionary and imperialist eras was not simply coincidence, they are critical of writers who portray missionaries as mere tools of secular imperialism and argue that much research on the links between the two movements remains to be done. Hutchison, *Errand to the World*, ch. 4 and passim, highlights some of the complexities.

7 Neill, *A History of Christian Missions*, 251–2; Beaver, 'Missionary Motivation through Three Centuries,' 126–7.

8 Regarding Livingstone, see Neill, *A History of Christian Missions*, 325, and Moorhouse, *The Missionaries*, chs 7 and 8. For Moody, see James F. Findlay, Jr, *Dwight L. Moody*, especially 32–6 and ch. 10. In speaking of theological liberals and conservatives, here and elsewhere in this book, I draw chiefly on distinctions provided by Hutchison in *The Modernist Impulse in American Protestantism*.

9 Beaver, 'Missionary Motivation through Three Centuries,' 148. For the founding and development of the SVM see Hopkins, *John R. Mott*.

10 Hutchison, *The Modernist Impulse in American Protestantism*, 57

11 Handy, *A History of the Churches in the United States and Canada*, 293; see also Hutchison, *Errand to the World*, ch. 4.

12 Stephen Neill, for instance, refers to the emergence of women in foreign missions in the nineteenth century as a 'revolutionary change' and observes that their numerical dominance on the mission fields 'has not been alto-

gether to the benefit of the work' (*A History of Christian Missions,* 255–6).
Yet these seemingly significant comments are followed by an almost total
silence about the part played by women in missions. Like Neill, most
historians of missions and religion have, until recently, made only passing
reference to women's role in the movement. Hardest to understand is R.
Pierce Beaver's devoting an entire book (*All Loves Excelling*) to American
women's participation and then, in the same year, ignoring the motivational significance of that participation in his article 'Missionary Motivation
through Three Centuries.' Hutchison's *Errand to the World* provides a
welcome break from these patterns in the attention it pays to the broad
significance of women's part in missions.

13 Neill, *A History of Christian Missions,* 256; Drewery, *William Carey,* 44, 52,
82, 145; Moorhouse, *The Missionaries,* 116–20

14 Beaver, *American Protestant Women in World Mission,* 53

15 Ibid., 49, 60, 89–90, 124, 131–3, 145–9; Bliss, *The Service and Status of Women
in the Churches,* 36–7

16 Quoted in Boyd and Brackenridge, *Presbyterian Women in America,* 3

17 Beaver, *American Protestant Women in World Mission,* ch. 1; Berg,
The Remembered Gate, 185–9; Pichanick, *Harriet Martineau,* 95–6; Cott,
The Bonds of Womanhood, 141

18 See Boyd and Brackenridge, *Presbyterian Women in America,* 8, for the
concern about groups of praying women; Phillips, *Protestant America and
the Pagan World,* 308–9, for the ABCFM quotation; and Beaver, *American
Protestant Women in World Mission,* ch. 1, for the typical organizational
pattern.

19 Montgomery, *Western Women in Eastern Lands,* 13–14

20 Beaver, *American Protestant Women in World Mission,* 54

21 Quoted in ibid., 51

22 Brumberg, *Mission for Life;* Beaver, *American Protestant Women in World
Mission,* 55–6; Phillips, *Protestant America and the Pagan World,* 309

23 Beaver, *American Protestant Women in World Mission,* 33, 60, 68, 71

24 Ibid., ch. 3, and 87. On the role of Mount Holyoke see also Green, *Mary
Lyon and Mount Holyoke,* 117, 240ff.

25 Beaver, *American Protestant Women in World Mission,* ch. 4; Hill, *The World
Their Household,* 44–54. For details of the Presbyterian pattern see Boyd
and Brackenridge, *Presbyterian Women in America,* ch. 3.

26 Gracey, 'Women and Missions,' 165; Boyd and Brackenridge, *Presbyterian
Women in America,* 15

27 Rev. E.M. Wherry, ed., *Woman and Missions,* 91; Montgomery, *Western
Women in Eastern Lands,* 10

28 For example, Hill, *The World Their Household*, 36–8, and Hunter, *The Gospel of Gentility*, 12. See also Scott, 'On Seeing and Not Seeing,' 12–13.

29 Hunter, *The Gospel of Gentility*, 13

30 Boyd and Brackenridge, *Presbyterian Women in America*, ch. 2

31 For the number and total membership of women's missionary societies see Hill, *The World Their Household*, 3; for the content and circulation of their periodicals, Brumberg, 'Zenanas and Girlless Villages'; and, for American missionaries' pioneer work, Beaver, *American Protestant Women in World Mission*, 110–11, 124, 133.

32 The notion of American women's foreign missionary work as redemptive social housekeeping is highlighted in the first part of the title of Patricia Hill's monograph – *The World Their Household*. See *The World Their Household*, 60, for the use of the 'household' metaphor in a popular missionary hymn.

33 Platt, *The Story of the Years*, 7, 14; WMS, *Our Jubilee Story*, ch. 2, and E.L. Macdonnell, 'The Woman's Foreign Missionary Society,' *KCM* 15 (Mar. 1892), 175; Cummings, *Our Story*, 13–14. Among Baptists, however, some of the borrowing patterns were reversed, with Maritime women leading the way; see Beaver, *American Protestant Women in World Mission*, 97–8, and, for their work, Merrick, *These Impossible Women*.

CHAPTER 2 Home-base bureaucrats

1 UCA, FMC, Minutes, 2: 5 Oct. 1875, 6; Macdonnell, 'The Woman's Foreign Missionary Society,' 175. On Presbyterian union see Johnston, 'The Canadian Presbyterian Union of 1875,' 61–106.

2 George Monro Grant, 'A History of What Was the Synod of the Maritime Provinces in Connection with the Church of Scotland,' *Presbyterian Record* 1 (Jan. 1876), 15–17; Moir, *Enduring Witness*, 146–9, 153

3 Neill, *A History of Christian Missions*, 274–6; Moir, *Enduring Witness*, 149–50; *Record* 1 (July 1876), 190, 191

4 For a church-sponsored account of Mackay's life see MacGregor, *The Black Bearded Barbarian*. Information on the careers of Fairweather and Rodger is provided in chs. 4 and 5.

5 On the allocation of mission fields, see *APP*, 1875, Minutes, 6, and 1876, Appendix, 157–72; for an attempt to defuse criticism of foreign missions prior to union see 'Foreign Missions,' *British American Presbyterian*, 2 Feb. 1872, 1; for the quotation, Beaver, *American Protestant Women in World Mission*, 87.

6 *APP*, 1878, Appendix, lxxvii

7 For a complaint about being scooped see UCA, FMC, General Correspondence, box I, file II, Scott to Hamilton Cassels, 25 Apr. 1892; for admonitions to readers, *Record* 2 (Feb. 1877), 29, and (Apr. 1877), 89.

8 FMC members were listed annually in *APP*. Biographical data on many members may be found in Morgan, ed., *The Canadian Men and Women of the Time*. For clergy see also UCA biographical files. For an account of MacKay's life by his missionary son-in-law see Thomson, *The Life and Letters of Rev. R.P. MacKay*.

9 Grant, *The Church in the Canadian Era*, 57

10 UCA, *The Woman's Missionary Society of the Presbyterian Church in Canada (Eastern Division)*, 2, 13; Mrs Florence Dodge, 'The W.F.M.S., Eastern Division,' *Record* 25 (June 1899), 186 (for the 'naked savages' reference); WMS, *Our Jubilee Story*, chs 1 and 2. The reference to the Montreal branch of the Woman's Union Missionary Society is in *Record* 2 (Feb. 1877), 32.

11 *The Woman's Missionary Society of the Presbyterian Church in Canada (Eastern Division)*, 2–3; WMS, *Our Jubilee Story*, ch. 1. First called the Halifax Woman's Missionary Society of the Presbyterian Church in Canada, the Maritime society's name was changed in 1884 to the Woman's Foreign Missionary Society of the Presbyterian Church in Canada, Eastern Section, to signify that it had moved beyond its Halifax base. In this book, references to the Woman's Foreign Missionary Society and to WFMS are to the Western Division society unless otherwise indicated. The Montreal organization similarly went through several name changes before styling itself the Woman's Missionary Society (Home, French and Foreign) at the turn of the century.

12 For the WFMS mandate and organizational structure see WFMS, *First Annual Report*, 1877, constitution, 23–9. The object of a presbyterial society, which normally met only once or twice a year, was to promote the organization of auxiliaries in all the congregations of a presbytery and 'to diffuse intelligence and excite Missionary interest, among the women and children of the Church' (28). Good overviews of the society's development during the early years are provided in Macdonnell, 'The Woman's Foreign Missionary Society,' and in Agnes F. Robinson, 'The Woman's F.M.S., Western Division,' *Record* 25 (June 1899), 189.

13 Regarding the McLarens' involvement in foreign missions see *Foreign Missionary Tidings* 26 (Sept. 1909), 57, and (Apr. 1910), 193, and UCA biographical file on William McLaren. WFMS board and executive members are listed in the society's annual reports.

14 Blaisdell, 'The Matrix of Reform'; Boyd and Brackenridge, *Presbyterian Women in America*, ch. 6

15 WFMS, *Fifth Annual Report*, 1881, 10–11
16 WFMS *First Annual Report*, 1877, 8; *Eleventh Annual Report*, 1887, 13
17 Macdonnell, 'The Woman's Foreign Missionary Society,' 176–7; Mrs George Hunter Robinson, 'A Great Auxiliary: A Sketch of the Woman's Foreign Missionary Society,' *Westminster* 1 (June 1896), 19; Mrs Eleanor Parker, 'W.F.M.S. of Winnipeg Presbytery,' *Record* 29 (Jan. 1904), 30; WFMS, *Thirty-Eighth Annual Report*, 1913–14, 11
18 See MacMurchy, *The Woman – Bless Her*, 16–17, for a profile of contemporary women's organizations that highlights these characteristics. As a member of the prominent, missions-minded MacMurchy family, the Toronto journalist was well acquainted with the WFMS. Assumptions about the middle-class status of the society's membership were reflected in advertisements and fictional articles in the periodical *Foreign Missionary Tidings*.
19 *Tidings* 30 (June 1914), 238–9
20 Montgomery, *Western Women in Eastern Lands*, xiii. Rijnhart and her book are discussed in ch. 3.
21 Quoted in ibid., 51
77
22 WFMS, *Eighteenth Annual Report*, 1893–4, presidential address, 14–17
23 A graph prepared by the WFMS and published in 1913 indicated that 43.5 percent of its total expenditure still went to its work in India; see *Pre-Assembly Congress*, Appendix.
24 WFMS, *Eighth Annual Report*, 1884, 2–4; 'A Patriotic Work,' *Westminster* 22 Mar. 1902, 359–60. Letters attempting to arouse the board's interest in work with Canadian Indians had in fact begun arriving in the late 1870s.
25 WFMS, *Eighth Annual Report*, 1884, 3–4; WMS, *The Story of Our Missions*, ch. 10
26 For the founding of the two China missions, see WMS, *The Story of Our Missions*, chs 3 and 4. For the Montreal society's desire to have its own missionaries, see UCA, Montreal Woman's Missionary Society, uncatalogued correspondence, Mrs Dunton to RPM, 18 Jan. 1902, and RPM to Mrs Dunton, 24 and 31 Jan. 1902. The Montreal society also briefly supported medical missionary Susie McCalla in Central India.
27 Mackay had explained his unconventional marriage to his fellow Presbyterians in terms of commitment to the cause: 'I am thinking how I can do most for Jesus'; MacKay, *Life of George Leslie Mackay*, 33–4.
28 FMC, General Correspondence, box 3, file 50, resolution of FMC Eastern Division, 21 Apr. 1909; *APP*, 1914, Appendix, 144. The WFMS had established a precedent for assisting the Eastern Division some years earlier by

providing financial help for its educational work in Trinidad and the New Hebrides.

29 'Woman's Work for Missions,' *KCM* 4 (Dec. 1885), 76–80

30 Gordon, 'The Woman's Foreign Missionary Society as a Conserving Influence,' *KCM* 10 (May 1889), 39–44; FMC, General Correspondence, box 2, file 31, typed manuscript dated 19 Aug. 1899, by F.F. Ellinwood, 25

31 *Westminster* 7 May 1898, 452; 13 May 1899, 513–14

32 *Westminster* 6 May 1899, 477

33 Macdonald in *Westminster* 6 May 1899, 477; Gordon, 'Influence,' 40

34 For reference to problems associated with special-object giving, see, for example, UCA, FMC, RPM Letterbook (hereafter Letterbook with name of writer), 1893–4, letter to Miss Lydia Meikle, 21 Dec. 1893, 286; and *Record* 29 (Aug. 1904), 343. The WFMS board's firm opposition to the practice reflected lessons it had learned from problems faced by American societies during their early years; see Hill, *The World Their Household,* 94–100.

35 'Canadian Women and Foreign Missions,' *KCM* 6 (May 1887), 44–5

36 Hill, *The World Their Household,* ch. 3; WFMS, *Twentieth Annual Report,* 1895–6, 40

37 UCA, FMC, CIM, General Correspondence (hereafter CIM Correspondence), box 2, file 26, J.F. Campbell to Thomas Wardrope, 23 Jan. 1885, and box 4, file 42, Norman Russell to RPM, June 1893; FMC, General Correspondence, box 1, file 15, Dr Morrison to RPM, 27 July 1893; UCA, WFMS Board of Management, Minutes (hereafter WFMS Board, Minutes), 10: 1 Aug. 1893; WFMS, *Twenty-Seventh Annual Report,* 1902–3, 23

38 Letters from WFMS members, *Review* 14 Mar. and 4 Apr. 1895, 801, 873

39 For the quotation see R.P. MacKay, 'W.F.M.S. and Mission Funds,' *Review* 28 Mar. 1895, 841 (the words were his paraphrase of a criticism). For the Montreal society's complaints see FMC, General Correspondence, box 2, file 34, 'Memorandum in connection with "Woman's Missionary Society" (Montreal),' undated, and box 3, file 50, Mrs E.B. Busteed to RPM, 14 June 1909; WFMS Board, Minutes, 7: 6 Jan. 1891, and FMC, Minutes, 19: 13 May 1907, 112. At the end of the century the Montreal women made an unsuccessful bid to claim all Quebec as their turf.

40 WFMS, *Answers*; RPM, 'W.F.M.S.,' 841; WFMS Board, Minutes, 12: 16 June 1896, 25–8

41 *Canada Presbyterian* 25 July 1883, 476, letter of T.F. Fotheringham; FMC, Minutes, 4: 8 Oct. 1889, 90–1. Home missions, as defined by Western missions superintendent James Robertson in 1896, were directed only at settlers of Protestant stock. In 1912, however, the definition would formally

broaden to include all mission enterprises in Canada west of the New
Brunswick border with the exception of work among Chinese immigrants;
Review 11 June 1896, 1170, and *Record* 39 (Jan. 1914), 19.

42 WFMS Board, Minutes, 6: 4 June 1889; 7: 14 Feb. 1891, and 11: 3 July 1894;
FMC, Minutes, 4: 11 June 1889, 76

43 Hill, *The World Their Household*, 51

44 UCA, Woman's Foreign Missionary Society, Western Division, *A Manual for
the Use of Women Offering for Foreign Mission Work*

45 For a case of the board's pressing the FMC to explain why it had rejected
two board-approved candidates, see WFMS Board, Minutes, 11: 5 and 8
June and 3 July 1894; see Minutes, 6: 7 Jan. and 14 Oct. 1890, and 8: 4 Apr.
1891, for evidence of its unease with the application of Dr Wilhelmina
G. Fraser.

46 *Westminster* 16 Oct. 1897, 295–6, and 16 May 1898, 399; WFMS Board,
Minutes, 6: 1 Apr. 1890

47 WFMS Board, Minutes, 8: 4 Apr. and 22 Dec. 1891; see also WFMS, *Sixteenth
Annual Report*, 1891–2, 9, 55–8.

48 McLeod-MacKay Letterbook, D.D. McLeod to Mrs Harvie, 3 Nov. 1891,
76, and RPM to Mrs Harvie, 24 Jan. 1893, 307; FMC, Minutes, 7: 12 Feb. and
17 May 1895, 83, 106, and 8: 20 Sept. 1895; WFMS Board, Minutes, 11: 12
Feb. 1895

49 FMC, Minutes, 9: 14 Sept. 1897, 14–16 (for the quotation); WFMS Board,
Minutes, 10: 19 Apr. 1893, and 12: 12 Jan. 1897

50 D.M. Buchanan, 'The Strength and Weakness of the W.F.M. Movement,'
KCM 18 (June-July 1894), 95–102

51 For Catherine Ewart's advocacy of and contributions towards the home see
WFMS Board, Minutes, 12: 18 May 1897, 158; for an account of the official
opening, *Review*, 14 Oct. 1897, 291; and, for the management structure
established in 1897, WFMS *Twenty-Second Annual Report*, 1897–8, 14. The
management arrangements and the name of the home changed several times
after 1908, when it became formally responsible for training deaconesses
as well as missionaries.

52 CIM Correspondence, box 10, file 115, RPM to Mr Sharrard, 6 Nov. 1912

53 UCA, WFMS, Correspondence, 1888–1913, Mrs Shortreed to RPM, 18 May
and 29 June 1898, and Mrs Shortreed to Rev. R.H. Warden, 26 Jan. 1899;
WFMS Board, Minutes, 12: 16 June 1896, 25–8. Board members continued
to pay their own travel expenses until 1906, the first year their annual
meeting was held outside Ontario.

54 FMC, Minutes, 5: 15 Nov. and 28 Dec. 1892, 300, 338

55 RPM Letterbook, 1893–4, letter to Rev. Harvey Grant, 9 Apr. 1894, 447
56 For example, RPM Letterbook, 1894–6, letter to Mrs Harvie, 13 Oct. 1894, and to Rev. Norman Russell, 24 Aug. 1895; FMC, Minutes, 9: 29 Sept. 1896
57 FMC, General Correspondence, box 6, file 78, Moore to RPM, 17 Oct. 1900. Moore's concern in this instance was both needless and ironic, for what the Montreal WMS objected to was not the ultimate authority of the FMC but rather the possibility that the WFMS would have a say in the control of 'their' missionary.
58 FMC, General Correspondence, box 5, file 76, RPM to W. Henry Grant, 24 Oct. 1913
59 CIM Correspondence, box II, file 118, RPM to Mrs James Steele, 2 May 1913
60 WFMS Board, Minutes, 13: 30 Jan. 1900, 276
61 See Macdonnell, 'The Woman's Foreign Missionary Society,' 177–8, for one insider's acknowledgment of occasional feminist tendencies within the society and for her explanation of why they were not the norm.
62 WFMS Board, Minutes, 21: 1 Oct. 1912, 181. In the U.S., by contrast, as the societies grew in size and complexity, a number of full-time, salaried positions were created, while some volunteer administrators received expense money; see Hill, *The World Their Household*, 84.
63 MacMurchy, *The Woman – Bless Her*, 20–1; H. Cassels Letterbook, 1887–90, Cassels to Mrs MacMurchy, 23 July 1889; tribute to the late Mrs Steele, *Missionary Messenger* II (Feb. 1924), 100
64 WFMS Board, Minutes, 19: 18 May and 9 Nov. 1909, 124–5, 222–3; MacMurchy, *The Woman – Bless Her*, 18–19, 22–6. MacMurchy was particularly critical of officers who refused to respond to calls for a decentralization of decision making.
65 Davy, ed., *Women, Work and Worship in the United Church*, 18–19, 137–8
66 UCA, 'Local Church Records,' contains the minutes of some WFMS presbyterials and auxiliaries. Accounts of meetings were sometimes published in WFMS and other church periodicals.
67 Robinson, 'The Woman's F.M.S.,' 189
68 WFMS Board, Minutes, 10: 20 Feb. 1894, and II: 14 and 21 May 1895; Strong-Boag, *The Parliament of Women*, 78–9
69 For example, WFMS Board, Minutes, 12: 3 Nov. 1896, 79. The 1896 decision not to send a delegate to the WCTU annual meeting was a controversial one, however.
70 For example, WFMS Board, Minutes, II: 14 and 21 May 1895; I: Nov. 1876; 9: 6 Sept. 1892
71 WFMS Board, Minutes, 10: 9 May 1893, and II: 8 and 15 Oct. 1895, 290–1, 295

72 Hill, *The World Their Household,* 56–7; WFMS Board, Minutes, 17: 13 Nov.
1906, 285–6, for clear evidence that WFMS leaders were influenced by their
American counterparts' experience on this subject

73 *Review* 21 Jan. 1886, 21, and 20 June 1889, 1451

74 Letters of 'Fidelia' and of 'Indignant Member of the WFMS' in *Canada
Presbyterian* 27 Jan. 1886, 70, and 27 June 1889, 1462; WFMS Board,
Minutes, 5: 2 Feb. 1886, and 6: 1 Oct 1889

75 'A Good Investment,' and 'Home Missions,' *Record* 21 (Mar. 1896), 62, and
22 (Dec. 1897), 316–17

76 *Record* 25 (Jan. 1899), 2, and 25 (Mar. 1899), 65; *Westminster* 2 Apr. 1898,
323–5, and 7 May 1898, 440–1

77 Letter from Dickey, *Westminster* 22 Jan. 1898, 90; WFMS, *Twenty-Second
Annual Report,* 1898, 15; UCA, WHMS, Minutes of Board Meetings (hereafter WHMS Board, Minutes), box 12, vol. 1, minutes of meetings of 'Presbyterian Ladies of Toronto,' St Andrew's Church, 15 Mar. and 6, 8, 11, and
13 Apr. 1898. On Lady Aberdeen's appeal and the response see also *Westminster* 12 Feb., 5 Mar., and 2 Apr. 1898, 174, 236, 352–3.

78 Gordon, *The Life of James Robertson,* 399–400

79 *Record* 26 (June 1901), 226

80 For example, *Westminster* 10 May 1902, 577, and *Presbyterian* 9 and 16 May
1903, 586, 618. (In July 1902, the Westminster Press had begun publishing
the *Westminster* as a monthly, supplemented by a new weekly called the
Presbyterian.)

81 'A Patriotic Work,' *Westminster* 22 Mar. 1902, 359–60; WFMS Board, Minutes,
15: 21 Mar. 1902, 84–5, containing inserted form letter

82 For reference to the Eastern Division attack see WFMS, *Twenty-Seventh
Annual Report,* 1902–3, 22–3, and for a belated report of an inside revolt,
letter from T.H. Mathieson, *Presbyterian* 31 May 1906, 705. For an overview
of the founding of the WHMS see *Home Mission Pioneer* 1 (Dec. 1903), 4–5.

83 For claims that the WHMS complemented the WFMS and drew on a distinct
constituency see 'W.H.M.S Second Annual Meeting' and 'How We Formed
a Woman's Home Missionary Society,' *Record* 30 (Apr. 1905), 147, and 29
(May 1904), 204; for MacKay's comment see FMC, General Correspondence, box 4, file 52, RPM to Rev. R.G. MacBeth, 18 Mar. 1910; for reports
of Western unrest, WFMS Board, Minutes, 19: 5 Jan. 1909, 50, and 31 Jan.
1910, 256–60, and WFMS, *Twenty-Ninth Annual Report,* 1905, 62.

84 For the field secretary's claim see notes of meeting between representatives
of WFMS, WHMS, and General Assembly Committee, 5, inserted with WFMS
Board, Minutes, 17: 13 Nov. 1906. For the overture and its aftermath see
Presbyterian 10 May and 21 June 1906, 605, 794, and 4 July 1907, 7.

85 For membership figures see WFMS, *Thirty-First Annual Report,* 1907, 75, and, for the joint meeting, WFMS Board, Minutes, 18: 19 Feb. 1907, 56–8.

86 WFMS Board, Minutes, 19: 8 Apr. and 4 June 1909, 104–6, 140–1, and *Tidings* 26 (June 1910), 236–40

87 WFMS Board, Minutes, 19: 13 Apr. and 18 May 1909, 106, 127

88 WFMS Board, Minutes, 19: 31 Jan. 1910, 256–60

89 Letter of R.G. MacBeth, *Presbyterian* 10 May 1906, 605; WFMS Board, Minutes, 21: 4 June 1913, 313

90 *Record* 37 (Dec. 1912), 534, and 39 (Jan. 1914), 19–21

91 Moir, 'Canadian Presbyterians and the Laymen's Missionary Movement,' 1–19; *The Woman's Missionary Society of the Presbyterian Church in Canada (Eastern Division),* 28; *Presbyterian* 10 May 1906, 605

92 FMC, General Correspondence, box 4, file 53, MacBeth to RPM, 8 Apr. 1910

93 WFMS Board, Minutes, 20: 12 Apr. 1910, 35; also WFMS, Correspondence, RPM to Mrs Shortreed, 11 Apr. 1910

94 WFMS, *Thirty-Fourth Annual Report,* 1910, 12

95 WFMS Board, Minutes, 20: 31 May 1910, 66–7, for plans to meet with the WHMS; 9 and 11 May 1911, 217, 234, regarding Shortreed and Steele; and 6 May 1910, 51–5, for earlier evidence of the latter's more flexible approach. Ill health was given as the official reason for Mrs Shortreed's resignation at the 1911 annual meeting – her twenty-fifth – but R.P. MacKay and others recognized that it was prompted by her failure to win the battle against amalgamation; CIM Correspondence, box 9, file 109, RPM to Kate Campbell, 1 May 1911.

96 *Tidings* 27 (Mar. 1911), 180–1, and WFMS, *Thirty-Fifth Annual Report,* 1910–11, 12

97 WFMS Board, Minutes, 21: 23 Apr. and 13 May 1912, 119, 129–31; WFMS Correspondence, Mrs Steele to RPM, 22 Oct. 1912

98 WFMS Board, Minutes, 21: 21 May 1912, 136; *Tidings* 30 (June 1913), 19

99 For an account of the Knox church meeting see *Tidings* 30 (June 1914), 230–5

100 For the new society's constitution and its first slate of officers see WFMS, *Thirty-Eighth Annual Report,* 1913–14, 220–31 and 4; for the continuing motto see WMS, *The Story of Our Missions,* cover.

101 FMC, General Correspondence, box 3, file 42, R.G. MacBeth to Professor McLaren, 2 Apr. 1906

102 Rubio and Waterston, eds, *The Selected Journals of L.M. Montgomery,* 112, 91

103 WFMS, *Thirty-Eighth Annual Report,* 1914, 14

CHAPTER 3 The context of a calling

1 Biographical information on missionaries as reported in this chapter and in Appendix B comes from a variety of sources of which the most important are UCA, FMC, Applications for Mission Work (hereafter Applications); UCA biographical files; WFMS and church publications; university archives, and Canada Census records.
2 Bainbridge, *Around the World Tour of Christian Missions*, 208
3 Based on data for 97 of the missionaries; see Appendix B, cols 1 and 7.
4 For illustrations, see Applications, 1894, box 1, file 8, correspondence regarding Mary Leach; and 1910, box 2, file 24, WFMS form completed by Mabel Maclean, 1. Eastern Division officials appear to have followed a similar age policy with respect to Korea appointments; their Trinidad field was a somewhat special case, however, as is explained below.
5 UCA, FMC, Minutes, 4: 1 Nov. 1888, 206, and 5: 18 May 1892, 28. For Scott's subsequent career as a missionary wife, teacher, and doctor, see Buck, *The Doctor Rode Side-Saddle*.
6 For Harris's background and appointment see Applications, box 1, file 3, Harris to FMC, 13 Apr. 1889, and three letters of reference, Apr. 1889; CIM Correspondence, box 3, file 35, Margaret Rodger to Thomas Wardrope, 19 Feb. 1890; and MacKellar, *Amelia J. Harris*. For the WFMS response to her death see WFMS, *Sixteenth Annual Report*, 1892, 27.
7 Applications, 1893, box 1, file 7a, correspondence regarding Janet White, and UCA biographical file on White
8 The average age of newly appointed Western Division missionaries before 1896 (based on data for 26 women) was 28.07; after 1896 (based on data for 58 women), it was 30.08. The upward trend in age appears to reflect deliberate policy: though it is admittedly sparse, the information on applicants and enquirers who were *not* appointed does not indicate an overall trend towards older candidacies in the later period.
9 *Tidings* 25 (Apr. 1909), 194; McCully, *Our Share in Korea;* UCA biographical files on Louise and Elizabeth McCully; *Record* 33 (Dec. 1908), 531-2
10 Appendix B, cols 4 and 2. Missionaries came from families in which the average number of children was 6.15 (based on data for 72 women). By comparison, the national average in 1891 was 5.2; Canada, *Census of Canada, 1890-91,* vol. 1 (Ottawa: S.E. Dawson 1893), table 3, 116.
11 For Presbyterian populations in Nova Scotia and the West see Grant, *The Church in the Canadian Era,* 3, 51, and, for the 1913 study, MacDougall, *Rural Life in Canada.*
12 Appendix B, col. 3

13 For examples of patterns described in this paragraph see CIM Correspondence, box 10, file 112, John Buchanan to RPM, 29 Feb. 1912, and Buck, *The Doctor Rode Side-Saddle*, 22–7 (interrupted schooling); WFMS Board, Minutes, 6: 1 Oct. 1889 (financial assistance); *Review* 3 Oct. 1889, 1574, and *Tidings* 29 (Oct. 1912), 81–2 (self-financing missionaries); Oliver, *Dr. Margaret MacKellar*, 38 (sending money home).

14 Ontario, Legislative Assembly of Ontario, *Report of the Minister of Education for the Year 1896* [with the Statistics of 1895] (Toronto: Warwick Bros. and Rutter 1897), Appendix 3, table C, 18–19

15 See Appendix B, col. 6, for the missionaries' pre-service work experience.

16 This pattern challenges Veronica Strong-Boag's suggestion that medical missionaries' careers came about in response to the missions propaganda to which they were exposed while at the medical colleges; see her 'Canada's Women Doctors,' 120.

17 FMC, Minutes, 2: 17 Oct. 1882, 162–3, 166a, and 166b; Travill, 'Early Medical Co-Education,' 68–89; Applications, box 1, file 4, G.M. Grant to Miss Shaver, 18 Mar. 1890

18 Rosemary R. Gagan's study of Methodist missionary women's backgrounds during roughly the same period reveals a broadly similar pattern of high educational achievement; Gagan, ' "Here I Am, Send Me." '

19 Johnston, 'The Canadian Mission in Trinidad,' ch. 5

20 The gap between male and female missionaries' salaries was greater in Trinidad than in any other overseas field. In 1896 all ordained Trinidad missionaries received $1,460 per year, while 'lady teachers' received only $400. By comparison, in Central India in the same year single male missionaries got $800 plus $90 'hill [vacation] expenses'; women missionaries got $730. See *APP*, 1896, Appendix 6, iv.

21 Martell, 'The Canadian Presbyterian Mission to Trinidad's East Indian Population,' ch. 5, refers to the frustration and disappointment felt by some women in the mission over the lack of support for, and recognition of, their work. For a moving illustration see the statement by Annie Blackadder in *Record* 26 (Dec. 1901), 494.

22 For example, FMC, Minutes, 3: 12 May 1886, 72–3, reference to Matilda Bray, and T. Wardrope Letterbook, letter to Bray, 21 May 1886, 312. See also Applications, box 1, file 4, G.M. Grant to Miss Shaver, 18 Mar. 1890.

23 FMC, Minutes, 4: 24 Sept. 1890, 142, in reference to Miss Victoria Angus; WFMS Board, Minutes, 8: 1 Dec. 1891

24 WFMS Board, Minutes, 12: 6 Oct. 1896, 63; FMC, Minutes, 9: 15 Oct. 1896. Like a number of other rejected candidates, Dr MacKay applied to another missionary agency and eventually received an appointment.

25 As reprinted in *Monthly Letter Leaflet* 8 (Feb. 1892), 202–5

26 On faith missions generally see Neill, Anderson, and Goodwin, eds, *Concise Dictionary of the Christian World Mission,* 206; and Austin, *Saving China,* ch. I, for discussion of the China Inland Mission, the best known such agency in Canada. For Presbyterian officials' opposition to the faith-missions approach, see *Review* 14 Mar. 1895, 793–4, and Applications, box 3, file 26a, RPM to D.F. Smith, 17 Mar. 1914. For their appeals to their colleges and to other Presbyterian boards for staff, see FMC, General Correspondence, box 5, file 77, AEA to D.M. Gordon, 19 Dec. 1913, and box 4, file 68, AEA to R.W. Ross, 9 Nov. 1912; CIM Correspondence, box 10, file 115, AEA to William Dale, 9 Nov. 1912.

27 Walls, 'The British,' 60; Webster, *The Christian Community and Change,* 27; Grant, *Moon of Wintertime,* 232

28 For 'half-way people' see CIM Correspondence, box I, file 9, Fairweather to William McLaren, 14 May 1877; for 'the subtle Hindoo,' *Canada Presbyterian* 5 Mar. 1880, 277–8.

29 See RPM Letterbook, RPM to Miss Hislop, 7 Jan. 1893, to Annie Childerhose, 22 Apr. 1893, and to Agnes Cowan, 26 May 1899, for candidates being redirected to the Northwest; and RPM to Mildred Turnbull, 6 Nov. 1902, for the quotation.

30 UCA, WFMS, Correspondence, Margaret Craig to RPM, 20 Nov. 1900, writing in reference to Elizabeth McLennan, BA

31 Regarding Dinwoody, see WFMS, Correspondence, AEA to Mrs Gray, 22 Sept. 1911; for Dickson, FMC, General Correspondence, box 4, file 64, 1912, RPM to C.S. Lord.

32 FMC, Minutes, 9: 20 May 1897, 108–9

33 WFMS, Correspondence, RPM to Mrs Steele, 20 Jan. 1913

34 For example, FMC, General Correspondence, box 2, file 34, Agnes I. Dickson to RPM, 21 Mar. 1902; Applications, box 2, file 14, the Rev. J.H. Ratcliffe to RPM, II Jan. 1900, writing on behalf of Dr Susie McCalla; CIM Correspondence, box 8, file 104, A.M. MacKay to RPM, 13 Jan. 1910, writing on behalf of Lizzie Robertson

35 For early curriculum and instructors see MDTH, 'Ewart Woman's Missionary Training Home of the Presbyterian Church in Canada, (Western Division),' leaflet for 1898–9; for the coeducational experiment see UCA, Ewart Missionary Training Home Management Committee, Minutes (hereafter Training Home, Minutes), 19 Mar. and 23 May 1901, 20 Sept. 1906, and 3 Apr. 1908.

36 MDTH, 'The Ewart Missionary and Deaconess Training Home, Toronto, 1908–09,' descriptive pamphlet, 6–7, and 'Calendar of the Presbyterian Missionary and Deaconess Training Home Session of 1924–25,' 6–7

37 WFMS Board, Minutes, 10: 21 Nov. 1893

38 For the pamphlet on Ewart objects see MDTH, 'The Ewart Missionary Training Home,' nd, 4, and, for the attendance and surveillance issues, Training
Home, Minutes, 7 Apr. 1902, 27 Mar. 1903, and 5 Feb. 1909.

39 Applications, box 2, file 23a, RPM to Rae Mowatt, 26 Feb. 1909

40 Regarding Smith see Applications, box 3, file 26a, J.N. Brinton [sp.?] to
AEA, 13 Sept. 1912; for schoolteachers' independent religious initiatives
see Applications, 1898, box 1, file 12, information regarding Dr Margaret
Wallace, and 1906, box 2, file 20, information regarding Mary Thomson;
box 1, file 3, Maggie Jamieson to FMC, 19 Apr. 1889. Further discussion of
the types of organized religious activity in which missionary candidates
had participated is provided later in this chapter.

41 One Interested, 'The Woman for the Foreign Field,' KCM 12 (July 1890),
160

42 RPM Letterbook, letter to Norman Russell, 9 Nov. 1894

43 See Appendix C for a list of the twenty-seven ministers and nine laymen
who served in India during this period. Among the laymen were six doctors,
an agricultural specialist, a Bible school graduate, and an American with
full-time experience in YMCA work. Data on male missionaries' backgrounds
come chiefly from Applications files, CIM Correspondence, and UCA biographical files.

44 UCA biographical file on John E. McFayden, particularly a clipping preserved there from the Evening News 5 Nov. 1901, and Moir, Enduring
Witness, 174–5; FMC, General Correspondence, box 2, file 30, Anna Ross to
Mrs Robinson, 15 Apr. 1899, and file 31, John E. McFayden to Dr Moore,
17 Oct. 1899

45 FMC, General Correspondence, box 3, file 51, RPM to Jonathan Goforth,
27 Nov. 1909; CIM Correspondence, box II, file 119, RPM to Jean Sinclair
MacKay, 27 June 1913

46 CIM Correspondence, box 4, file 49, Bella Ptolemy to RPM, 9 Sept. 1895

47 See Appendix C for a list of the wives of India male missionaries in this
period. This paragraph excludes a consideration of those who were originally career missionaries and those who were European residents of India.
Data have been drawn chiefly from Applications files and from UCA biographical files on the women's husbands. Little information is available for some
wives, particularly the early ones.

48 See, for instance, Murdoch, Indian Missionary Manual, 526.

49 See Applications, 1910, box 2, files 24 and 24a, for correspondence regarding
the appointment of W. John Cook; also box 1, file 5, G.M. Grant to
Hamilton Cassels, 17 Nov. 1891, regarding the application of China volunteer T.B. Scott and the importance attached to his fiancée's strengths.

50 One Interested, 'The Woman,' 160–1; see also M.H.P., 'Am I Called to Foreign Missionary Work?' *Review* 3 Oct. 1889, 1571.

51 Prentice, 'The Feminization of Teaching,' 5–20; Hacker, *The Indomitable Lady Doctors,* and Strong-Boag, 'Canada's Women Doctors'; Cook and Mitchinson, eds, *The Proper Sphere,* ch. 4

52 Evered Poole, 'Woman's Duties at Home,' *Review* 12 Dec. 1895, 539

53 Austin, ed., *Woman; Her Character, Culture, and Calling,* especially the pieces by J.T. Gracey, J.B. Aylesworth, and Austin himself

54 J.A.M., 'A Trained Nurse for Honan,' *KCM* 8 (July–Aug. 1888) 179; see also William Frizzell, 'Woman's Place in the Church,' *KCM* 19 (Oct. 1895), 201–9.

55 See, for example, WFMS, *Tenth Annual Report,* 25, in regard to Mary McGregor's school work, and *Leaflet* 8 (Feb. 1892), 200–1, for Dr Marion Oliver's speech on the opening of a new women's hospital.

56 Appendix B, col. 7, and, regarding Sutherland, WFMS, *Fourteenth Annual Report,* 1889–90, 29

57 Rabe, *The Home Base of American China Missions,* 97. The average age at marriage for 'brides' in Canada in 1921 was 25.5; M.C. Urquhart and K.A.H. Buckley, eds, *Historical Statistics of Canada,* 2nd ed. (Ottawa: Statistics Canada 1983), B75–81.

58 Hunter, *The Gospel of Gentility,* 79; Bainbridge, *Around the World Tour of Christian Missions,* 206

59 For the contract see Applications, box 2, file 14, 1900, copy signed by Belle Choné Oliver, 6 Dec. 1901. For responses to missionary marriages see *Tidings* 27 (Jan. 1911), 135; CIM Correspondence, box 8, file 100, Kenneth G. MacKay to RPM 5 Jan. 1909; FMC, Minutes, 23: 7 Sept. 1910, 23–24.

60 Welter, 'The Feminization of American Religion,' 143

61 For two of many contemporary comments on the much greater appeal of foreign, than home, missions, see J.A. Macdonald, 'Seven New Missionaries,' *KCM* 10 (June 1889), 105–8; and editorial, 'Home Missions,' *Review* 24 Oct. 1889, 1598.

62 Collins, *Real People*

63 For example, Mrs Margaret Caven Wilson, 'From Neemuch to the Himalyas,' *KCM* 11 (Feb. 1890), 207–15, and 'Calcutta,' *KCM* 12 (June 1890), 102–10

64 Rijnhart, *With the Tibetans in Tent and Temple;* UCA biographical file for Dr Susie Carson Rijnhart

65 *Leaflet* 11 (Apr. 1895), 319–20

66 'A Native Khana,' *Record* 32 (Sept. 1907), 399–400

67 For China appointments see Appendix B, and UCA, Brown, 'History of the

Honan (North China) Mission,' vol. 2, ch. 30. The increase of course reflected official policy as well as volunteers' interest.

68 L.M. Montgomery, *Anne of Green Gables* (New York: Bantam Books 1976, orig. ed., 1908), 191–2

69 Chown, *The Stairway,* 12–13

70 For two very different examples of this genre see Gracey, *Eminent Missionary Women,* and Montgomery, *Western Women in Eastern Lands.*

71 For an illustration of the new procedures see Applications, 1890, box 1, file 4, data for Lizzie McWilliams, including fitness questionnaire. For an excellent example of a candidate who seemed to be seeking martyrdom see FMC, General Correspondence, box 1, file 15, Walter Gowans to President, Board of Foreign Missions, 16 Mar. 1893, and, for concern about the health of workers in the field, WFMS, Correspondence, resolution of WFMS Board to FMC, 31 May 1892.

72 WFMS, *Sixteenth Annual Report,* 1892, 27; *Leaflet* 8 (Mar. 1892), 216–18, (Apr. 1892), 239, and 9 (June/July 1892), 66

73 *Leaflet* 8 (Apr. 1892), 239. See also MacKellar, *Amelia J. Harris.*

74 See Applications, files for 1891–4, and, for Harris's cousin, 1893, box 1, file 7a, correspondence regarding W. Jane Gordon.

75 FMC, General Correspondence, box 2, file 20, W.D. Ballantyne to RPM, 26 Oct. 1894

76 For a vivid example related to the Boxer Rebellion see FMC, General Correspondence, box 2, file 32, John MacDougall to RPM, 31 Aug. and 12 Sept. 1900. MacDougall, himself a former China missionary, was sharply critical of MacKay for not making more of the near-martyrdom of the North Honan missionaries, who had been forced temporarily to abandon their field and return to Canada.

77 See, for instance, *Westminster* 10 May 1902, for its editor's restrained coverage of the circumstance surrounding the dismissal of India veteran John Wilkie.

78 CIM Correspondence, box 3, file 40, Gandier to RPM, 14 Oct. 1892

79 On this risk see Isabella Thoburn, 'An Open Letter to a Missionary Candidate,' *Tidings* 2 [new series] (Aug. 1898), 135.

80 For illustrations of the aspects of pre-departure ceremonies discussed in this paragraph see Oliver, *Dr. Margaret MacKellar,* 30–31; Dr Lucinda Graham, Diary, 5–18 Sept. 1892, privately held; 'Miss Mair's Farewell,' *The Tribune* Campbellton, New Brunswick, 14 Nov. 1905, as preserved in PANS, Maritime Missionaries to Korea Collection, MGI (hereafter Korea Collection), vol. 2339, no. 14; *Leaflet* 1 (Sept. 1884), 56.

81 UCA, 88-029C, Glenna Jamieson Collection, Belle Choné Oliver Papers,

untitled autobiographical notes describing pre-missionary years, 3. See
also Oliver, *Dr. Margaret MacKellar*, 31.

82 WFMS Board, Minutes, 12: 28 Apr. 1896; CIM Correspondence, box 4,
file 46, Lizzie McWilliams to RPM, 10 Aug. 1894

83 'Westminster Table Talk,' *Westminster* July 1896, 91

84 CIM Correspondence, box 5, file 70, Rachel Chase to RPM, 16 Apr. 1899

85 For Chase's decision to remain in Canada see CIM Correspondence, box 5,
file 73, Chase to RPM, 16 Oct. 1899, and, for details of her designation
service, undated newspaper clipping preserved with WFMS Board, Minutes,
10. Regarding O'Hara's 1898 departure service see *Westminster* 29 Oct.
1898, 456. FMC Convenor William Moore, the young Methodist Salem G.
Bland, and three other ministers were in attendance. On the arrangements
for Mackay see *APP*, 1882, Appendix, lxxxi.

86 For example, CIM Correspondence, box 3, file 38, Charles H. Cooke to
Hamilton Cassels, 12 Nov. 1891; and Korea Collection, 'Miss Mair's
Farewell'

87 *APP*, 1882, Appendix, lxxxi; R.P. MacKay *Life of George Leslie Mackay;*
Austin, *Saving China*, 30–5, 90; McLaurin, *Mary Bates McLaurin;* Bahr,
Least of All Saints

88 On McWilliams and Dow see Applications, box 1, file 4, McWilliams to
Thomas Wardrope, 25 Dec. 1890, and file 5, Dow to Wardrope, 24 Apr.
1891. On Mair see Korea Collection, vol. 2257, letters of Catherine Mair to
Edith Sutherland (later Mrs Duncan McCrae), especially no. 43, 28 June
1898; 16 Feb. [1901]; no. 45, 12 Jan. 1902; and no. 47, 16 Nov. 1903; and
vol. 2339, 'Miss Mair's Farewell.'

89 Reid, *The Presbyterian Church St. Andrew's and Lachute, Quebec,* 43–5; Scott,
McClure: The China Years, Prologue and ch. 7

90 India missionary Dr Susie McCalla went to China in 1902 as the wife of the
Rev. Harvey Grant. Her sister Jeanette McCalla Ratcliffe, a minister's
widow, joined her there in 1911.

91 See Applications, 1898, box 1, file 12, correspondence to/from Dr Joseph
A. Hall, especially Hall to RPM, 11 Apr. 1899, and FMC, General Correspondence, box 2, file 30, Dr Frederic B. Duval to RPM, 24 Jan. 1899, for evidence
of the FMC's reluctance to have three members of the dynamic Russell
family in its Central India field.

92 Berger, *The Sense of Power; Record* 1 (Jan. 1876), 16, for Grant, and 2 (July
1877), 189, for MacMurchy

93 For example, FMC, Minutes, 3: 14 Feb., 3 June, and 12 June 1884; *APP*,
1882, Appendix, lxxxi

94 J.H. Brown, 'Anglo-Saxon Supremacy and Missions,' *KCM* 19 (Mar. 1896), 569–76

95 Applications, box 1, file 3, Jamieson to Dr Wardrope, 20 Feb. 1889

96 Applications, box 1, file 5, Jeanie Dow to Dr Wardrope, 24 Apr. 1891

97 *Record* 9 (Mar. 1884), 57–8, and MacTavish, ed., *Missionary Pathfinders*, ch. 14; Buchanan, *My Mother*, 1

98 Applications, 1896, box 1, file 10, Thomson's response on WFMS application form; UCA biographical file for Margaret H. Brown, handwritten autobiographical notes. The few applicants who reported the opposite pattern – active family opposition to their candidacies – were generally not encouraged by foreign missions officials.

99 For the beginning and end of the *Children's Record* see *Presbyterian Record* 17 (Apr. 1892), 85, and 25 (Nov. 1899), 332–3. For missionary letters to children's church groups see, for example, Marion Fairweather to St Andrew's Church Bible Class, *Record* 4 (Feb. 1879), 44–5; and W.A. Wilson to 'My Dear Children,' *Review* 17 Jan. 1889, 1273.

100 See *APP*, 1896, Appendix 22, iii, for data on sex ratios in young people's societies, and, for mission study techniques, *Review* 2 Apr. 1896, 934, and 28 May 1896, 1126. See also Leila Gay Mitchell McKee, 'Voluntary Youth Organizations in Toronto,' especially ch. 4.

101 For an illustration of heavy-handed clerical recruitment see FMC, General Correspondence, box 1, file 14, E.B. Chestnut to RPM, 21 Nov. 1892, and, for Scott's successes at St John's, *Tidings* 25 (Jan. 1909), 138.

102 Austin, *Saving China*, 5; Oliver, *Dr. Margaret MacKellar*, 16; 'A Few Objections to Revivals Considered,' *Review* 16 Dec. 1886, 400

103 Pederson, ' "The Call to Service" '

104 For the SVM and its origins see Hopkins's, *John R. Mott*, and, for the Mott quotation, John R. Mott's *The Decisive Hour of Christian Missions*, 135. Regarding MacKellar, see Oliver, *Dr. Margaret MacKellar*, 25–6, and, on leakage, General Correspondence, box 4, file 65, AEA to W.B. Smith, 6 May 1912. For evidence of WFMS support for the SVM see *Tidings* 29 (Mar. 1913), 190, and MDTH, Training Home, Minutes, 26 Jan. 1898.

105 Vickery, *The Young People's Missionary Movement*, 12–30; FMC, General Correspondence, box 3, file 43, Report of Whitby Conference and Conference on Missions and Sunday Schools, July 1906

106 Autobiographical notes in UCA biographical file for Jane Kinney; Applications, 1912, box 3, file 26a, data on Esther N. Smith

107 See Beaver, *American Protestant Women in World Mission*, 32–3, regarding

early use of the special-obligations argument, and Bainbridge, *Around the World Tour of Christian Missions*, 56, for an interesting variation on it.

108 Banner, *Elizabeth Cady Stanton*, 161–5; Gage, *Woman Church and State;* Austin, ed., *Woman; Her Character, Culture and Calling*, ch. 15; Speer, *Missionary Principles and Practice*, ch. 40, especially 464–5

109 WFMS, *Second Annual Report*, 1878, 11

110 *Tidings* 30 (June 1914), 234

111 *The Message* 18 (July 1909), 12

112 For example, *Leaflet* 11 (Oct. 1894), 151; *Tidings* 27 (Oct. 1910), 87–8

113 Applications, 1909, box 2, file 23, response no. 15 on form completed by Hall

114 Oliver, *Dr. Margaret MacKellar*, 19–20

115 J.A. Macdonald, 'Canadian Women and Foreign Missions,' *KCM* 6 (May 1887), 43

116 WFMS, *Sixteenth Annual Report*, 1892, 15; Aylesworth, in Austin, ed., *Woman; Her Character, Culture and Calling*, 190. See also MacTavish, ed., *Harvests in Many Lands*, 276.

117 Applications, box 1, file 6a, Riddell to FMC, 16 May 1892; McLeod-MacKay Letterbook, D.D. McLeod to Riddell, 30 May 1892

118 Hunter, *The Gospel of Gentility*, ch. 2

119 Ibid., 51

120 Ibid.

121 Murray, *At the Foot of Dragon Hill*, vii–xii

CHAPTER 4 Women's work in Central India

1 Malcolm, *A Memoir of Central India;* Wolpert, *A New History of India*, 170, 178, 203–5; Thompson, *The Making of the Indian Princes*, 278 and ch. 45

2 Aberigh-Mackay, *The Chiefs of Central India*, vol. 1, i–ii; India, Census, 1881, *Central India*, 9

3 Aberigh-Mackay, *The Chiefs of Central India*, xxvii, lxv–lxxvi; Russell, *New Days in Old India*, 6

4 India, Census, *Central India*, 10

5 Dhar, *The Indore State*, 33, 56; Aberigh-Mackay, *The Chiefs of Central India*, clxxxiv, cc; O'Dwyer, *India as I Knew It*, 161; CIM Correspondence, box 3, file 35, Amy Harris to Hamilton Cassels, 1 Jan. 1890

6 On languages and religions in Central India see Malcolm, *A Memoir of Central India*, vol. 1, ch. 12; India, Census, *Central India*, 10, 15; Taylor, *In the Heart of India*, 48–54; and Naik, *Impact of Education on the Bhils*, 23–4.

On the high rate of female illiteracy, even by Indian standards, see data cited in Balfour and Young, *The Work of Medical Women in India*, 8.
7 Two useful case studies of village life in the region are Mathur, *Caste and Ritual in a Malwa Village*, and Mayer, *Caste and Kinship in Central India*. David Kinsley's chapter 'Village Goddesses' in his *Hindu Goddesses* suggests the complexity of village religious practices and the important role that local goddesses played in them.
8 On the administrative policy of Malcolm and his successors see Malcolm, *A Memoir of Central India*, vol. 2, ch. 16, especially 301, 303–4, Thompson, *The Making of the Indian Princes*, 264, 272–5, and Wilson, *The Redemption of Malwa*, 35, 37. For the Cowley Fathers see Taylor, *In the Heart of India*, 61.
9 Beach and Fahs, eds, *World Missionary Atlas*
10 CIM Correspondence, box 1, file 5, Lowry to 'My Dear Friends,' 13 Dec. 1873; file 6, Fairweather to Lowry, 20 Mar. 1874, and file 7, Fairweather to William McLaren, 16 Aug. 1875; *APP*, 1877, Appendix, lxix–lxx
11 See, for example, CIM Correspondence, box 1, file 8, Fairweather to Lowry, 7 Aug. 1876.
12 Christensen and Hutchison, eds, *Missionary Ideologies in the Imperialist Era*, Introduction
13 See, for example, 'Door to Door Zenana Work in the City of Peking,' *Canada Presbyterian* 19 Jan. 1887, 57.
14 'Zenana Work,' *Canada Presbyterian* 18 and 25 Nov. 1885, 761, 777
15 WFMS, *Second Annual Report*, 1878, 11, and *Fourth Annual Report*, 1880, 14
16 WFMS, *Third Annual Report*, 1879, 19
17 'Zenana Work,' *Canada Presbyterian* 18 Nov. 1885, 761; CIM Correspondence, box 7, file 98, Janet White to AEA, 31 July 1908
18 For Fairweather's views and zenana visiting experiences see *Record* 2 (June 1877), 155–6, and also *Canada Presbyterian* 26 July 1878, 611–12. For a colleague's account of similar frustrations see UCA, FMC, CIM, box 23, item 290, Mission Reports (hereafter CIM Reports, with year), 1897, report of Jessie Grier, 51–2.
19 Mrs G.H. Menzies, 'Two Zenana Wives in Neemuch,' *Record* 32 (June 1907), 260–1
20 *Tidings* 22 (May 1905), 46–8
21 CIM Correspondence, box 5, file 53, Duncan to RPM, June 1896; WFMS report in *Tidings* 17 (June 1900), 34–8
22 *APP*, 1898, Appendix, 197
23 RPM Letterbook, RPM to O'Hara, 9 Sept. 1895
24 CIM Correspondence, box 4, file 50, O'Hara to RPM, 8 Oct. 1895

25 For example, Malcolm, *A Memoir of Central India,* vol. 2, ch. 14. Writer E.M. Forster, who in 1921 briefly served as private secretary to the maharaja of Dewas State Senior (some twenty-three miles from Indore), was struck by the gap between what he had heard about 'Oriental seclusion' and the reality of his own experience: '[W]hat strikes me is Oriental publicity.' He ate with the palace residents, he reported, sat chatting in their bedrooms, and called on the maharaja's wives; *The Hill of Devi,* 64–5.

26 By contrast, some male workers were anxious to undermine the myth of the zenana in order to promote their own mission agendas; for example, CIM Correspondence, box 2, file 20, John Wilkie to William McLaren, 22 Nov. 1881, 'private,' and file 26, J. Fraser Campbell to Thomas Wardrope, 23 Jan. 1885.

27 O'Malley, *Modern India and the West,* 449–50, and Balfour and Young, *The Work of Medical Women in India,* Introduction

28 WMS, *The Story of Our Missions,* ch. 2

29 W.A. Wilson, 'Itinerating in Central India,' *KCM* 12 (Aug. 1890), 223. See also Russell, *Village Work in India.*

30 CIM Correspondence, box 7, file 96, Jean Sinclair MacKay to RPM, 18 Dec. 1907; Russell, *Village Work in India,* 55, 63; Margaret Caven Wilson, 'District Work in Central India,' *KCM* 5 (Apr. 1887), 338–44; Taylor, *In the Heart of India,* 71–2; UCA, Jessie Duncan, 'India,' undated MS, 10

31 Russell, *Village Work in India,* 45; Dr Margaret O'Hara in *Tidings* 1 [new series] (Feb. 1898), 300–3, and Wilson, *The Redemption of Malwa,* 43

32 Taylor, *In the Heart of India,* 111ff, 164–5; Frank Russell, *New Days in Old India,* 9, 42; *Tidings* 30 (June 1914), 240–3, 245–6. Though they spoke of their field as Central India, it was only the Malwa portion that the missionaries tried to work. See Appendix D for a list of mission stations established before 1915 and map (page 93) for their locations.

33 CIM Correspondence, box 1, file 15, report by J. Fraser Campbell, 30 Mar. 1880; Margaret Caven Wilson, 'District Work,' 338–44

34 See CIM Correspondence, box 7, file 91, Sinclair to RPM, 16 Jan. 1905, for the China visit; file 96, Sinclair MacKay to RPM, 18 Nov. 1907, for 'pure preaching'; and box 8, file 102, 13 July 1909, for Mandesaur.

35 Dr Elizabeth McMaster, 'Some Touring Scenes,' *Record* 32 (June 1907), 263, and Russell, *Village Work in India,* 55; CIM Correspondence, box 8, file 104, Sinclair MacKay to RPM, 2 Feb. 1910; and Sinclair MacKay in *Record* 33 (Apr. 1908), 153–5

36 Sinclair MacKay, in *Record* 33 (Apr. 1908), 153–5; Wilson, 'Itinerating,' part 2, *KCM* 12 (Sept. 1890), 263–7; Jessie Weir, 'Mhow,' *Record* 32 (June 1907), 265

37 O'Hara, *Leaf of the Lotus,* 139–40; Duncan, 'India,' 10; McMaster, 'Touring Scenes,' 263, and MacKellar, 'Incidents of Medical Work,' *Record* 32 (June 1907), 266; *APP,* 1905, Appendix, III–12. For a much different pattern see Orchard, *Canadian Baptists at Work in India,* ch. 3, 'The Field Lady Missionary,' by K.S. McLaurin.

38 *APP,* 1914, Appendix, 133, 134; WFMS, *Thirty-Eighth Annual Report,* 1914, 23

39 UCA, WFMS, Women's Council of the Canadian Presbyterian Mission in Central India, Minutes (hereafter Women's Council Minutes), 8 July 1911, and 20 Feb. 1912

40 For details of the opposition see CIM, Miscellaneous Documents, box 26, file 305; for the imperial perspective, NAI, Government of India, Foreign Department, Proceedings, Secret – 1, Oct. 1883, Mar. 1884, and Nov. 1884; and, for Lord Dufferin's intervention, Wilson, *The Redemption of Malwa,* 37.

41 WFMS, *Tenth Annual Report,* 1886, 24

42 *Leaflet* 3 (May 1886), 7–8

43 For the banyan-tree and mud-hut schools see, respectively, CIM Correspondence, box 1, file 16, Wilkie to McLaren, 30 June 1880, and box 5, file 54, Norman Russell to RPM, 28 July 1896; for Jamieson's Neemuch school see account by Russell in *Review* 27 July 1893, 43.

44 CIM Correspondence, box 3, file 36, Amy Harris to Hamilton Cassels, 27 Oct. 1890

45 S.R. Shirgaonkar, 'The Education of Girls in Maharashtra,' 354; CIM Correspondence, box 5, file 59, W.A. Wilson to RPM, 7 June 1897

46 FMC, Minutes, 13: 26 Sept. 1900, 24; Women's Council Minutes, 23 Nov. 1897, 1 Mar. 1898, 20 Nov. 1900

47 On integrated schools see WFMS, *Tenth Annual Report,* 1886, 25, and Janet MacGillivray, 'Fruitage of Woman's Work in Central India,' *Record* 35 (Oct. 1910), 451; on calling women see WMS, *The Story of Our Missions,* 30. For the use of inducements in other India missions see Charlotte Dennett Staelin, 'The Influence of Missions on Women's Education in India,' 136, and Marchioness of Dufferin and Ava, *Our Viceregal Life in India,* 34. For Duncan's use of pice see 'India,' 7.

48 Women's Council Minutes, 1 Dec. 1899, 14, and 20 July 1909; WFMS Board, Minutes, 16: 15 Sept. 1903, 29

49 Reprinted speech by Jessie Duncan in *Tidings* (May 1900), 5; report by Mary Leach, in *Tidings* 20 (Nov. 1903), 150; CIM Correspondence, box 2, file 24, Isabella Ross to Thomas Wardrope, 8 Sept. 1883, and letter from Mrs Margaret Caven Wilson in *Canada Presbyterian* Dec. 1885, 809

50 CIM Reports, report of Isabella Ross, 1884, 27, and 1887, 13–14, and of Mary Dougan, 1897, 65; WFMS, *Tenth Annual Report,* 1886, 26

51 CIM Correspondence, box 3, file 32, Wilkie to Wardrope, 16 Aug. 1887; A.W. Wilkie to Mrs Harvie, 20 May 1885, in UCA biographical file on John Wilkie; WFMS, *Tenth Annual Report,* 25–6. See also CIM Correspondence, box 3, file 34, Mrs Margaret Caven Wilson to Mrs MacMurchy, 30 July 1889.

52 WFMS, *Tenth Annual Report,* 25–6

53 CIM Correspondence, box 3, file 33, Wardrope to W.A. Wilson, 15 Mar. 1889

54 WFMS, *Sixteenth Annual Report,* 1892, 25; *Eighteenth Annual Report,* 1894, 33

55 CIM Correspondence, box 4, file 49, 'Report of A.P. Mitchell, Inspector of Schools (European), C.P. & C.I.'; box 6, file 77, Sinclair to RPM, 13 July 1900, official and unofficial letters; Taylor, *In the Heart of India,* 124, and Duncan, 'India,' 18

56 Staelin, 'The Influence of Missions on Women's Education in India,' Appendix 4, 312; Orchard, *Canadian Baptists at Work in India,* ch. 4

57 WFMS, *Thirty-Eighth Annual Report,* 1914, 22–3 (attendance patterns and extras); Duncan, 'India,' ch. 6, and UCA, Duncan, 'India's Womanhood on the March,' vol. 1, 77–8 (Parsi students); Taylor, *In the Heart of India,* 124 (science classes); Women's Council Minutes, 31 Dec. 1912, and WMS, *Fourth Annual Report,* 1917, 89 (normal school training); CIM Correspondence, box 8, file 104, information form regarding the high school, Indore, 1910 ('Special table')

58 Duncan, 'India,' 24; see also CIM Correspondence, box 14, file 167, AGG O.V. Bosanquet to Miss White, 22 Oct. 1917.

59 CIM Correspondence, box 4, file 41, Jan.–Mar. 1893, W.A. Wilson, statement of views as requested by FMC, undated and unsigned, and file 47, letter of N. Russell accompanying Council Minutes of 21 Mar. 1895

60 Ibid., box 5, file 52, Wilkie to RPM, 2 Apr. 1896

61 Ibid., Oliver, Jessie Grier, and Maggie MacKellar to RPM, 30 Mar. 1896, and Oliver to Mrs Harvie, 15 Apr. 1896

62 See, for example, ibid., Wilkie to RPM, 2 Apr. 1896; *Tidings* 1 (May 1897), 7, and 4 (Jan. 1900), 250.

63 CIM Correspondence, box 5, file 52, W.A. Wilson to RPM, 22 Apr. 1896; FMC report in *Review* 4 June 1896, 1150; *APP,* 1899, Appendix, 164

64 CIM Correspondence, box 17, file 244, Report of Survey of Educational Work of Central India Mission by R.A. King, Mar. 1924

65 Ibid., box 4, file 44, letter of Dr O'Hara, 2 Oct. 1893, written from Ceylon, and file 50, O'Hara to RPM, 8 Oct. 1895, especially 7–8

66 UCA biographical file on the Rev. J. Fraser Campbell; Buchanan, *My Mother*

67 CIM Correspondence, box 6, file 87, King to RPM, 7 July 1903; box 10, file 112, J.A. Sharrard to RPM, 26 Apr. 1912

68 Ibid., box 8, file 104, J. Fraser Campbell to RPM, 10 Mar. 1910; file 106, King
to RPM, 23 Aug. 1910; box 11, file 117, 'Annual Report of the Canadian
Mission College and Schools for the year 1912'

69 APP, 1895, Appendix 13, Central India staff list

70 Beaver, American Protestant Women in World Mission, 133–5

71 For Fairweather's information and advice see CIM Correspondence, box 1,
file 6, Fairweather to William McLaren, 5 Nov. 1874; file 8, to Thomas Lowry,
7 Aug. 1876, and file 9, to McLaren, 14 May 1877. For non-professionals
practising medicine see box 2, file 20, J.M. Douglas to Convenor, 26 Aug. 1881,
and letter of Mary McGregor in Canada Presbyterian 7 Oct. 1881, 630.

72 Hacker, The Indomitable Lady Doctors, 58–9, 68–9; WFMS, Ninth Annual
Report, 1885, 20; Jean Sinclair MacKay, tribute to the late Dr Beatty in
Missionary Monthly 14 (May 1939), 207–8

73 Wilson, The Redemption of Malwa, 48; Margaret MacKellar, tribute to Beatty,
Missionary Monthly 14 (May 1939), 208, also obituary, United Church Observer
15 Mar. 1939, 30; Marchioness of Dufferin and Ava, Our Viceregal Life in
India, 138. Lady Dufferin did not identify the dinner guests by name but
referred to three of them as fellow passengers on the voyage from England.

74 WFMS, Twelfth Annual Report, 1888, 23

75 As reprinted in Leaflet 8 (Feb. 1892), 200–1

76 For the initial Dhar contacts see Taylor, In the Heart of India, 75, and CIM
Correspondence, box 2, file 29, Marion Oliver to WFMS, 14 Mar. 1887; for
the quotation and O'Hara's move to Dhar, see Russell, Village Work in India,
157, 158–63. On the unique drawing power of women doctors see also CIM
Correspondence, box 2, file 26, Wilson to Wardrope, 26 Mar. 1885.

77 Quoted in Taylor, In the Heart of India, 129–30

78 FMC, General Correspondence, box 3, file 50, Captain Meaden to RPM, 6
Dec. 1909; O'Hara, Leaf of the Lotus, 130–1; Tidings 30 (June 1914), 241;
CIM Correspondence, box 8, file 101, Margaret MacKellar to Inspector-
General of Civil Hospitals, 18 June 1909

79 WFMS, Twentieth Annual Report, 1896, 24; APP, 1899, Appendix, 168

80 WFMS, Twenty-Fifth Annual Report, 1901, 23; CIM Correspondence, box 11,
file 117, Thomson to RPM, 29 July 1913; WMS, The Story of Our Missions, 52

81 Balfour and Young, The Work of Medical Women in India, 112–17; WFMS
Board, Minutes, 20: 15 Nov. and 13 Dec. 1910, 136, 153; Oliver, Dr.
Margaret MacKellar, 36–7, 39; WFMS Twenty-Fifth Annual Report, 1901, 28

82 McMaster, 'Touring Scenes,' 263, and O'Hara, Leaf of the Lotus, 159–60,
171; CIM Correspondence, box 7, file 89, Dr Josephine Eltzholtz to RPM,
10 Feb. 1904; Oliver, Dr. Margaret MacKellar, 34–5. See also Balfour and
Young, The Work of Medical Women in India, ch. 6.

83 Luard, comp., *Indore State Gazetteer,* vol. 2, 65; Dr Agnes Turnbull, 'Desolation Wrought by Plague,' *Tidings* 20 (Jan. 1904), 196–9; WFMS, *Twenty-Eighth Annual Report,* 1904, 26; *Record* 32 (Feb. 1907), 51

84 CIM Correspondence, box 10, file 112, Margaret O'Hara to RPM, 26 Mar. 1912; FMC, General Correspondence, box 2, file 36, 1902, 'Summary of a Day as a Medical Missionary,' unsigned handwritten account

85 CIM Correspondence, box 7, file 97, Oliver to RPM, 18 May 1908; Women's Council Minutes, 5 Mar. 1902, and 3 Dec. 1907

86 *Leaflet* 2 (Oct. 1885), 7; WFMS, *Fifteenth Annual Report,* 1891, 16; *Sixteenth Annual Report,* 1892, 24

87 Ibid., 23, and *Thirty-Eighth Annual Report,* 1914, 21, 26, 28; MacKay, *Dr. Marion Oliver,* 30; Dr Susie McCalla, 'Letter from India,' *Record* 26 (June 1901), 242–3

88 CIM Correspondence, box 3, file 39, Wilkie to Mrs Harvie, 20 Apr. 1892, and file 40, Wilkie to RPM, 27 Oct. 1892; also in file 40, responses by MacKellar and other missionaries to circular letter on MacKellar's posting, sent to Canada, 21 Dec. 1892, and Oliver to Cassels, 15 Dec. 1892

89 I have avoided using the word 'converts' in connection with the orphans who came into Christianity at this time, since some of them were very young when they were rescued from the famine and probably had little recollection of any other faith.

90 Regarding Fairweather's orphanage see her letter in *Record* 4 (June 1879), 155–6, and that of James Douglas in *Canada Presbyterian* 8 Nov. 1878, 21; for its closure see CIM Correspondence, box 1, file 16, John Wilkie to McLaren, 'private,' 16 Apr. 1880. On the rescue work of Jamieson and Johory see WMS, *The Story of Our Missions,* 36–8, and, for Wilkie's role in the latter, his article in *Review* 14 Feb. 1895, 703.

91 Letter by Jean Sinclair in *Tidings* 1 (May 1897), 25–6

92 Ibid.; CIM Report, 1898; *Review* 8 July 1897, 11; RPM Letterbook, RPM to Jessie Duncan, 5 Feb. 1897; UCA, FMC, CIM, box 19, Presbytery Minutes, July 1897, 152ff

93 UCA, FMC, CIM, box 19, Presbytery Minutes, July 1897, 152ff

94 CIM Correspondence, box 5, file 60, Campbell to RPM, 7 July 1897; RPM Letterbook, RPM to Campbell, 7 Sept. 1897; CIM, box 19, Presbytery Minutes, 12 Nov. 1897, 171

95 Margaret MacKellar, 'Catherine Campbell,' *Missionary Monthly* 12 (Mar. 1937), 114

96 CIM Correspondence, box 5, file 60, Sinclair to RPM, 12 Sept. 1897; file 61, O'Hara to RPM, 21 Sept. 1897

97 The famine was part of an India-wide phenomenon. Combined with the

plague and depression that followed, it caused the country's population to decline absolutely in the decade 1895–1905; see Wolpert, *A New History of India,* 267, and, for missionaries' overviews of the situation in Malwa, Taylor, *In the Heart of India,* ch. 5, and Wilson, *The Redemption of Malwa,* 21–2.

98 CIM Correspondence, box 5, file 74; box 6, file 75, letter of 28 Jan. 1900

99 Women's Council Minutes, 7–8 Mar. 1900

100 CIM Correspondence, box 6, file 75, O'Hara to RPM, 24 Jan. 1900; O'Hara, *Leaf of the Lotus,* 121

101 MacKellar in *Tidings* 4 [new series] (Jan. 1900), 267–71, also 271–3

102 CIM Correspondence, box 6, file 77, J.T. Taylor to RPM, 13 July 1900

103 Women's Council Minutes, 1 May 1900; FMC, Minutes, II: 15 May 1900, 77; *APP,* 1900, 34

104 CIM Correspondence, box 6, file 78, John Buchanan to members of presbytery committee on famine relief, 31 Dec. 1900; file 79, J.T. Taylor to RPM, 6 Apr. 1901

105 Ibid.

106 Women's Council Minutes, 20 Nov. 1900; see also MacKellar, 'Campbell,' 114.

107 Women's Council Minutes, 14 Aug. 1903, and 3 Jan. 1905

108 On the placement of rescued children and widows see CIM Correspondence, box 6, file 81, statistical table by J.T. Taylor showing dispersal by station, 1 Mar. 1902, and WMS, *The Story of Our Missions,* 32–8, 41. On the origins of the Victorian Orphanage see CIM Correspondence, box 5, file 59, Frank Russell to RPM, 22 June 1897, and box 6, file 81, clipping from *Manitoba Morning Free Press* 1 Mar. 1902. Regarding students for the boarding school see FMC, Minutes, 13: 26 Sept. 1900, 27; letter by Jean Sinclair in *Tidings* 17 (Sept. 1900), 95; and Women's Council Minutes, 5 Mar. 1902.

109 On the boys' orphanage see Taylor, *In the Heart of India,* 105–11, and Wilson, *The Redemption of Malwa,* 59–60; regarding the widows' homes see Wilson, *The Redemption of Malwa,* 61, and WMS, *The Story of Our Missions,* 37–9.

110 CIM Correspondence, box 7, file 90, 11 Aug. 1904

111 For reference to work routines in the orphanage, see, for example, ibid.; also file 91, Campbell to RPM, 31 Jan. 1905, and file 95, Campbell to AEA, 25 Apr. 1907; letter from Mrs D.G. Cock in *Message* 12 (Oct. 1903), 14–15. Regarding the Bombay conference see Women's Council Minutes, 5 Mar. 1901.

112 CIM Correspondence, box 7, file 91, Campbell to RPM, 7 Apr. 1905
113 Letter from Campbell in *Tidings* 4 (Jan. 1900), 273; CIM Correspondence, box 7, file 91, Campbell to RPM, 20 Mar. and 7 Apr. 1905. Because a number of the girls came into the orphanage bearing the same name, the missionaries resorted to the practice of using an identifying number along with the girl's name in writing about each one.
114 CIM Correspondence, box 7, file 91, Campbell to RPM, 7 Apr. 1905
115 Regarding runaway boys see ibid., box 6, file 86, J.T. Taylor to RPM, 11 June 1903, and file 88, Taylor to RPM, 11 Nov. 1903.
116 Ibid., box 7, file 91, Campbell to RPM, 20 Mar. 1905
117 Murdoch MacKenzie, 'Some First Impressions of India,' *Record* 26 (May 1901), 194
118 *Record* 29 (July 1904), 297
119 Ibid., 31 (Mar. 1906), 108–11, (Apr. 1906), 156–7, 162; CIM Correspondence, box 7, file 93, King to 'My Dear Friends,' 23 Mar. 1906. The revival was part of a spiritual phenomenon that had originated in a Welsh mission and spread to orphanages and boarding schools in other parts of India.
120 For Campbell's accounts of revival activity see CIM Correspondence, box 7, file 93, Campbell to RPM, 15 Jan., 6 Feb., and 17 Apr. 1906, and file 95, Campbell to AEA, 25 Apr. and 9 May 1907. For retrospective views see MacKellar, 'Campbell,' 115, and Duncan, 'India,' 20–1.
121 WMS, *The Story of Our Missions,* 33–5, and WFMS, *Thirty-Eighth Annual Report,* 1914, 20. Regarding marriages, see Duncan, 'India,' 15–16, and Jamieson Collection, letters of Dr Belle Choné Oliver to 'Dear Dr. [MacKellar],' 7 and 14 May 1910.
122 Taylor, *In the Heart of India,* 110
123 Christensen and Hutchison, eds, *Missionary Ideologies in the Imperialist Era,* Introduction, 6, 9; see also Hutchison, *Errand to the World,* 101–2
124 Brown, 'History of the Honan (North China) Mission'; Staelin, 'The Influence of Missions on Women's Education in India'; Orchard, *Canadian Baptists at Work in India*
125 Paul, 'Presbyterian Missionaries and the Women of India,' 20–6; Flemming, 'New Models, New Roles,' 35–57; Webster, *The Christian Community and Change*
126 Women's Council Minutes, 17 Mar. 1914. The Council's transfer of Kate Campbell from the Neemuch orphanage to full-time evangelistic work in Banswara was a significant step in this regard; see MacKellar, 'Campbell,' 114–15.

CHAPTER 5 Gender politics in a mission

1 Murdoch, *Indian Missionary Manual,* 552
2 CIM Correspondence, box 1, file 15, Fairweather to William McLaren, Mar. 1880
3 Ibid., file 8, Fairweather to Thomas Lowry, 7 Aug. 1876; Fairweather, 'Seven Years in the Indian Mission Field,' *Canada Presbyterian* 10 Sept. and 22 Oct. 1880, 708–9, 740; *APP,* 1878, Appendix, lxxv; Fairweather to Hamilton WFMS as printed in *Record* 3 (June 1878), 155
4 See Fairweather, 'Seven Years,' 12 Nov. 1880, 852, and Fairweather to Mrs Harvie, as printed in *Canada Presbyterian* 9 Aug. 1878, 644–5, for her work with educated Indian men; CIM Correspondence, box 1, file 9, Fairweather to McLaren, 14 May 1877, for her early views on such work, and Fairweather to WFMS Secretary as printed in *Canada Presbyterian* 5 Mar. 1880, 277–8, for the later emphasis on an intelligent approach. For the criticism from a supporter see CIM Correspondence, box 1, file 15, Rev. Oscar D. Watkins to Fairweather, 22 Feb. 1880.
5 *APP,* 1878, Appendix, lxxiv
6 CIM Correspondence, box 1, file 12, Madhi Hoosein to McLaren, 4 May 1879, and McGregor to McLaren, 12 June 1879, enclosing copy of undated notes from Mrs J. Douglas to McGregor; FMC Minutes, 2: 17 June 1879, 93–4
7 For their comments on the rumours see CIM Correspondence, box 1, file 13, Campbell to McLaren, 7 and 21 Aug. 1879; McGregor to McLaren, 12 Aug. 1879; Rodger to McLaren, 20 Aug. 1879. For their complaints about Douglas as an administrator see file 11, Campbell to McLaren, 5 Feb. 1879; file 12, Rodger to McLaren, 25 June 1879; file 13, Campbell to McLaren, 28 Aug. 1879.
8 Ibid., file 13, D. McPherson and R. Jeffrey to McLaren, 12 Sept. 1879; Beaumont to Douglas, 6 Aug. 1879, co-signed by John D. Morrison, Chaplain, Church of Scotland, Mhow, and — [illeg.], and forwarded to the FMC. See also Beaumont to McLaren, 14 Aug. 1879.
9 FMC, Minutes, 2: 23 Oct. 1879, 106–8; CIM Correspondence, box 1, file 15, McLaren to Lowry, 27 May 1880
10 For testimonials to Fairweather's worth see, for example, CIM Correspondence, box 1, file 15, James Larey [sp.?] to Fairweather, 9 Jan. 1880, and Oscar D. Watkins to Fairweather, 22 Feb. 1880. For her defence see Fairweather to McLaren, Mar. 1880, and file 17, Fairweather to McLaren, 14 Aug. 1880.
11 Wilkie's criticisms of Fairweather were most frequent in 1880, but as late

as 1885 he was still holding her partly accountable for the mission's continuing troubles; for example, ibid., box 2, file 26, Wilkie to Wardrope, 24 Aug.
1885.

12 For 'staying power' see ibid., file 19, Wilkie to McLaren, 15 Jan. 1881; for
'*too clever*,' box 1, file 16, Wilkie to McLaren, 27 May 1880, 'private.'

13 For references to gossip, still-unknown rumours, and British opposition see
ibid., box 1, file 16, Wilkie to McLaren, 3 June 1880, 'private,' and box 2,
file 19, Wilkie to McLaren, 15 Jan. 1881. For Fairweather's allegedly negative
influence on the mission staff, including Douglas, see box 1, file 16, Wilkie
to McLaren, 16 Apr. 1880, 'private,' and box 2, file 19, Wilkie to McLaren,
4 May and 23 June 1881.

14 Regarding his fears of a return by Fairweather see ibid., box 2, file 23, Wilkie
to McLaren, 14 May 1883. On his efforts to undermine Douglas see ibid.,
box 1, file 16, Wilkie to McLaren, 6 and 16 Apr. 1880, and box 2, file 20,
Wilkie to McLaren, 23 July 1881, 'private.' See *APP,* 1883, Appendix, ci,
regarding Douglas's 1882 recall.

15 FMC, Minutes, 2: 10 June 1880, 122; also *APP,* 1880, Appendix, lxxxiv–lxxxv.
In 1887 Fairweather returned to India to work under the Lady Dufferin
medical plan, having previously trained as a doctor in Chicago. She remained
only briefly before marrying a widowed doctor and returning with him to
the United States; see Brouwer, ' "Far Indeed from the Meekest of
Women." '

16 FMC, Minutes, 2: 4 Apr. 1879, 81–6 (quotation 85), and, for background, 2:
22 Apr. 1878, 265. See also CIM Correspondence, box 1, file 9, James
Douglas to McLaren, 26 Oct. 1877; and Kemp and Farries, eds, *Handbook
of the Presbyterian Church,* 296–300.

17 The 1879 regulations provided for the FMC to determine salaries for the
women missionaries 'after conference with the Mission Council.' New
regulations on this subject in 1883 did involve some consultation with the
women concerned, but vagueness about what constituted allowable
expenses still left plenty of room for disputes. See FMC, Minutes, 2: 4 Apr.
1879, 78–81; 18 Apr. 1883, 193–4; and 3: 14 Feb. 1884, 10.

18 CIM Correspondence, box 2, file 20, Wilkie to McLaren, 'private', 9 Nov.
1881, and 22 Nov. 1881

19 Ibid., box 2, file 23, McGregor to FMC, 13 Mar. 1883; see also McGregor to
Wardrope, 16 Aug. 1883.

20 Thomas Wardrope Letterbook, Wardrope to McGregor, 9 July 1883; CIM
Correspondence, box 2, file 23, Wilkie to McLaren, 28 Mar. 1883, and file
26, Wilkie to Wardrope, 29 Jan. 1885

21 CIM Correspondence, box 2, file 27, McGregor to Wardrope, 26 Jan. 1886;

W.A. Wilson to FMC, 5 May 1886; and McGregor to Wardrope, 19 May 1886

22 For the accusations see ibid., file 23, Wilkie to McLaren, 28 Mar. and 24 Apr. 1883, and FMC, Minutes, 3: 21 May 1885, 38; for Wilkie's use of the mission press, Wardrope Letterbook, Wardrope to Wilkie, 10 May 1883; and, for his warning to the FMC, CIM Correspondence, box 2, file 25, Wilkie to Wardrope, 21 Nov. 1884.

23 Wardrope Letterbook, Wardrope to Wilkie, 10 May 1883; CIM Correspondence, box 2, file 26, Wilkie to Wardrope, 29 Jan. and 30 Dec. 1885; H. Cassels to Wardrope, 29 May 1885; file 27, Builder to Wardrope, 21 Jan. 1886; FMC, Minutes, 3: 1 May 1886

24 CIM Correspondence, box 2, file 28, McGregor to Wardrope, 10 and 19 July 1886, and W.A. Wilson to Wardrope, 12 Aug. 1886; file 29, McGregor to Wardrope, 2 Mar. 1887; FMC, Minutes, 3: 4 Jan. 1887, 119, 120

25 CIM Correspondence, box 2, file 27, letter of commendation to McGregor signed by various Indian officials, 20 Jan. 1886, with undated newspaper clipping, and McGregor to Wardrope, 26 Jan. 1886; file 28, printed correspondence from J.S. Milton, and file 30, McGregor to Wardrope, 16 Sept. 1887; FMC, Minutes, 3: 21 and 22 Sept. 1887, 147, 150, 154

26 Regarding Ross, see CIM Correspondence, box 3, file 31, Ross to Wardrope, 11 Jan. 1888; file 32, Ross to Cassels, 20 Sept. 1888, and Ross to McLaren, 22 Nov. 1888. For the FMC's findings see FMC, Minutes, 3: 15 and 17 May 1888, 174, 177, 182–5.

27 UCA, Murdoch MacKenzie Personal Papers, Diary, 21 May 1902

28 FMC, Minutes, 3: 17 May 1888, 189

29 Wardrope Letterbook, Wardrope to McGregor, 17 Dec. 1887; FMC, Minutes, 3: 17 May 1888, 185; 4: 25 Sept. 1888, 7; WFMS Board, Minutes, 6: 6 Nov. 1888

30 CIM Correspondence, box 2, file 28, Rev. R.C. Murray to Wardrope, 4 May 1886; Wilson, *The Redemption of Malwa*, 91–2

31 A key reason for having the two bodies (it was common practice in many India missions) was so that, as Indian men were ordained and admitted to presbytery, they would not have a say in the spending of funds from the home church; see Webster, 'Introduction,' *Journal of Presbyterian History* 62 (Fall 1984), 191, and CIM Correspondence, box 3, file 34, W.A. Wilson to Cassels, 10 Aug. 1889.

32 FMC, Minutes, 4: 25, 26 Sept. 1888, 6, 20–1. UCA, FMC CIM, Mission Council Minutes (hereafter CIM Council Minutes), box 24, item 291, Mar. 1884, 3; CIM Correspondence, box 2, file 30, Builder to Wardrope, 29 Sept. 1887, and box 3, file 37, Oliver to Cassels, 26 Mar. 1891

33 FMC, Minutes, 4: 25 Sept. 1888, 6; CIM Correspondence, box 3, file 32, Wilkie
to Cassels, 26 Dec. 1888. Since Wilkie was to remain such an important
figure in the women missionaries' lives, it is worth noting some of the means
by which he established and maintained his inordinate influence with
home-base officials and publicists. He was remarkably gifted at self-promo-
tion, especially in person, and, conscious of this fact, arranged several trips
back to Canada over and above his regular furloughs in order to promote
his causes. Both in writing and in person he presented highly optimistic reports
about his past work and future prospects. Meanwhile, colleagues who challenged his inflated claims or questioned the wisdom of his methods almost
invariably appeared jealous or inflexible. This was the case, for instance,
when they tried to point out that college work in an Indian mission,
whatever its other merits, was not an effective agency for obtaining converts.
Because he was far more successful than they at getting funds for his
projects, Wilkie was able to build up a large missionary infrastructure at his
station. This, in turn, contributed to the impression that he had established
a large and vital congregation, one capable of reaching out itself in a
missionary way. Since they served his own goals, he advocated two broad
missionary policies that the FMC found congenial: making one station –
Indore – the site of the mission's chief institutions; and leaving the FMC
rather than the Mission Council with responsibility for major mission decisions. In general, however, he eschewed a firm commitment to particular
mission policies and thus was able to respond to changing situations in a
pragmatic and flexible way.

34 CIM Correspondence, box 2, file 30, Campbell to Wardrope, 3 Sept. 1887

35 Rodger to Mrs Harvie as printed in *Leaflet* 1 (Nov. 1884), 6; CIM Correspondence, box 2, file 26, Wilkie to Wardrope, 22 June 1885, and 24 Sept. 1885

36 CIM Correspondence, box 2, file 30, Campbell to Wardrope, 3 Sept. 1887,
and Builder to Wardrope, 7 Oct. 1887; see also box 3, file 33, replies to
council's circular letter on proposed boarding school and women's hospital,
2, 15, 21 May 1889.

37 Ibid., box 2, file 28, Rodger to Wardrope, 13 Sept. 1886, and box 3, file 34,
Rodger to Mrs MacMurchy, 20 July 1889; Wardrope Letterbook, Wardrope to Rodger, 2 Oct. 1888, and 9 Nov. 1889

38 CIM Correspondence, box 3, file 38, Wilkie to Cassels, 3 Dec. 1891

39 Wardrope Letterbook, Wardrope to Campbell, 24 Sept. 1887, and CIM
Correspondence, box 2, file 30, Builder to Wardrope, 29, 30 Sept. 1887

40 CIM Correspondence, box 2, file 29, Oliver to Mrs Harvie, 14 Mar. 1887, and
to Wardrope, 26 Aug. 1887; Beatty and Oliver to WFMS, 16 Mar. 1887

41 FMC, Minutes, 4: 25 Sept. 1888, 4–5, and 29 May 1889, 61; CIM Correspon-

dence, box 2, file 30, Oliver and Wilkie to FMC on behalf of Dr Beatty, 26 Aug. 1887, and Builder to Wardrope, 29 Sept. 1887

42 CIM Correspondence, box 3, file 34, Wilkie to Cassels, 7 Oct. 1889

43 Ibid., Campbell to Cassels, 2 Sept. 1889

44 Ibid., Wilson to Cassels, 10 Aug. 1889; file 35, council resolution of 21 Aug. 1889, as forwarded by Campbell to Wardrope, 18 July 1890

45 Ibid., file 34, Beatty to Cassels, 31 Aug. 1889, and Rodger to Cassels, 24 Aug. 1889

46 Ibid., Oliver to Cassels, 12 Sept. 1889

47 Ibid., Beatty to Cassels, 31 Aug. 1889, and file 37, Oliver to Cassels, 26 Mar. 1891, forwarding the women missionaries' joint petition

48 Hacker, *The Indomitable Lady Doctors,* 58; Strong-Boag, ed., '*A Woman with a Purpose,*' 282, 289

49 CIM Correspondence, box 3, file 37, 1 May 1891. By the time she wrote these words MacKellar herself was being drawn into the disputes.

50 For the McKelvie-Wilkie dispute see ibid., McKelvie to Cassels, 16 Apr. 1891; FMC, Minutes, 5: 18 May 1892; D.D. McLeod–R.P. MacKay Letter-book, RPM to Principal Grant, 19 Oct. 1892. Regarding Wilson see CIM Council Minutes, box 24, 13–14, 28 Nov. 1890, 120, 124–7; and CIM Correspondence, box 3, file 36, Wilson to Cassels, 9 Dec. 1890.

51 CIM Council Minutes, box 24, 13–14, 28 Nov. 1890, 120, 127

52 UCA, Presbyterian Church in Canada, *Regulations for Foreign Mission Work,* especially 6

53 CIM Council Minutes, box 24, 10 Nov. 1891, 147

54 CIM Correspondence, box 4, file 41, Jan.–Mar. 1893, unsigned and undated statement from Wilson to FMC, 6–8. In opposing Campbell on the particular matter cited by Wilson, the women missionaries were probably protesting Campbell's treatment of Dr Minnie Fraser, who had, in effect, been dismissed from his station shortly after being posted there in 1891; box 3, file 37, Campbell to Wardrope, 22 Apr. and 21 May 1891.

55 CIM Council Minutes, box 24, 26 July 1893, 201–3

56 CIM Correspondence, box 4, file 45, Russell to RPM, 12 Mar. 1894

57 Ibid., Report of 'The Committee of Presbytery' accompanying Russell to RPM, 12 Mar. 1894; CIM Council Minutes, box 24, 1–3 Mar. 1894, 220–3, with Minutes of Canadian Finance Committee, 5 Mar. 1894, 224–5

58 CIM Correspondence, box 4, file 45, Russell, Buchanan, and Wilson to RPM, 4 Apr. 1894

59 Ibid., 'Reply' by Campbell to FMC request of 23 May 1894, for information on the mission troubles; see also RPM Letterbook, RPM to Campbell, 12 July 1894.

60 RPM Letterbook, RPM to Wilkie, 13 July 1894, and RPM to N. Russell, 14 Sept. and 18 Oct. 1894

61 Ibid., RPM to N. Russell, 27 Sept. 1894

62 For Oliver see FMC, Minutes, 7: 13 Sept. 1894, 27; for the threats from the field, CIM Council Minutes, box 19, file 269, 31 Oct. 1894, 4; and, for Fraser's response, CIM Correspondence, box 4, file 46, Fraser to Mrs Harvie, 29 Aug. 1894, and Fraser to RPM, 21 Dec. 1894.

63 RPM Letterbook, RPM to MacKellar, 9 Feb. 1895

64 CIM Correspondence, box 4, file 48, MacKellar to MacKay, 11 Apr. 1895

65 Ibid., file 47, Sinclair to RPM, 24 Jan. 1895

66 Ibid., file 46, M. O'Hara, M.A. Dougan, Kate Calder, and M.A. Jamieson to RPM, 15 Dec. 1894; Calder to RPM, 1 Nov. 1894

67 Ibid., file 46, Russell to RPM, 8 Nov. 1894; file 47, Wilkie to RPM, 5 Jan. 1895

68 For Calder's quarrels with co-workers see ibid., file 47, Wilkie to RPM, 5 Jan. 1895; also Minnie Fraser to RPM, 7 Jan. 1895, and Isabella Ross to RPM, 10 Jan. 1895. For Jamieson's views see file 46, Maggie Jamieson to RPM, 9 Oct. 1894, from Quebec.

69 Ibid., file 47, O'Hara to RPM, 24 Jan. 1895, and Wilkie to RPM, 5 Jan. 1895; file 49, Russell to RPM, 24 July 1895. In his letter, one of a series in his campaign to prevent O'Hara from opening work in Dhar, Wilkie advised the FMC that only a male missionary should begin work in a new station.

70 For the regulations see FMC, Minutes, 8: 25 Sept. 1895, 33–6, and, for complaints about them, CIM Council Minutes, box 19, file 269 [Mar. 1896], 10–11.

71 CIM Council Minutes, box 19, file 269 [Mar. 1896], 3; FMC, Minutes, 8: 25 Sept. 1895, 33

72 CIM Council Minutes, box 19, file 269, letter to FMC, 11 Aug. 1896, signed by ten missionaries, with postscript (iv) by O'Hara

73 FMC, Minutes, 8: 19 May 1896, 81–2, and 9: 30 Sept. 1896, 21–3

74 Ibid., 11 Dec. 1896, 44; CIM Correspondence, box 5, file 54, W.A. Wilson to RPM, 12 Aug. 1896, and file 56, Wilson to RPM, 9 Nov. 1896

75 For the views of those consulted see CIM Correspondence, box 5, file 58, Memorial to General Assembly from Indore Presbytery, 1897, Appendix c.

76 Ibid., 20, 21

77 Ibid., letter of W.A. Wilson to RPM, 25 Mar. 1897, quoting McInnes. Underlining in original

78 Ibid., Memorial, 17

79 Ibid., 4, 5, and letter of A.P. Ledingham to RPM, 18 Mar. 1897; FMC, Minutes, 9: 9 and 27 Apr. 1897, 66ff, 77–8, 85

80 CIM Correspondence, box 5, file 60, M. Oliver and five other missionaries to RPM, 16 Aug. 1897; also Sinclair to RPM, 16 Aug. 1897, and Duncan to RPM, 18 Aug. 1897. They were especially anxious to repudiate the idea that they had any inclination to involve themselves in unseemly, presbytery-type matters.

81 FMC, Minutes, 9: 9 Apr. 1897, 66–73, and 19–20 May 1897, 96–9

82 RPM Letterbook, RPM to Wilkie, 26 May 1897

83 FMC, Minutes, 9: 20 May 1897, 97–9; FMC, General Correspondence, box 1, file 14, Grant to Cassels, 5 Dec. [1892]. Grant's long-standing friendship with J. Fraser Campbell may well have made him cautious about Wilkie.

84 For the text of the new regulations see FMC, Minutes, 10: 15 Sept. 1897, 20–5, and, for the deliberations leading up to them in the General Assembly, APP, 1897, 18–20, 25–6, 37.

85 CIM Correspondence, box 5, file 64, formal response to General Assembly from W.A. Wilson *et al*

86 RPM Letterbook, RPM to Oliver, 3 July 1897; see also RPM to Wilkie, 26 May 1897, to Sinclair, 3 July 1897, and to Duncan, 3 July 1897.

87 CIM Correspondence, box 5, file 64, letter from nine members of Women's Council to RPM, 8 Mar. 1898, and Wilkie to RPM, 24 Mar. [1898]

88 Ibid., formal response to General Assembly from O'Hara, Maggie Jamieson, and Kate Calder, 9 Mar. 1898; file 65, Ledingham to RPM, 11 May 1898

89 APP, 1898, 31–2

90 Dr Minnie Fraser, Isabella Ross, and Kate Calder, who had been stationed in Mhow, left the mission before 1900 and subsequently married.

91 CIM Correspondence, box 5, file 63, Janet White to RPM, 28 Feb. 1898; O'Hara, *Leaf of the Lotus*, 120; CIM Correspondence, box 4, file 43, Sinclair to Cassels, 16 Aug. 1893, 'private'

92 Women's Council Minutes, 29, 30 Nov. and 1 Dec. 1899; 20 Nov. 1900; 5 Mar. and 10 July 1901

93 CIM Correspondence, box 6, file 79, Leach to RPM, 17 Jan. 1901

94 Perhaps because the amendment ending that right had come from the General Assembly rather than the FMC, they did not formally protest against it.

95 WFMS, Correspondence, Mrs Shortreed to RPM, 29 June 1898, and Mrs Shortreed to Rev. R.H. Warden, 26 Jan. 1899. The WFMS board had strongly supported the majority faction of women missionaries in their bid to preserve a joint council in which they had full rights. That effort having failed, the board was anxious to ensure that the Women's Council would have effective control over all women's work sponsored by WFMS funds.

96 CIM Correspondence, box 10, file 115, Campbell to RPM, 10 Nov. 1911

97 The proposed appointment of Robson provoked an extensive correspondence in 1912 and early 1913. For evidence of Robson's acceptance of the arrangement see ibid., Robson to RPM, 11 Oct. 1912.

98 Ibid., box 6, file 77, Sinclair to RPM, 13 July 1900. See also Sinclair's official letter to MacKay of the same date for more specific details about the controversy between her and Wilkie over her efforts to upgrade the boarding school and, for Wilkie's version, file 80, Wilkie to RPM, 1 Aug. and 5 Dec. 1901.

99 Ibid., box 6, file 77, Oliver to Mrs Bell, 17 Aug. 1900, accompanying Oliver's own article, 'Industrial Home at Indore'

100 Ibid., file 81, Oliver to RPM, 16 and 31 Mar. 1902, and file 80, Taylor to Oliver, 9 Dec. 1901. See also file 81, Oliver to RPM, 14 Mar. 1902, enclosing extracts from personal letters written by other missionaries in Central India. This and later correspondence suggested that some other mission workers had similar suspicions.

101 FMC, Minutes, 14: 10–13 June 1902, 118, 120–3, 126–7; 15: 9 Sept. 1902, 15, and 12 Nov. 1902, 41–2. See also CIM Correspondence, box 6, file 81, RPM to Wallace, 27 June 1902, and file 83, Wallace to RPM, 11 Sept. 1902.

102 FMC, Minutes, 14: 12 June 1902, 125, and, for background to its decision, 2 May 98–9, and 10–12 June 118–25

103 CIM Correspondence, box 6, file 81 [Murdoch MacKenzie], 'Statement of the Situation in India before the For. Mis. Co.,' unsigned and undated. MacKenzie was almost as circumspect in his diary as in this formal statement. Nevertheless, his increasing disillusionment with Wilkie is clear. See, for example, MacKenzie Papers, Diary, 21 May and 5, 10–11, and 14 June 1902.

104 In subsequent private letters to R.P. MacKay, Oliver stood by her suspicions about drug use by Wilkie and implied that he had become addicted to cocaine tablets intended for hospital use; see CIM Correspondence, box 6, file 84, letter of 24 Nov. 1902, and file 85, letter of 25 Feb. 1903.

105 Regarding the memorial see FMC, Minutes, 15: 24 Apr. 1903, 108; a copy is held by the author. Regarding the Commission see UCA, FMC, CIM, Wilkie Case Documentation, box 25, item 301.

106 UCA, FMC, CIM, Organization of Gwalior Mission for Wilkie, box 25, item 302; Record 29 (Feb. 1904), 50–1

107 CIM Correspondence, box 7, file 91, King to RPM, 26 May 1905; Wilson to RPM, 12 Jan. [1905]

108 APP, 1918, Appendix, 98–9

109 Duncan, 'India's Womanhood on the March,' 86

110 CIM Correspondence, box 11, file 117, Oliver to RPM, 6 Feb. 1913

111 UCA, FMC, CIM, Minutes of the Mission Council on Women's Work, 1920–4,

box 26, item 309, Oct. 1923, 5–6, and Minutes of the [united] Mission Council, 18–23 July 1924, 3–6

112 Hunter, *The Gospel of Gentility,* ch. 6, especially 225–8

CHAPTER 6 Beyond the romance of missions

1 'Extract from a Private Letter from Dr. Elizabeth Beatty,' *Leaflet* 4 (Feb. 1888), 3

2 *Record* 20 (June 1895), 151

3 Wilson, *The Redemption of Malwa,* 72. In 1915 the WMS put the 'total Christian community' in Central India at 3,048, but this figure obviously included unbaptized children and adults; WMS, *The Story of Our Missions,* 27.

4 For example, Jamieson Collection, Choné Oliver Diary, 31 Oct. 1905; and MacKay, *Voices from India,* 121–4

5 *APP,* 1878, Appendix, lxxv; Fairweather, 'Seven Years,' 10 Dec. 1880, 916–17; CIM Correspondence, box 10, file 114, R. Schofield to RPM, 26 Sept. 1912. For brief references to *Brahmo Samaj* and *Arya Samaj* see Brown, *Modern India,* 77, 154–5, and, for more detail on the latter society, which was the more important in Central India, Jardens, 'Dayananda Saras-vati,' 34–47.

6 For Wilkie's view see *Review* 30 May 1889, 1430, and, for Russell's, CIM Correspondence, box 4, file 41, Russell to RPM, 22 Mar. 1893.

7 Wilson, 'Itinerating,' no. 2, 263–7; McCalla, 'Letter,' 243; letter of Alexander Armstrong Scott, 5 Sept. 1914, preserved in 'Touchstone,' in Alexander A. and Mrs. Minnie Shaw Scott Papers, privately held

8 'A Visit to India,' *Record* 38 (June 1913), 250

9 For Goodfellow see *Tidings* 19 (Oct. 1902), 108; and, for the Jamieson quotation, *Record* 18 (Nov. 1893), 297.

10 *Record* 33 (Apr. 1908), 155. Interestingly, however, once-common references to fields 'white unto the harvest' became infrequent as the missionaries' experience grew. Coupled with the scriptural line 'The harvest truly is plenteous, but the labourers are few,' it had created an image of spiritual fruit ripe for the picking that even the most optimistic missionary was no longer prepared to perpetuate.

11 Oliver, comp., *Tales from the Inns of Healing,* 63; CIM Correspondence, box 3, file 40, Norman Russell to Hamilton Cassels, 13 Sept. 1892; see also box 4, file 44, Russell to RPM, 14 Nov. 1893.

12 It is worth recalling that though he had a very different goal in view, Karl Marx, too, had been confident that changes taking place under British

imperialism would erode ancient traditions and prepare the ground for a transformed, improved, India; see Marx's 'The Future Results of British Rule in India,' 583–8.

13 Mott, *The Decisive Hour of Christian Missions,* 85–90; Gandhi, *Christian Missions,* especially 73ff; *Record* 26 (Oct. 1901), 416, and Thoburn, *The Christian Conquest of India,* 228–9

14 CIM Correspondence, box II, file 117, Oliver to RPM, 6 Feb. 1913

15 Ibid., McMaster to RPM, 6 Feb. 1913

16 The complexities that could result when 'clients' became emotionally attached to missionaries is effectively suggested in Gerald Hanley's novel *The Journey Homeward* (London: Abacus 1984): Miss Bullen's three 'converts' after forty years in the isolated Muslim village of Kangla are three men who, with the connivance of the village elders, initially feign conversion in order to prevent her from becoming discouraged. Under her powerful influence, they gradually become genuine Christians. When they confess this fact to the elders after she has left the village, the latter agree that they should go and tell her in order to bring her back. The elders are as hostile as ever to Christianity, but they cannot bear to lose the old woman, whom they have come to think of as their own.

17 Wilson, *The Redemption of Malwa,* 46

18 For Jean Sinclair MacKay's proud reference to the fact that her husband was 'slow to baptize,' see CIM Correspondence, box 14, file 168, Sinclair MacKay to RPM, 15 Feb. 1917. See also 'Presbyterian Missions' in Neill, Anderson, and Goodwin,, eds, *Concise Dictionary of the Christian World Mission,* 495.

19 For some among numerous examples available see Norman Russell, 'The Workers in Mhow,' *Record* 18 (Nov. 1893), 299; Jamieson Collection, Choné Oliver to 'Dear Dr.,' 7 May 1910; O'Hara, *Leaf of the Lotus,* 156–7.

20 CIM Correspondence, box 4, file 44, Dougan to RPM, 24 Nov. 1893; 'Letter from Margaret MacKellar,' *Record* 18 (Nov. 1893), 297–8

21 For example, CIM Correspondence, box 8, file 103, Jean Sinclair MacKay to RPM, II Nov. 1909; and report by Kate Calder in *Tidings* 16 (Aug. 1899), 119–20

22 O'Hara, *Leaf of the Lotus,* 103

23 See, for example, MacGillivray, 'Fruitage,' 449–53, for a summary of such reports.

24 Margaret A. Coltart, 'Vellore: Venture of Faith and Cooperation,' *Missionary Monthly* 21 (June 1946), 250; *Tidings* 22 (Sept. 1905), 90, and 25 (Nov. 1908), 107–8; Duncan, 'India's Womanhood on the March,' 77–8

25 'Letter from Miss Jamieson,' *Record* 18 (Nov. 1893), 296; Margaret Coltart,

'Some Data about Early Life of Margaret Coltart,' 7, in Coltart Papers, privately held

26 O'Malley, *Modern India and the West,* 464

27 Oddie, *Social Protest in India;* Liddle and Joshi, *Daughters of Independence;* Luard, comp., *Indore State Gazetteer,* Vol. 2, 16–20, and Lebra-Chapman, *The Rani of Jhansi*

28 Duncan, 'India's Womanhood on the March.' See also MacGillivray, 'Fruitage,' especially 451–2; 'Mrs. Taylor, Indore,' *Tidings* 24 (June 1907), 22–3; and *Messenger* 4 (Dec. 1917), 326.

29 On Indian Christian girls' academic achievements see Pathak, *American Missionaries and Hinduism,* especially 156, and Webster, *The Christian Community and Change,* 228–9. On nursing and medical education see Hocking, ed., *Re-Thinking Missions,* 211, 268; also Balfour and Young, *The Work of Medical Women in India.*

30 O'Hara, *Leaf of the Lotus,* 125–6, 127–8

31 CIM Correspondence, box 6, file 79, J.R. Harcourt to RPM, 3 Jan. 1901. Italics in original.

32 For the expression see Allen, *Plain Tales from the Raj,* 281; for its use by adult orphans raised by the missionaries see MacKellar, 'Campbell,' 113.

33 Murdoch, *Indian Missionary Manual,* 526; Mrs Minnie Shaw Scott [5 Sept. 1914], in Scott Papers

34 For concern over immorality see Choné Oliver Diary, 2 Aug. 1909; on missionaries blacklisting unsatisfactory workers see CIM Correspondence, box 3, file 36, Jean Sinclair to Hamilton Cassels, 4 Dec. 1890, and *APP,* 1893, Appendix II, cxi.

35 CIM Correspondence, box 3, file 37, Sinclair to Hamilton Cassels, 2 Feb. 1891; box 11, file 117, Harriet Thomson to RPM, 29 July 1913

36 See, for example, ibid., box 4, file 41, printed report for Mhow station by Norman Russell, and MacKellar, 'Incidents,' 266.

37 The most memorable portrayals of Englishwomen's snobbish attitudes towards Indians occur in fiction, most notably in E.M. Forster's *A Passage to India* and in the novels in Paul Scott's *Raj Quartet,* but the historical literature abounds with examples. Two specialized works that support the stereotypes while providing interesting exceptions are Barr, *The Memsahibs,* and MacMillan, *Women of the Raj.*

38 Russell, *Village Work in India,* 149, 161–2

39 O'Hara, *Leaf of the Lotus,* 90–3, 107–8, 147–8, 157; *Record* 22 (Sept. 1897), 235–6, and 53 (June 1928), 164; CIM Correspondence, box 7, file 96, printed copy of reply to addresses delivered to H.H. Raja Udaji Rao Powar Sahib Bahadur

40 Mrs Mary E. Addison, 'Honor to Dr. Margaret O'Hara,' *Record* (May 1920), 143–4

41 Beaver, *American Protestant Women in World Mission,* 135; Johnston, ed., *Report of the Centenary Conference on the Protestant Missions of the World,* 176–7; CIM Correspondence, box 6, file 83, Marion Oliver to RPM, 19 Aug. 1902

42 For an excellent example of this see CIM Correspondence, box 2, file 29, Marion Oliver to WFMS, 14 Mar. 1887.

43 S. Satthianadhan, *Missionary Work in India from a Native Christian Point of View,* 21, as quoted in Oddie, 'India and Missionary Motives,' 71; Allen, *Plain Tales from the Raj,* 228

44 CIM Correspondence, box I, file 16, Wilkie to McLaren, 3 June 1880, 'private'; obituary for Janet White, *Missionary Monthly* (Nov. 1921), 263

45 Letter of Kate Builder to WFMS, 21 Feb. 1884, in UCA biographical file for the Rev. Joseph Builder (regarding Mhow); Duncan, 'India's Womanhood on the March,' 18, and CIM Correspondence, box II, file 117, John Buchanan to RPM, 27 Aug. 1913 (regarding Neemuch); box 7, file 93, O'Hara to RPM, 6 and 7 June 1906 (regarding Dhar)

46 Regarding this decoration see *British Orders and Awards,* rev. ed. (London: Kaye and Ward 1968; orig. ed. by Major Lawrence L. Gordon), 30; for figures on recipients in the Central India mission see Choné Oliver in *Tidings* 30 (June 1914), 241; on Buchanan's work see Taylor, *In the Heart of India,* 113–14, 117, and, for his award, CIM Correspondence, box II, file 121, Janet White to RPM, 4 Dec. 1913. Buchanan received the gold rather than the silver version of the medal for his extensive famine relief work among the Bhils, an honour seldom bestowed on a missionary, according to White.

47 Janet White, 'What the Kaiser-I-Hind Medal Means,' *Tidings* 23 (Oct. 1906), 90–2

48 O'Hara, *Leaf of the Lotus,* 131

49 Report by Herdman in *Tidings* 29 (Feb. 1913), 156–7; CIM Correspondence, box 10, file 113, RPM to Colonel Roberts, 3 May 1912; box 7, file 92, White to RPM, 1 Dec. 1905

50 CIM Correspondence, box 9, file 50, Captain Meaden to RPM, 6 Dec. 1909

51 Ibid., file III, Dr Alex Nugent to RPM, 2 Nov. 1911; box 10, file 112, 1912, copy of address by AGG M.F. O'Dwyer

52 Ibid., box 8, file 104, J.R. Harcourt to RPM, 29 July 1910, I, 5–6; file 107, J.T. Taylor to RPM, 29 Oct. 1910. By contrast, to the north in Jaora State, where nationalism was evidently not then a concern, a British official gave the Rev. F.J. Anderson temporary use of the opium agent's bungalow when he was opening mission work there in 1913; *APP,* 1914, Appendix, 137.

53 On the Mhow school difficulty see CIM Correspondence, box 9, file 109, Taylor to RPM, 7 Apr. 1911; also RPM to Frank Russell, 22 May 1911, and to Robert King, 25 May 1911. Regarding the Indore College grant see box 10, file 114, King to High Commissioner for the Dominion of Canada, 28 Aug. 1911, and King to RPM, 22 Sept. 1911; file 112, King to RPM, 1 Feb. 1912, and AGG O'Dwyer to RPM, 7 Feb. 1912. King was outraged by the AGG's action, since he considered himself a loyal spokesman for the Empire.

54 For example, ibid., box 7, file 96, Jean Sinclair MacKay to RPM, 18 Dec. 1907. Even after this period, when Indian nationalism became a much more pressing issue, the women missionaries seldom commented on the subject; Ruth Compton Brouwer, 'Canada, India and the Missionary Link: The Presbyterian Missionary Community and the Growth of Indian Nationalism, 1914–1925,' paper prepared for symposium on 'The Presbyterian Contribution to Canadian Life and Culture,' part 2, Toronto, 17 May 1989.

55 Aberigh-Mackay, *The Chiefs of Central India,* lxxvi; Luard, *Indore State Gazetteer,* Vol. 2, 153; Oddie, *Social Protest in India,* 221, 226

56 Oliver to Mrs Greer, as printed in *Record* 22 (July 1897), 183; CIM Correspondence, box 4, file 46, Russell to RPM, 17 Sept. 1894; Oddie, *Social Protest in India,* 236, for Hughes' criticism, and ch. 8 generally for British missionaries' diverse positions on the opium question

57 Hunter, *The Gospel of Gentility,* 70–9, and accompanying substantive notes; Smith-Rosenberg, 'The Female World of Love and Ritual,' in her *Disorderly Conduct,* 53–76. This article was first published in 1975. See also her 'Hearing Women's Words,' in ibid., 11–52, for Smith-Rosenberg's more recent thoughts on the significance of Victorian women's friendships and the language they used to describe them.

58 Murdoch, *Indian Missionaries Manual,* ch. 20, and One Interested, 'The Woman,' 163–4; CIM Correspondence, box 2, file 26, John Wilkie to Thomas Wardrope, 24 Sept. 1885

59 For example, CIM Correspondence, box 6, file 83, Oliver to RPM, 1 Sept. 1902

60 MacKay, *Dr. Marion Oliver*

61 Jamieson Collection, Choné Oliver, untitled autobiographical MS. A few of Oliver's letters to MacKellar have been preserved in this collection.

62 Choné Oliver to Mrs Coltart, 22 Dec. 1916, in Coltart Papers; Jamieson Collection, Choné Oliver Diary, 18 Nov. 1940, and Glenna Jamieson and Choné Williams, 'Dr. Belle Choné Oliver, Woman Doctor: Healing the Whole Person / Body, Mind and Soul,' undated MS; CIM Correspondence, box 14, file 162, Oliver to RPM, 25 May 1917; Oliver, *Dr. Margaret MacKellar*

63 For the birthday quotations see Choné Oliver Diary, 25 Jan. 1930; for

reference to staff opposition, 14 Jan. 1930; and, for information about Oliver's appointment to the new job, handwritten outline of events in her career, Coltart Papers, 3–4.

64 Choné Oliver Diary, 14 Jan. 1934

65 Obituary in UCA biographical file for Oliver; Diary of Alan Oliver for 16, 19, 21, and 23 May 1947, in possession of Glenna Jamieson and Choné Williams

66 For dinner parties and other get-togethers see, for example, Choné Oliver Diary, 31 Mar. 1904, and A.A. Scott to 'Dear Mother,' 12 Dec. 1912, and 12 Sept. 1913, in Scott Papers. For Christmas celebrations see CIM Correspondence, box 7, file 89, Mrs Wilson to RPM, 31 Jan. 1904, and box 8, file 103, Harriet Thomson to RPM, 31 Dec. 1909.

67 CIM Correspondence, box 8, file 119, Taylor to RPM, 23 June 1913

68 In 1896, women missionaries received $300 furlough allowance, as compared with a salary of $730 in India. By 1913, the gap had narrowed, with the allowance raised to $500. Even so, their income was lowest at the very time when their need for money was often most acute. By contrast, single male missionaries' furlough allowance approximated their annual field salary. For data see *APP*, 1896, Appendix 6, iv, and 1913, Appendix, 147–8.

69 The gradual development of a sense of alienation from the homeland and the role of a furlough in bringing it to a head are movingly conveyed in Pearl Buck's biography of her missionary mother, *The Exile.*

70 CIM Correspondence, box 7, file 91, Sinclair to RPM, 16 Jan. 1905

71 Jamieson Collection, Choné Oliver Diary, 23 Feb. 1908, and copy of 'On Furlough' by Mary E. Allbright. See also *Messenger* (Nov. 1921), 268, for MacKellar's use of the poem to express her feelings as she prepared to return to India in 1921.

72 See, for instance, Choné Oliver Diary, 14 and 27 Jan. and 20 and 30 Mar. 1906.

73 Regarding Menzies, see Jamieson Collection, Menzies to 'My dearest Dr. McKellar [*sic*],' 17 May 1910. For Goodfellow, see CIM Correspondence, box 9, file 108, Dr Alex Nugent to RPM, 2 Mar. 1911, and box 10, file 114, statement of Dr C.D. Parfitt, 27 Aug. 1912; *Tidings* 27 (Mar. 1911), 177; WMS, *Fifth Annual Report*, 1918, 14, 109.

74 *Leaflet* 11 (Apr. 1895), 315

75 *Missionary Monthly* 21 (Dec. 1946), 545. The lines as reproduced in the tribute vary slightly from the original stanza by Whitman.

CHAPTER 7 'A sphere less injurious'

1 As Edward S. Said has pointed out, ideas about the East continued to have

a powerful hold in the West even when they were at odds with the dominant reality. 'Orientalism,' he asserts, 'has less to do with the Orient than it does with "our" world'; Said, *Orientalism*, 12.

2 'Women and Missions,' *Canada Presbyterian* 20 Apr. 1887, 264–5; Rev. L.H. Jordan in *Review* 21 Nov. 1889, 1632

3 Brouwer, 'The Canadian Methodist Church and Ecclesiastical Suffrage for Women,' especially 14–15, 19. Methodist WMS leaders were by no means militants on the subject, but when Alexander Sutherland, the General Secretary of missions in the church, told the 1906 General Conference that they were uninterested in such rights, they promptly passed a pro-suffrage resolution in order to set the record straight. The issue was potentially a much more significant one than that of female ordination, since what was at stake was the right of women to participate as lay members in all areas of church government and administration. Clearly, all active churchwomen stood to be affected by it.

4 Bacchi, *Liberation Deferred?*, 7, table 3

5 UCA, Woman's Missionary Society of the Methodist Church, Canada, *Thirty-Third Annual Report*, 1913–14, Manitoba Conference, 121

6 Banner, *Elizabeth Cady Stanton*, ch. 8; Gage, *Woman Church and State;* Bacchi, *Liberation Deferred?*, 67–8

7 MacMurchy, *The Woman – Bless Her,* 15; also Mitchinson, 'Canadian Women and Church Missionary Societies'

8 Bliss, *The Service and Status of Women in the Churches,* 183

9 For an indication of how remarkable an event this was considered to be see 'Westminster Table Talk,' *Westminster* 1 (July 1896), 91, written, probably, by editor J.A. Macdonald.

10 FMC, General Correspondence, box 3, file 5, RPM to M. MacGillivray, 9 Nov. 1909

11 Dr Maggie MacKellar and Dr Maggie O'Hara were granted honorary LLDs by Queen's University in 1929 and 1932, respectively; Queen's University Alumni Files. When O'Hara died in 1940, some thirteen years after her retirement, the principal of Queen's and several other university officials travelled to Smiths Falls for her funeral; *Record* 65 (Oct. 1940), 292–4.

12 It was not until the early 1920s that the first requests for the ordination of women were presented to the Presbyterian General Assembly; some Saskatchewan clergy called for the change in the face of a shortage of ordained men for home mission work. In 1936 their gifted candidate, Lydia Gruchy, was finally ordained in the United Church of Canada. Ironically, but perhaps not surprisingly, the WMS initially opposed the move; Hallett, 'Nellie McClung and the Fight for the Ordination of Women,' 2–16.

13 On missionaries and church union see Moir, *Enduring Witness,* 229–30; for one missionary's offhand comment on the suffrage issue see CIM Correspondence, box 11, file 117, Marion Oliver to RPM, 7 Feb. 1913.

14 WFMS, Board of Management, Minutes, 21: 18 June 1912, 146

15 For example, letter from Marion Fairweather to Kingston WFMS as printed in *Record* 3 (Apr. 1878), 103–4

16 *Review* 4 Oct. 1886, 319; see also CIM Correspondence, box 2, file 28, Marion Oliver to Thomas Wardrope, 17 Aug. 1886, for her dread of her upcoming designation service.

17 Quoted in Griffith, *Jean Dow,* 19

Select bibliography

The bibliography that follows is made up almost exclusively of works cited in the Notes. A more extensive guide to sources can be found in Ruth Compton Brouwer, 'Canadian Women and the Foreign Missionary Movement: A Case Study of Presbyterian Women's Involvement at the Home Base and in Central India, 1876–1914' (PHD diss., York University, Toronto 1987).

Primary sources

NATIONAL ARCHIVES OF INDIA, NEW DELHI

Government of India. Proceedings of Foreign Department, 1833–4, with *Index to Proceedings of Foreign Department,* 1883–4, 1885–9, 1900, 1902

PRIVATELY HELD PAPERS

Coltart, Margaret. Personal Papers
Graham, Lucinda. Diary
Scott, Alexander A., and Scott, Mrs Minnie Shaw. Personal Papers
Taylor, John T., and Taylor, Mrs Harriet Copeland. Personal Papers

PUBLIC ARCHIVES OF NOVA SCOTIA, HALIFAX

Maritime Missionaries to Korea Collection
Woman's Foreign Missionary Society, Eastern Division, Presbyterian Church in Canada. *Annual Reports*

UNITED CHURCH/VICTORIA UNIVERSITY ARCHIVES, TORONTO

I. Records generated by the Presbyterian Church in Canada

The Acts and Proceedings of the ... [ordinal] General Assembly of the Presbyterian Church in Canada
Board of Foreign Missions. *Pre-Assembly Congress: Addresses delivered at the Presbyterian Pre-Assembly Congress held in Massey Hall, Toronto, Saturday, May 31st to Wednesday, June 4th., 1913, with Reports of Committees.* Toronto 1913
Deaconess Committee and Board of the Presbyterian Missionary and Deaconess Training Home (originally Ewart Woman's Missionary Training Home). Management Committee Minutes, Calendars, Reports, and other miscellaneous materials
Foreign Missions Committee, Western Section. Applications for Mission Work
– General Correspondence
– Letterbooks
– Minutes (printed from 1882)
Foreign Missions Committee, Western Section, Central India Mission. General Correspondence
– Mission Council Minutes, and Council, Finance and Indore Presbytery Minutes
– Mission Reports
– Wilkie Case Documentation
Pre-Assembly Congress. Toronto: Board of Foreign Missions, Presbyterian Church in Canada 1913
Regulations for Foreign Mission Work. Toronto: Presbyterian Printing 1891
Rules and Forms of Procedure in the Church Courts of the Presbyterian Church in Canada. Montreal: Drysdale 1899
Woman's Foreign Missionary Society, Western Division. *Annual Reports*
– *Answers to Erroneous Statements Concerning the W.F.M.S.* Toronto: Press of the Canada Presbyterian 1895
– Correspondence, 1888–1913
– List of Applicants for Service in the Foreign Field, 1889–1917
– *A Manual for the Use of Women Offering for Foreign Mission Work and for Missionaries in Connection with the Woman's Foreign Missionary Society of the Presbyterian Church in Canada (W.D.).* Toronto: Presbyterian News n.d.
Woman's Foreign Missionary Society, Western Division, Board of Management. Minutes

Woman's Foreign Missionary Society, Western Division, Women's Council of the Canadian Presbyterian Mission in Central India. Minutes

Woman's Foreign Missionary Society / Women's Missionary Society, Western Division. Minutes of the Candidate Committee, 1913–19

Woman's Missionary Society (Montreal). Correspondence, 1882–1914

– Executive Committee Meetings, 1882–1914

The Woman's Missionary Society of the Presbyterian Church in Canada (Eastern Division), 1876–1926. N.p., n.d.

Women's Missionary Society of the Presbyterian Church in Canada, Western Division. *Our Jubilee Story: 1864–1924* [Toronto 1924]

– *The Planting of the Faith: A Further Story of Our Missions*. N.p. 1921

– *The Story of Our Missions* [Toronto 1915]

2. Unpublished records by and about missionaries

Brown, Margaret H. 'History of the Honan (North China) Mission of the United Church of Canada, Originally a Mission of the Presbyterian Church in Canada: 1887–1951.' 2 vols. Typed. 1970

Duncan, Jessie. 'India.' Typed. N.d.

– 'India's Womanhood on the March.' 2 vols. Typed. N.d.

Glenna Jamieson Collection. Belle Choné Oliver Personal Papers

MacKenzie, Murdoch. Personal Papers

United Church of Canada Biographical Files

PERIODICALS

British American Presbyterian
The Canada Presbyterian
Foreign Missionary Tidings
The Home and Foreign Record of the Canada Presbyterian Church
The Home Mission Pioneer
Knox College Monthly (from 1887 *The Knox College Monthly and Presbyterian Magazine*)
The Message
The Missionary Monthly
Monthly Letter Leaflet
The Presbyterian
The Presbyterian Record
The Presbyterian Review
The Westminster

BOOKS AND BOOKLETS

Aberigh-Mackay, G.R. *The Chiefs of Central India.* Vol. I. Calcutta: n.p. 1879
Austin, B.F., ed. *Woman; Her Character, Culture and Calling.* Brantford: Book and Bible House 1890
– *Woman: Maiden, Wife and Mother.* Special Preface by the Countess of Aberdeen. Toronto: Linscott Publishing n.d.
Bainbridge, William F. *Around the World Tour of Christian Missions.* Boston: D. Lothrop 1882
Beach, Harlan P.; and Fahs, Charles H. *World Missionary Atlas.* New York: Institute of Social and Religious Research 1925
Buchanan, Ruth. *My Mother.* Toronto: Women's Missionary Society of the Presbyterian Church in Canada 1938
Canada's Missionary Congress: Addresses Delivered at the Canadian National Missionary Congress, Held in Toronto, March 31 to April 4, 1909, with Reports of Committees. Toronto: Canadian Council, Laymen's Missionary Movement 1909
Chown, Alice A. *The Stairway.* Boston: Cornhill 1921
Cummings, Mrs Willoughby. *Our Story: Some Pages from the History of the Woman's Auxiliary to the Missionary Society of the Church of England in Canada, 1885–1928.* Toronto: Garden City Press n.d.
Dufferin and Ava, Marchioness of. *Our Viceregal Life in India: Selections from My Journal.* London: John Murray 1893
Forster, E.M. *The Hill of Devi: Being Letters from Dewas State Senior.* London: Edward Arnold 1953
Gage, Matilda Joslyn. *Woman, Church and State.* Reprint of 1893 edition. Foreword by Mary Daly. Watertown: Persephone Press 1980
Gandhi, M.K. *Christian Missions: Their Place in India.* Ahmedabad, India: Navajivan Publishing House 1941
Gordon, A.J. 'The Ministry of Women,' *The Missionary Review of the World* 7 (Dec. 1894) 910–21
Gordon, Charles W. *The Life of James Robertson D.D.* Toronto: Westminster Press 1908
Gracey, J.T. 'Women and Missions,' in B.F. Austin, ed., *Woman; Her Character, Culture and Calling,* ch. 12. Brantford, Ont.: Book and Bible House 1890
Gracey, Mrs J.T. *Eminent Missionary Women.* New York: Eaton and Mains 1898
Grant, George Monro. *The Religions of the World.* Rev. and enl. ed. London: A. and C. Black 1895

Griffith, Margaret R. *Jean Dow, M.D.: A Beloved Physician.* Toronto: Woman's
Missionary Society of the United Church of Canada n.d.

Hocking, Ernest William. *Re-thinking Missions: A Laymen's Inquiry after One
Hundred Years.* New York: Harper and Brothers 1932

India. Census. 1881. *Central India* (Microfiche, Robarts Library, University of
Toronto)

Johnston, James, ed. *Report of the Centenary Conference on the Protestant
Missions of the World.* Vol. 2. London: James Nisbet and Company 1888

Kemp, A.F.; and Farries, F.W., eds. *Handbook of the Presbyterian Church in
Canada 1883.* Ottawa 1883

Luard, C.E., comp. *Indore State Gazetteer.* Vol. 2. Calcutta: Government
Publishing 1908

McCully, Elizabeth A. *Our Share in Korea.* Toronto: Woman's Missionary
Society of the United Church of Canada n.d.

MacDougall, John. *Rural Life in Canada: Its Trends and Tasks.* Introduction
by Robert Craig Brown. Toronto: University of Toronto Press 1973.

McGregor, Mary Esther [Marion Keith]. *The Black-Bearded Barbarian: The
Life of George Leslie Mackay.* New York: Missionary Education Movement
1912

MacKay, Jean Sinclair. *Dr. Marion Oliver: A Memoir.* Toronto: Women's
Missionary Society of the Presbyterian Church in Canada 1920

– *Voices from India.* Toronto: Woman's Missionary Society of the United
Church of Canada 1934

MacKay, R.P. *Life of George Leslie Mackay, D.D., 1844–1901.* Toronto: Board
of Foreign Missions, Presbyterian Church 1913

MacKellar, Margaret. *Amelia J. Harris: The Story of Her Life.* N.p. 1937

MacMurchy, Marjory. *The Woman – Bless Her.* Toronto: S.B. Gundy 1916

MacTavish, W.S., ed. *Harvests in Many Lands: Fruitage of Canadian Presbyterianism.* Toronto: William Briggs 1908

– *Missionary Pathfinders: Presbyterian Labourers at Home and Abroad.*
Toronto: Committee on Young People's Societies, Presbyterian Church
1907

– *Reapers in Many Fields.* Toronto: Committee on Young People's Societies,
Presbyterian Church 1904

Malcolm, John. *A Memoir of Central India including Malwa and Adjoining
Provinces with the History and Copious Illustrations of the Past and Present
Condition of That Country.* 2 vols. 1832. Reprint ed. New Delhi: Sagar
Publications 1970

Marx, Karl. 'The Future Results of British Rule in India,' in Robert C. Tucker,
ed., *The Marx-Engels Reader,* 583–8. New York: W.W. Norton 1972

Montgomery, Helen Barrett. *Western Women in Eastern Lands: An Outline Study of Fifty Years of Woman's Work in Foreign Missions*. New York: Macmillan 1911

Mott, John R. *The Decisive Hour of Christian Missions*. New York: Student Volunteer Movement 1910

Murdoch, John. *Indian Missionary Manual: Hints to Young Missionaries in India*. 3rd ed. London: James Nisbet and Company 1889

Murray, Florence J. *At the Foot of Dragon Hill*. New York: E.P. Dutton and Company 1975

O'Hara, Margaret. *Leaf of the Lotus*. Toronto: John M. Poole, Westminster Press 1931

Oliver, B. Choné. *Dr. Margaret MacKellar: The Story of Her Early Years*. Toronto: Women's Missionary Society of the Presbyterian Church in Canada 1920

– comp. *Tales from the Inns of Healing: Christian Medical Service in India, Burma and Ceylon*. Toronto: Committee on Missionary Education, United Church of Canada 1944

Orchard, Malcolm L. *Canadian Baptists at Work in India*. Toronto: Missionary Education Department 1922

Platt, Harriet Louise. *The Story of the Years: A History of the Woman's Missionary Society of the Methodist Church, Canada, 1881–1906*. Vol. 1. Toronto: Woman's Missionary Society, Methodist Church 1908

Rijnhart, Susie Carson. *With the Tibetans in Tent and Temple*. Chicago: Fleming H. Revell 1901

Rubio, Mary; and Waterston, Elizabeth, eds. *The Selected Journals of L.M. Montgomery*. Vol. 2, 1910–21. Toronto: Oxford University Press 1987

Russell, Frank H. *New Days in Old India*. Toronto: United Church of Canada 1926

Russell, Norman. *Village Work in India: Pen Pictures from a Missionary's Experience*. New York: Fleming H. Revell 1902

Smith, Elizabeth. *'A Woman with a Purpose': The Diaries of Elizabeth Smith, 1872–1884*. Edited, with an Introduction, by Veronica Strong-Boag. Toronto: University of Toronto Press 1980

Speer, Robert E. *Missionary Principles and Practice*. 4th ed. New York: Young People's Missionary Movement 1908

Taylor, J.T. *In the Heart of India: The Work of the Canadian Presbyterian Mission*. Toronto: Presbyterian Church in Canada 1916

– *Our Share in India: The Story of the Central India Mission of the United Church of Canada*. Toronto: United Church of Canada n.d.

Thoburn, James M. *The Christian Conquest of India*. New York: Missionary Education Movement 1906

Thompson, Andrew. *The Life and Letters of R.P. MacKay, D.D.* Toronto: Ryerson Press 1932

Vickery, C.V. *The Young People's Missionary Movement.* New York: Young People's Missionary Movement 1906

Wherry, E.M., ed. *Woman and Missions: Papers and Addresses Presented at the Woman's Congress of Missions, Oct. 2–4, 1893, in the Hall of Columbus, Chicago.* New York: American Tract Society 1894

Wilson, W.A. *The Redemption of Malwa: The Central India Canadian Presbyterian Mission.* Toronto: Arbuthnot and MacMillan 1903

Secondary sources

Allen, Charles, ed. *Plain Tales from the Raj: Images of British India in the Twentieth Century.* London: Futura Publications 1976

Austin, Alvyn J. *Saving China: Canadian Missionaries in the Middle Kingdom, 1888–1959.* Toronto: University of Toronto Press 1986

Bacchi, Carol Lee. *Liberation Deferred? The Ideas of the English-Canadian Suffragists, 1877–1918.* Toronto: University of Toronto Press 1983

Bahr, Robert. *Least of All Saints: The Story of Aimee Semple McPherson.* Englewood Cliffs, NJ: Prentice-Hall 1979

Bailey, Susan F. *Women and the British Empire: An Annotated Guide to Sources,* ch. 3. New York: Garland Press 1983

Balfour, Margaret I.; and Young, Ruth. *The Work of Medical Women in India.* London: Oxford University Press 1929

Banner, Lois W. *Elizabeth Cady Stanton: A Radical for Woman's Rights.* Boston: Little, Brown 1980

Barr, Pat. *The Memsahibs: The Women of Victorian India.* London: Secker and Warburg 1976

Bearce, George D. *British Attitudes towards India, 1784–1858.* London: Oxford University Press 1961

Beaver, R. Pierce. *American Protestant Women in World Mission: A History of the First Feminist Movement in North America.* Grand Rapids, Mich.: William B. Eerdmans 1980. Orig. pub., 1968, as *All Loves Excelling*

– 'Missionary Motivation through Three Centuries,' in Jerald C. Brauer, ed., *Reinterpretations in American Church History,* 113–51. Chicago: University of Chicago Press 1968

Berg, Barbara J. *The Remembered Gate: Origins of American Feminism / The Woman and the City, 1800–1860.* New York: Oxford University Press 1978

Berger, Carl. *The Sense of Power: Studies in the Ideas of Canadian Imperialism, 1867–1914.* Toronto: University of Toronto Press 1970

Blaisdell, Charmarie Jenkins. 'The Matrix of Reform: Women in the Lutheran and Calvinist Movements,' in Richard L. Greaves, ed., *Women in Protestant History,* 13–44. Westport, Conn.: Greenwood Press 1985

Bliss, Kathleen. *The Service and Status of Women in the Churches.* London: SCM Press 1952

Boyd, Lois A.; and Brackenridge, R. Douglas. *Presbyterian Women in America: Two Centuries of a Quest for Status.* Westport, Conn.: Greenwood Press 1983

Brouwer, Ruth Compton. 'The Canadian Methodist Church and Ecclesiastical Suffrage for Women, 1902–1914,' Canadian Methodist Historical Society *Papers.* Vol. 2. n.d.

– ' "Far Indeed from the Meekest of Women": Marion Fairweather and the Canadian Presbyterian Mission in Central India, 1873–1880,' in John S. Moir and C.T. McIntire, eds., *Canadian Protestant and Catholic Missions, 1820s–1960s: Historical Essays in Honour of John Webster Grant,* 121–49. New York: Peter Lang 1988

– 'Opening Doors through Social Service: Aspects of Women's Work in the Canadian Presbyterian Mission in Central India, 1877–1914,' in Leslie A. Flemming, ed., *Women's Work for Women: Missionaries and Social Change in Asia,* 11–34. Boulder, Col.: Westview Press 1989

Brown, Judith M. *Modern India: The Origins of an Asian Democracy.* Delhi: Oxford University Press 1985

Brumberg, Joan Jacobs. *Mission for Life: The Story of the Family of Adoniram Judson.* New York: Free Press 1980

– 'Zenanas and Girlless Villages: The Ethnology of American Evangelical Women, 1870–1910,' *The Journal of American History* 69 (Sept. 1982): 347–71

Buck, Pearl. *The Exile.* New York: Reynal and Hitchcock 1936

Buck, Ruth Matheson. *The Doctor Rode Side-Saddle.* Toronto: McClelland and Stewart 1974

Christensen, Torben; and Hutchison, William R., eds. *Missionary Ideologies in the Imperialist Era: 1880–1920.* Aarhuis, Denmark: Farlaget Aros 1982

Collins, Alice Roger. *Real People.* N.p., n.d. [booklet in United Church / Victoria University Archives biographical file for Dr Margaret MacKellar]

Cook, Ramsay; and Mitchinson, Wendy, eds. *The Proper Sphere: Woman's Place in Canadian Society.* Toronto: Oxford University Press 1976

Cott, Nancy F. *The Bonds of Womanhood: 'Woman's Sphere' in New England, 1780–1835.* New Haven: Yale University Press 1977

Davy, Shirley, ed. *Women, Work and Worship in the United Church of Canada.* N.p.: United Church of Canada 1983

Dhar, Sailendra Nath. *The Indore State and Its Vicinity.* Indore: Indian Science Congress 1936

Douglas, Ann. *The Feminization of American Culture.* New York: Knopf 1977

Drewery, Mary. *William Carey: Shoemaker and Missionary.* London: Hodder and Stoughton 1978

Fairbank, John K. *The Missionary Enterprise in China and America.* Cambridge, Mass.: Harvard University Press 1974

Findlay, James F., Jr. *Dwight L. Moody: American Evangelist, 1837–1899.* Chicago: University of Chicago Press 1969

Flemming, Leslie A. 'New Models, New Roles: U.S. Presbyterian Women Missionaries and Social Change in North India, 1870–1910,' in Leslie A. Flemming, ed., *Women's Work for Women: Missionaries and Social Change in Asia,* 35–57. Boulder Col.: Westview Press 1989

Forman, Charles W. 'The Americans,' *International Bulletin of Missionary Research* 6 (Apr. 1982): 54–6

Forrester, Duncan B. *Caste and Christianity: Attitudes and Policies on Caste of Anglo-Saxon Protestant Missionaries in India.* London: Curzon Press 1980

Foster, John William. 'The Imperialism of Righteousness: Canadian Protestant Missions and the Chinese Revolution, 1925–1928,' PHD diss., University of Toronto 1977

Gagan, Rosemary R. ' "Here I Am, Send Me": The Personnel of the Woman's Missionary Society of the Methodist Church of Canada, 1881–1925,' paper presented to Canadian Methodist Historical Society, Toronto, June 1985

Grant, John Webster. *The Church in the Canadian Era.* Updated and expanded ed. Burlington, Ont.: Welch Publishing 1988

– *Moon of Wintertime: Missionaries and the Indians of Canada in Encounter since 1534.* Toronto: University of Toronto Press 1984

– 'Presbyterian Women and the Indians,' paper presented to Canadian Society of Presbyterian History, Toronto 1978

Green, Elizabeth Alden. *Mary Lyon and Mount Holyoke: Opening the Gates.* Hanover, NH: University Press of New England 1979

Hacker, Carlotta. *The Indomitable Lady Doctors.* Paperback ed. Halifax: Formac 1984

Hageman, Alice. 'Women and Missions: The Cost of Liberation,' in Alice Hageman, ed., *Sexist Religion and Women in the Church,* 167–93. New York: Association Press 1974

Hallett, Mary E. 'Nellie McClung and the Fight for the Ordination of Women in the United Church of Canada,' *Atlantis* 4 (Spring 1979): 2–16

Handy, Robert T. *A History of the Churches in the United States and Canada.* Oxford: Oxford University Press 1976

Hill, Patricia R. *The World Their Household: The American Woman's Foreign*

Mission Movement and Cultural Transformation, 1870–1920. Ann Arbor: University of Michigan Press 1985

Hopkins, C. Howard. *John R. Mott.* Grand Rapids, Mich.: William B. Eerdmans 1979

Hunter, Jane. *The Gospel of Gentility: American Women Missionaries in Turn-of-the-Century China.* New Haven: Yale University Press 1984

Hutchison, William R. *Errand to the World: American Protestant Thought and Foreign Missions.* Chicago: University of Chicago Press 1987

– 'Introduction,' and 'Comment,' *International Bulletin of Missionary Research* 6 (Apr. 1982): 50–1, 64–5

– *The Modernist Impulse in American Protestantism.* Cambridge, Mass.: Harvard University Press 1976

James, Janet Wilson. 'An Overview,' in Janet Wilson James, ed., *Women in American Religion,* 1–25. Philadelphia: University of Pennsylvania Press 1980

Jardens, J.T.F. 'Dyananda Sarasvati and Christianity,' *Indian Church History Review* 15 (June 1981): 34–47

Johnston, Geoffrey Deane. 'The Canadian Mission in Trinidad, 1868–1939: Studies in a Colonial Church,' THD diss., Knox College 1976

– 'The Road to Winsome Womanhood: The Canadian Presbyterian Mission among East Indian Women and Girls in Trinidad, 1868–1939,' in John S. Moir and T.C. McIntire, eds., *Canadian Protestant and Catholic Missions, 1820–1939: Historical Essays in Honour of John Webster Grant.* New York: Peter Lang 1988

Johnston, John A. 'The Canadian Presbyterian Union of 1875,' *Canadian Society of Presbyterian History Papers* 1975

Kinsley, David. *Hindu Goddesses: Visions of the Divine Feminine in the Hindu Religious Tradition.* Berkeley: University of California Press 1986

Latourette, Kenneth Scott. *A History of the Expansion of Christianity.* Vol. 6: *The Great Century in Northern Africa and Asia, A.D. 1800–A.D. 1914.* New York: Harper and Brothers 1944

Lebra-Chapman, Joyce. *The Rani of Jhansi: A Study in Female Heroism in India.* Honolulu: University of Hawaii Press 1986

Liddle, Joanna; and Joshi, Rama. *Daughters of Independence: Gender, Caste and Class in India.* London: Zed Books 1986

McCully, Bruce Tiebout. *English Education and the Origins of Indian Nationalism.* Gloucester, Mass.: Peter Smith 1966

McKee, Leila Gay Mitchell. 'Voluntary Youth Organizations in Toronto, 1880–1930,' PHD diss., York University 1982

McLaurin, K.S. *Mary Bates McLaurin*. Toronto: The Women's Baptist Foreign
Missionary Society 1945

MacMillan, Margaret. *Women of the Raj*. New York: Thames and Hudson
1988

Malmgreen, Gail, ed. *Religion in the Lives of English Women, 1760–1930*.
Bloomington: Indiana University Press 1986

Martell, Anne. 'The Canadian Presbyterian Mission to Trinidad's East Indian
Population, 1868–1912,' MA thesis, Dalhousie University 1974

Mathur, K.S. *Caste and Ritual in a Malwa Village*. Bombay: Asia Publishing
House 1964

Mayer, Adrian C. *Caste and Kinship in Central India: A Village and Its Region*.
London: Routledge and Kegan Paul 1960

Merrick, Earl C. *These Impossible Women, 100 Years: The Story of the United
Baptist Woman's Missionary Union of the Maritime Provinces*. Fredericton:
Brunswick Press 1970

Mitchinson, Wendy. 'Canadian Women and Church Missionary Societies:
A Step towards Independence,' *Atlantis* 2 (Spring 1977): 57–75

Moir, John S. 'Canadian Presbyterians and the Laymen's Missionary Movement,' Canadian Society of Presbyterian History *Papers* 1983

– *Enduring Witness: A History of the Presbyterian Church in Canada*, 2nd ed.
N.p.: Presbyterian Church in Canada 1987

Moorhouse, Geoffrey. *The Missionaries*. London: Eyre Methuen 1973

Morgan, James Henry, ed. *The Canadian Men and Women of the Time: A
Handbook of Canadian Biography*. Toronto: William Briggs 1898, 2nd ed.
1912

Naik, T.B. *Impact of Education on the Bhils: Cultural Change in the Tribal Life
of Madya Pradesh*. New Delhi: Research Programme Committee 1969

Neill, Stephen. *Colonialism and Christian Missions*. New York: McGraw-Hill
1966

– *A History of Christian Missions*. Harmondsworth, Middlesex: Penguin Books
1964

– *The Story of the Christian Church in India and Pakistan*. Grand Rapids,
Mich.: William B. Eerdmans 1970

Neill, Stephen; Anderson, Gerald H.; and Goodwin, John, eds. *Concise Dictionary of the Christian World Mission*. London: Lutterworth Press 1970

Oddie, G.A. 'India and Missionary Motives c. 1850–1900,' *Journal of Ecclesiastical History* 25 (Jan. 1974): 61–74

– *Social Protest in India: British Protestant Missionaries and Social Reforms,
1850–1900*. New Delhi: Manohar 1979

O'Dwyer, Michael. *India As I Knew It: 1885–1925.* London: Constable and
Company 1925

O'Malley, L.S.S. *Modern India and the West.* London: Oxford University Press
1941; 1966 microfilm-xerography reprint

One Hundred Years of Erskine Church, Montreal. N.p. 1933

Pathak, Sushil Madhav. *American Missionaries and Hinduism: A Study of Their
Contacts from 1813 to 1910.* Delhi: Munshiram Manaharlal 1967

Paul, Glendora B. 'Presbyterian Missionaries and the Women of India during
the Nineteenth Century,' *Journal of Presbyterian History* 62 (Fall 1984):
20–6

Pederson, Diana. ' "The Call to Service": The YWCA and the Canadian College Woman, 1886–1920,' in Paul Axelrod and John G. Reid, eds., *Youth,
University and Canadian Society: Essays in the Social History of Higher Education,* 187–215. Kingston: McGill-Queen's University Press 1989

Phillips, J. Clifton. *Protestant America and the Pagan World: The First Half
Century of the American Board of Commissioners for Foreign Missions,
1810–1860.* Cambridge, Mass.: Harvard University Press 1969

Pichanick, Valerie Kossew. *Harriet Martineau: The Woman and Her Work,
1802–1876.* Ann Arbor: University of Michigan Press 1980

Prentice, Alison. 'The Feminization of Teaching in British North America
and Canada, 1845–1875,' *Histoire sociale/Social History* 8 (May 1975): 5–20

Prochaska, F.K. *Women and Philanthropy in Nineteenth-Century Britain.*
Oxford: Clarendon Press 1980

Rabe, Valentin H. *The Home Base of American China Missions, 1880–1920.*
Cambridge: Harvard University Press 1975

Reid, W. Harold. *The Presbyterian Church St. Andrews and Lachute, Quebec,
1818–1932.* N.p. 1979

Ridout, Katherine. 'A Woman of Mission: The Religious and Cultural Odys-
sey of Agnes Wintemute Coates,' *Canadian Historical Review.* Forthcoming,
June 1990

Said, Edward W. *Orientalism.* New York: Pantheon Books 1978

Scott, Ann Firor. 'On Seeing and Not Seeing: A Case of Historical Invisibility,'
Journal of American History 71 (June 1984): 7–21

Scott, Munroe. *McClure: The China Years.* Toronto: Canec Publishing 1977

Shenk, Wilbert R. 'The "Great Century" Reconsidered,' *Missiology: An International Review* 12 (Apr. 1984): 133–46

Shirgaonkar, S.R. 'The Education of Girls in Maharashtra,' in A.G. Pawar,
ed., *Maratha History Seminar, Papers,* 351–63. Kolhapur, India: Shivaji University 1971

Smith-Rosenberg, Carroll. 'The Female World of Love and Ritual: Relations between Women in Nineteenth-Century America,' and 'Hearing Women's Words: A Feminist Reconstruction of History,' in Caroll Smith-Rosenberg, *Disorderly Conduct: Visions of Gender in Victorian America,* 53–76. New York: Oxford University Press 1985

Staelin, Charlotte Dennett. 'The Influence of Missions on Women's Education in India: The American Marathi Mission in Ahmadnagar, 1830–1930,' PHD diss., University of Michigan 1977

Strong-Boag, Veronica Jane. 'Canada's Women Doctors: Feminism Constrained,' in Linda Kealey, ed., *A Not Unreasonable Claim: Women and Reform in Canada, 1880s–1920s.* Toronto: Women's Press 1979

– *The Parliament of Women: The National Council of Women of Canada, 1893–1929.* Ottawa: National Museums of Canada 1976

Thompson, Edward. *The Making of the English Princes.* London: Oxford University Press 1943

Travill, A.A. 'Early Medical Co-education and Women's Medical College, Kingston, Ontario, 1880–1894,' *Historic Kingston* 30 (Jan. 1982): 68–89

Walls, Andrew F. 'The British,' *International Bulletin of Missionary Research* 6 (Apr. 1982): 60–4

Warren, Max. *Social History and Christian Mission.* London: SCM Press 1967

Webster, John C.B. *The Christian Community and Change in Nineteenth Century North India.* Delhi: Macmillan Company of India 1976

– 'Introduction,' *Journal of Presbyterian History* 62 (Fall 1984): 190–8

Welter, Barbara. 'The Feminization of American Religion: 1800–1860,' in Barbara Welter, *Dimity Convictions: The American Woman in the Nineteenth Century,* 83–102. Athens, Ohio: Ohio University Press 1976

– 'She Hath Done What She Could: Protestant Women's Missionary Careers in Nineteenth-Century America,' in Janet Wilson James, ed., *Women in American Religion.* Philadelphia: University of Pennsylvania Press 1980

Wolpert, Stanley. *A New History of India.* 2nd ed. New York: Oxford University Press 1982

Index

King, Annie Murray 112, 222
King, Robert A. 111, 112, 127, 159, 222
Klondike gold field 45
Knox College, Toronto 62, 65, 76, 164
Knox College Monthly 33, 37
Korea: mission 6, 31; missionaries 55, 58, 79, 91, 200–1, 219–20

Ladies' Auxiliary Association (Montreal) 25, 30. *See also* Woman's Missionary Society (Montreal)
Lakshmibai, Rani, of Jhansi 171
Latourette, Kenneth Scott 11
Laymen's Missionary Movement 24, 49
Leach, Mary 72–3, 155, 176, 205
Ledingham, A.P. 154, 222
Livingstone, David 12, 14
Livingstone, Mary 14
Lowry, Thomas 96
Lyon, Mary 17

MacBeth, R.G. 48, 49, 51
McCalla, Susie 79, 205
McClung, Nellie 190, 191
McClure, Robert 79
McClure, William 79
McCully, Elizabeth 55, 79, 200
McCully, Louise 55, 79, 200
Macdonald, J.A. 45, 46, 68–9, 88; praises WFMS 32, 33
Macdonald, J.K. 159
McFayden, John E. 65
MacGillivray, Janet 51
McGregor, Mary 106, 206; and mission controversies 35, 132–3, 135–8, 182, 192
Machar, Agnes Maule 23

McInnes, John 151–2
Mackay, George Leslie 23, 30–1, 78–9
MacKay, James Sutherland 103, 222
MacKay, Jean Sinclair. *See* Sinclair, Jean
McKay, Kate 60
Mackay, Mary. *See* Buchanan, Mary Mackay
MacKay, Robert Peter 62, 85, 100, 103, 184; appointment of as FMC secretary 24; and controversies in Central India mission 147–8, 152, 153, 158; relations with WFMS 31, 32, 38–40, 49–50; on recruitment of missionaries 61, 75; on training of missionaries 37, 63, 65
MacKellar, Margaret (Maggie) 71, 85, 88, 116, 168, 206; attitude to medical work 118–19; designation service of 77, 183; and mission controversies 144, 148, 149, 158–9; missionary work 104, 122, 179; special friendships 183; tributes to 179, 268n11
McKelvie, George 142, 144, 222
MacKenzie, Murdoch 126, 137, 158, 256n27
McLaren, Marjory 26, 40–1, 45
McLaren, William 21, 24, 26, 36, 48, 133, 135
McMaster, Elizabeth 104, 166–7, 207
MacMurchy, Archibald 24
MacMurchy, Bessie 27
MacMurchy, Helen 27
MacMurchy, Marjory (daughter) 5, 41, 231n18
MacMurchy, Marjory (mother) 27, 41, 80
McMurrich, W.B. 24